→ Label over.

D1610905

Routledge Education Books

Advisory editor: John Eggleston
*Professor of Education
University of Keele*

Teachers and classes

A Marxist analysis

Kevin Harris

ROUTLEDGE & KEGAN PAUL
London, Boston and Henley

First published in 1982
by Routledge & Kegan Paul Ltd
39 Store Street, London WC1E 7DD,
9 Park Street, Boston, Mass. 02108, USA and
Broadway House, Newtown Road,
Henley-on-Thames, Oxon RG9 1EN
Printed in Great Britain by
St Edmundsbury Press
Bury St Edmunds, Suffolk

Library of Congress Cataloging in Publication Data

Harris, Kevin.
Teachers and classes.

(Routledge education books)
Bibliography: p.
Includes index.
1. Communism and education--Australia--New South
Wales.   I Title.   II. Series.
HX526.H35   371.1'04   81-8542
ISBN 0-7100-0865-1   AACR2

FOR ANN HALL
who provided me with the inspiration to begin this book and who,
along with Gary, Stephen and Rachel, also provided the material
conditions whereby I could complete it

Contents

Preface

In the course of undergoing teacher training, teaching for twelve years, reading for three degrees in education, and lecturing in teacher-training institutions for a further twelve years, I have come into contact with a vast number of books, papers, lectures and addresses concerned with the role and function of teachers. This book is a challenge to virtually everything I have encountered in that field, and a challenge to most of what today's students and teachers learn or accept about their role and social function as teachers or future teachers.

The book is introductory in two senses. It has been written essentially for those who are not deeply acquainted with Marxist theory or the methodology of Marxist analysis, and thus offers an elementary introduction to and application of certain aspects of the Marxist research programme. On the other hand it is also introductory in the sense that it offers the first sustained Marxist analysis of the role and function of teachers under contemporary corporate capitalism, or at least the first that I know of. A balance has therefore been sought - one between a simplified introduction to a particular mode of analysis, and at the same time a rigorous application of that mode of analysis to a relatively unexplored area. The overall aim has been to provide something which both sophisticated Marxists and those as yet unfamiliar with Marxism can take hold of and get their teeth into, such that theoretic production might advance and result in greater interest and more rigorous analysis in this area.

In compiling this book I have pillaged much from the unpublished works of many of my friends and colleagues. John Freeland, Michael Gallagher, Rachel Sharp, Peter Stevens and Ted Trainer will find large amounts of their material reproduced throughout the following pages. I have also benefited from discussions with Colin Evers and Carol O'Donnell concerning specific parts of the text, and especially from the invaluable comments provided by Jim Walker who critically read an earlier version of the complete text. In fairness to Jim I must note that I did not incorporate all of his suggested amendments, and that while this final version owes much to him, it is by no means a version that he would fully endorse. The final responsibility for what follows rests with me alone.

Biographical introduction

I was a child of the working class - the working class in its
strictest sense. My father had left school at a very early age,
and moved through a series of unskilled labouring jobs, at least
at those times when jobs were available. My mother had had
even less schooling, and, forbidden from working by my father's
ethos, occupied herself in 'keeping the house'. Consequently we
lived on or below the poverty line in a depressed little slum in
the inner-city Sydney area, dependent for our existence on
whatever wages my father could bring home in return for his
physical labour.

Amidst all of this my parents held to one unshakeable belief;
namely that the conditions of our existence were dependent
largely on their lack of education and skills; and they resolved
that the same would not be the case for their children. Thus,
from as early as I can remember, it was continually drummed
into me that I should work my hardest at school, continue my
education as far as possible, get good results, and thus finish
up with a good job, security, money, and a decent standard of
life outside of the slums.

For reasons which I could not possibly recall or untangle I
managed to satisfy their desires and expectations throughout
primary school; and in those days it was one's performance at
primary school which determined which type of high school one
entered. At the top there were selective high schools offering
five-year courses leading to university entry; in the middle
were junior high schools offering three years of a largely
academic programme; while at the bottom were the 'junior techs'.
My class photo of the final year of primary school has forty-
seven boys jammed into it: two of us made it to a selective high
school, and so proud was the headmaster that he called a special
assembly for the purpose of congratulating us and wishing us
well.

High school proved to be something of a different matter. There
were few kids around who came from homes or areas like mine,
most were better dressed and equipped than I was, for whatever
reasons I didn't get on well with the teachers, much of the work
didn't interest me (French and Latin were compulsory), and in
fact all I wanted to do was leave - this especially so as my neighbourhood friends reached their fifteenth birthday and went out
into the world of jobs, and money. My parents, however, would
not allow me to leave; and so, in quite an unmotivated manner,
I stuck it out, finally ending up with a mediocre pass which

1

earned me a Leaving Certificate and satisfied matriculation requirements by the barest minimum. My parents were delighted, and offered to continue to support me as I tackled university. I, however, had another idea.

Graduation from high school brought with it an immediate change in attitude towards my neighbourhood friends. Whereas two years earlier I envied their entry into the wage-earning work-force and the attendant conspicuous benefits like sharp clothes, money for cigarettes and movies, and so on; suddenly I saw them as my father had always described them - 'wage slaves who will never move out of this suburb'. On the other hand there was I, still with only a school uniform, but with the world literally at my feet. It was at that point that I made a spontaneous decision. The world and the university could wait: my calling was to become a schoolteacher, whereby I could lead others (those with less enlightened parents?) to the position I had arrived at.

After completing a two-year primary teachers' course I returned to a working-class primary school fully intent on liberating as many of the children as possible through the wondrous medium of education. For five years I passed on my father's message, constantly encouraging my pupils to do their best, to go onwards, and to raise themselves from their miserable conditions: I stood before them as the shining example that it could be done, and offered every encouragement within my power. And at the end of each of those years one or two or three from the senior year gained entry into a selective high school. It appeared to me as though my efforts with the junior classes were eventually paying off.

At the beginning of 1962 the state education system was radically restructured. The three-tier secondary school system was replaced with geographically based comprehensive schools, whereby all children in a particular area would go to the same high school and *there*, after an initial common programme, 'sort themselves out' into different levels and/or areas of interest. The new schools, however, did not suddenly materialise as physical entities, nor were the smaller three-year junior high schools and 'techs' simply rased to the ground. What happened was that a transition period was set into operation: all schools ostensibly taught the same curriculum, all pupils sat for the same exams, and those children in junior schools who wanted to go on were to be simply offered places in the existing senior schools. Thus a child sent to a 'junior tech' (now renamed, but bearing its past history) was theoretically in the same position as a child sent to a selective school (also renamed, but also bearing its past history). Theory and practice, however, didn't coincide. The junior schools tended to have less qualified teachers, they were traditionally in depressed areas, they were relatively ill-equipped, and they continued to bear the stigma of what they once were - the bottom of the heap. Simply calling a school 'Downtown High' changed little when the signs and engravings still said 'Downtown Junior Technical School', when half the school was set out in workshops for wood and metal, when science laboratories and libraries were either absent or obviously secondary appendages, when the very pupils were either the younger siblings or progeny of those who attended and remembered the *real* Downtown Tech, and especially when the first intakes of the new 'high' schools were almost equivalent to what they would have been had the tri-partite system remained.

It seemed to me that there was a particularly important job to be done at that time; namely convincing the pupils of these new 'high' schools that they had the same opportunities as pupils at 'established' high schools, and also offering the same opportunities. This was my second calling. I applied for, and was appointed to the very 'junior tech' I had bypassed twelve years earlier.

My initial concern at this school was with the new intake of first-formers, and I passed on the same message that I had emphasised throughout my primary-school career: 'Work hard, study, pass your exams, go on to a full high school, university etc. and escape your conditions.' I was fortunate enough to be able to keep contact with this group right through the new four-year junior course, as well as picking up new classes as they entered the school. Conditions were certainly different from teaching primary school: interest was harder to maintain, motivation was lower, there were far more discipline problems, pupils left as jobs beckoned from outside, and so on. But my main concern was to keep as many pupils on as possible, to assist them through their fourth-year exam, and to encourage them to then go further. Of the initial intake of just over 160 pupils, less than thirty entered fourth form, eight passed their junior exam, five went on to a full high school, and one matriculated and eventually graduated from university. In subsequent years the numbers varied marginally, mainly in response to a slight change in the first-form intake procedures. I remained at the school for seven years, thus witnessing the full progress through the school of four intakes. Nearly 700 pupils entered the school, less than fifty graduated with a junior certificate and went on to senior years: I suspect there would be no more than five university graduates among them. At the end of the seventh year I resigned from teaching.

Those were the seven hardest-working years of my life. They were shared with a staff as dedicated as you might ever hope to find. And yet somewhere we failed, and failed miserably. I do not think that we were bad teachers - certainly our inspection reports were never unfavourable, and those that have remained in the service are now in senior positions. On the other hand, I do not think we were lumbered with bad children. It seems to me now that the failure, the miserable failure, was in large part inevitable, being built into the very structure of the situation in a way which I did not understand, and which none of us understood. It seems to me also that the situation was not and is not peculiar to the particular conditions of that school at that time (although some aspects may have been). I recall the celebrations when my teachers succeeded with two of us back in 1949. I recall, with some dismay, that the successes I counted as a primary-school teacher were of the same low order, and that I never really added up the failures. I suspect very strongly that the propensity for teacher-failure, while it might vary slightly according to particular contingencies, is deeply inherent within the very structure of schooling under capitalism, such that teachers, by and large, are destined to fail. The purpose of this book is to advance our understanding of why this is so, and to suggest strategies whereby the problem might be overcome.

A coda might be in order here. In one sense my parents were perfectly right. It was those extra two years of secondary schooling, followed by teacher training (itself made possible by those extra years) which were very largely instrumental in my gaining the sort of job, and income, which facilitated an escape from the slums and the shedding of many burdens carried by the working class. And later it was the furthering of my schooling in the form of taking three university degrees which directly enabled me to now occupy an extremely privileged social position. I am perfectly well aware that it was education, as provided within particular social conditions, which opened the doors for me. But I am now just as well aware that it was the same educational and social system which closed the doors on the vast majority of my peers and my pupils; and I am by no means convinced that they, and the millions like them, are less worthy or less deserving human beings. I trust that I shall not be misunderstood as being irrationally ungrateful in my commitment to the overthrow of the very social conditions which enabled me to attain my position of relative, personal, individual privilege.

Chapter 1
Teachers and education

INTRODUCTION

Given that this book has kicked off with the dismal notion of teacher-failure, it is important right at the outset to indicate clearly just what it is that teachers are being charged with failing at. The Introduction might have made it appear that the failure in question was a matter of not getting all children through senior high school or university. Well, teachers certainly do fail to do that; but I take this to be a contingency related rather distantly to the far more fundamental issue which I am concerned to examine. Put bluntly and crudely (the charge will be sharpened and refined later), teachers fail to Educate.

Now the charge, of course, lacks substance until we indicate what is meant by 'Educate' – the capital E is deliberate – and clarification here is all the more necessary because of the different ways in which the terms 'educate' and 'education' are commonly used today.

There was a time when 'education' was used only in a generalised way to refer to any process or occurrence which influenced a person's development, but over the last century particularly we have seen the emergence of a far more specific application of the term. In 1867, John Stuart Mill drew a distinction between a *wide* meaning of 'education' – 'whatever helps to make the individual what he is, or hinders him from being what he is not' – and a *narrow* meaning referring to the 'culture' *purposely* transmitted to new generations, 'in order to qualify them for at least keeping up, and if possible for raising the level of improvement which has been attained'.[1] In the following years educational theorists produced many variations on the theme of the 'narrower' meaning. For instance R.M. Livingstone spoke of educational activities as being tinged with a 'vision of greatness'; T.P. Nunn declared that 'the primary aim of all educational effort should be to help boys and girls to achieve the highest degree of individual development of which they are capable';[2] A.N. Whitehead looked to education to produce people 'who possess both culture and expert knowledge in some special direction. Their expert knowledge will give them the ground to start from, and their culture will lead them as deep as philosophy and as high as art';[3] D.H. Lawrence asserted that, 'Education means leading out the individual nature in each man and woman to its true fullness';[4] and R.M. Hutchins insisted that, in contrast to the family and the church, 'Education deals with the development

5

of the intellectual powers.'[5] And a century after Mill, R.S. Peters, in more complicated fashion, drew much the same distinction between an 'undifferentiated' sense of 'education' referring to socialisation processes in general, and a 'differentiated' normative sense associated with the production of the educated man (sic), who could be identified thus:[6]

(i)   An educated man is one whose form of life – as exhibited in his conduct, the activities to which he is committed, his judgments and feelings – is thought to be desirable.

(ii) Whatever he is trained to do he must have knowledge, not just knack, and an understanding of principles. His form of life must also exhibit some mastery of forms of thought and awareness which are not harnessed purely to utilitarian or vocational purposes or completely confined to one mode.

(iii) His knowledge and understanding must not be inert either in the sense that they make no difference to his general view of the world, his actions within it and reactions to it *or* in the sense that they involve no concern for the standards immanent in forms of thought and awareness, as well as the ability to attain them.

Now, regardless of the excesses and extravagances that tend to creep into such discourse, it is clear that we do have two different general senses of 'education' in common usage today. On the one hand there is that sense which is largely synonymous with socialisation (and this we shall refer to as education with a small 'e'); while on the other hand there is a sense which points specifically *beyond* socialisation, usually in the direction of full personal development with special emphasis being placed on cognitive or intellectual development – and it is this *general* sense (for we are hardly endorsing any of the specific statements quoted above) that we are gracing with the capital 'E'.

With the distinction now made we can re-state our central thesis thus: teachers in general educate in that they act as agents of socialisation, but they fail to Educate in the sense of going beyond socialisation to bring out and develop the full capabilities of their charges.

How much bite this thesis has, however, is dependent largely on what it is that teachers are called upon or looked upon as doing: and there can be little doubt that the general body of rhetoric concerning the aims, duties and functions of teachers points well beyond mere socialisation and, if not quite to the heights envisaged by Livingstone or Whitehead, then at least in much the same direction. Academic education texts, curricula preambles, graduation addresses, and teachers' journals continually represent the teacher as a figure leading (or striving to lead) children in the highest cultural, personal, and intellectual directions possible: and, while the function of socialisation often gets mention, it tends to be raised as a general and incidental process which teachers necessarily assist with, but which teachers qua teachers should proceed beyond. In fact it is often

this 'something extra' which is used to differentiate teachers
from all those other people who are influential in the formation
of children as social beings; and teachers themselves appear to have
been caught up in and by the rhetoric, for, as numerous studies
show, they perceive their work primarily in intellectual and moral
terms, and look on the task of general social training with comparative indifference.[7]

Teachers are charged (theoretically) with the task and responsibility of Educating – of going beyond socialisation – and this they
fail to do. But it remains to be seen now whether they could
possibly go beyond socialisation within the conditions placed upon
them.

SCHOOLING, EDUCATION AND *EDUCATION*

Teachers, or at least the teachers this book is concerned with,
work in schools. Now what goes on in schools is, at a basic
operational level of definition, schooling. In our ordinary, everyday language, however, we tend to refer to what goes on in
schools as education; so much so that the two terms tend to be
taken as synonymous or coextensive. We speak of going to school
to get an education; the level of people's education is commonly
measured by or equated with the number of years they have
attended school and the awards gained there; schools themselves
are generally categorised and described in terms of being part of
the education system; and schools of course come under the control and auspices of education departments, local education
authorities, and ministers of education. The school/education
nexus is an extremely strong one; so strong in fact that the
equivalence of 'schooling' and 'education' is largely taken for
granted.

When we consider conjunctions which have come to be taken for
granted, or as part of 'the way things are', we often find that
both the strength and the tenuousness of the nexus become more
clearly revealed by the effect brought about when the nexus is
deliberately broken. This is particularly so with regard to the
schooling/education nexus. George Bernard Shaw complained
that his education was interrupted by his schooling; and Margaret
Mead has noted that her grandmother wanted her to have a good
education and so kept her out of school. These statements emerge
as credible and startling. Their credibility lies in the fact that
they were made by people generally considered to be highly
Educated; they are startling because they turn on the paradox
that schooling is antagonistic to, rather than compatible with,
Education. The statements entail far more than a begrudging
notion which any of us might make about 'not getting much of an
education at school' – they point to a distinct incompatibility between the institution of schooling and the notion of Education;
an incompatibility so surprising on first contact that the actual
statements themselves have achieved the status of modern epi-

grams, and tend to appear regularly on desk calendars, as
epigraphs to books and articles, and among lists of 'quotable
quotes'.

Now there are really two points at issue here; points which
actually concern different sides of the same coin. First, there is
the problem of the very conflation of 'schooling' and 'education',
and turning with this is the issue of which particular sense of
'education' is being conflated with 'schooling'. Consider carefully the following two statements. The first is by Herbert Gintis,
and has been extracted from a broadly Marxist context: [8]

The function of education in any society is the socialisation of
youth into the prevailing culture. On the one hand, schooling
serves to integrate individuals into society by institutionalizing
dominant value, norm and belief systems. On the other hand,
schooling provides the individual competencies necessary for
the adequate performance of social roles. Thus education
systems are fundamental to the stability and functioning of any
society.

The second is by I.L. Kandel, a liberal conservative, commonly
charged with being an essentialist: [9]

The earliest and most persistent reason for the establishment
of schools as formal agencies of education is the desire on the
part of a group, society, or state to conserve and transmit its
cultural heritage to the younger generation and to equip this
generation with those habits, skills, knowledges and ideals that
will enable it to take its place in a society and contribute to
the stability and perpetuation of that society.

There are three things there deserving of particular note. First,
although they are speaking from quite different and opposed contexts, both Gintis and Kandel spell out the same message – that
the function of education is conservative, being directed towards
integrating new generations into the prevailing culture, and providing knowledge and skills geared towards ensuring social stability and perpetuation of the status quo. Second, both authors
use the words 'schooling' and 'education' interchangeably (and
in doing so they are anything but unusual or exceptional). Third,
it is abundantly clear that what they are really talking about is
socialisation: the point both authors are making is that schooling
is basically a socialising agency or institution.

Now I take it (without providing any argumentation at this
point) that Gintis and Kandel are perfectly correct in this regard.
Schools are agents of socialisation, and they always have been –
at least they have been ever since they became compulsory and
universal. Thus we find that the schooling/education nexus holds.
But where does Education come into the picture?

As far as our discourse is concerned it is largely smuggled in
through a sort of halo effect (of considerable ideological force)
arising out of our imprecise usage of a single word to refer to
two distinct processes – both of which relate to the development
of human beings, and more especially to development in the areas
of knowledge, values and skills, and thus to the daily practice

of schooling – but which relate in quite different ways. Schooling
has much to do with socialisation and the production of socialised
beings, but very little to do with Education or the production of
Educated people.[10]

It is, of course, one thing to make such assertions and quite
another thing to provide convincing arguments for them. Now one
way to provide support for the assertions would be to undertake
a detailed analysis of the schooling process in order to see
whether what goes on there is more ascribable to socialisation or
Education. This very common form of empirical analysis, however,
is fraught with problems. On the one hand, due consideration
would have to be given to everything that went on in schools.
We would have to be aware that things like how movement takes
place around the building, the existence of separate staff and
student toilets, the dynamics of decision making, and the different rituals of interpersonal relations (depending on who is relating with whom) are just as much a part of schooling as the teaching and learning that goes on in the classroom is. Virtually all
empirical studies of schooling have assumed the teaching-learning
aspect to be central, and not surprisingly have assisted in building up an image of schooling as a place primarily concerned with
those activities more closely related to the notion of Education.
What has been sadly lacking, however, is attention to what has
recently become known as the hidden curriculum of the school.
But even if it were possible to study every aspect of schooling
another huge problem then arises; that of interpretation. It is
very dangerous to take empirical data at face value: appearances
have to be interpreted and penetrated, and different observers
might see different things, interpret them in different ways, and
penetrate them to different degrees. What is seen by one observer
as a class learning its seven-times table might be seen by another
observer as a highly structured exercise in participating in a
complex social ritual centred around compliance with authority.
Again it is not surprising that empirical studies of this type tend
to reinforce the preconceptions of the investigators rather than
throw light on the object under investigation.[11]

A second means of supporting our assertions could be to
examine the products or graduates of schooling in order to determine whether they have been socialised or Educated; and given
that we have fairly tight criteria for determining each, this
should not be too much of a problem. We could attempt to see
whether schooled people are able merely to perform social roles
and have the habits, skills, knowledge, beliefs, ideals, values
and norms that will contribute to social stability, or whether
they measure up to (say) Nunn's fully developed people or the
Peters prototype of an Educated person. And if this proved too
much of a task we could at least tune in to expert commentary on
the matter, where, despite the occasional principals who get
carried away with their own perceived achievements on speech
nights, the general drift of informed educational commentary
tends to bemoan the fact that our schools are either not Educating

enough people or not Educating people well enough, or both. The
same R.S. Peters, for instance, openly laments the fact that the
majority do not care about the ideals embodied in the concept of
'Education' and pursue ways of life which are 'largely the outcome of habit, social pressure, sympathy and attraction towards
what is immediately pleasurable': [12] and in tandem with P.H.
Hirst he sets up the Educated person 'in stark contrast' to the
ideal and orientation towards consumption which, it is claimed,
has become the *'predominant feature* of Western society'.[13] It
would appear, then, that our schools are doing a pretty bad job
of Educating (and a pretty good job of socialising); and I for
one have yet to read the work which heaps all praise on their
current Educative effects.

This proposed study of school graduates, however, might not
take us as far as we wish; for it could easily be argued that the
poor success rate of schools in Educating is a result of contingent
factors (like lack of funds) and that, given the prevailing circumstances, schools are really doing an excellent job. The fact that
they seem to be producing socialised people rather than Educated
people means only that they are contingently agents of socialisation, and nothing has been said which seriously challenges the
view that their real purpose is one of Educating. In the face of
this objection a new tack must obviously be sought.

A third possibility for supporting our assertions lies in analys-
ing the function that schooling performs within the total dynamics
of reproduction of social relations. This is the tack we shall, in
fact, be taking, albeit at a much later stage in this work. But
two preliminary remarks have to be made here. First, it might
appear that the dice have already been loaded in that we are
going to work within a context of reproduction of social relations;
a context which appears to exclude development, change or
betterment. This, however, is not so. 'Reproduction of social
relations' refers to the continuance of the same basic form of a
society, wherein there could be marked historical transformations
occurring, and not to an endless repetition of the same daily ways
replayed by each succeeding generation. For the last (say) 200
years Britain, America, and the Boro Indians have each been
engaged in the reproduction of particular social relations, but
while things have hardly changed at the day-to-day level for
the Boro there has, of course, been demonstrable change and
development within the other two societies even while the basic
social relations have been constantly reproduced. Second, such
a tack requires setting down a categorisation of social relations,
and elaboration of a theory of the dynamics whereby these social
relations are reproduced. Again this will be filled out later; but
we can at least note here that we shall be categorising social
relations (or characterising the 'basic form' of a society not in
terms of governmental types (aristocracy, oligarchy, monarchy,
democracy) nor in terms of dominant types of production
(agrarian societies or industrial societies) but rather in terms
of modes of production (slavery, serfdom, capitalism, socialism);

and also that our following discussion will be concerned primarily
with the context of contemporary capitalism.

TEACHERS, EDUCATION AND *EDUCATION*

We asked earlier whether teachers could possibly go beyond
socialisation within the conditions placed upon them, and we have
now recognised two of those conditions as the context of schooling
and the context of capitalist social relations. Now schooling is a
process in which the directive agents are teachers, such that
certain claims made regarding the schooling process can also
generally apply to or be connected with teachers; and schooling
is also a process which (as we shall see later) is structured by
dominant social relations. We can therefore now amend our (un-
supported) claim regarding schooling having much to do with
socialisation but little to do with Education to read: 'Teachers,
under contemporary capitalist social relations, have much to do
with socialisation and very little to do with Education': which
gets us back, with a little more precision, to where we were
earlier. While the process of schooling can not (and will not) be
ignored, we must not lose sight of the fact that teachers are the
immediate agents of the process under consideration, and our
discussion must focus on and continually return to the work they
do and the function they perform.[14]

It should also be emphasised very strongly here that the
extremely negative claim we have made about teachers is not intended to constitute a personal indictment against them, especially
at the individual level, nor is it intended to slight the great
amount of effort many put into their day-to-day work – especially
that effort which is directed, even if circuitously – towards the
end of Educating. The claim that teachers fail to Educate does
not necessarily point to teacher-incompetence, and the argument
and analysis which follows has nothing to do with that. It may,
of course, be the case that some teachers are incompetent, lazy,
or merely serving time, but that is not our concern. What we
shall argue is that, even given the most able, enthusiastic and
idealistic teachers, teacher-failure-in-general is inevitable in
that it is brought about through the conditions placed upon
teachers or the structural circumstances within which they work.
Paradoxically, then, our analysis will actually serve to exonerate
teachers to a large extent from some of the more simplistic charges
of failure (and incompetence) which are commonly levelled against
them.

Teachers might not take kindly at first to the charge that they
are failing to Educate, but on the other hand they are also not
likely to deny it. Teachers, more than anybody, know that their
lot is not always a happy one, and that the job of educating can
be difficult and frustrating, and the job of Educating often near
to impossible. This is more the case in state or government schools
than in private schools, in lower-secondary forms rather than

upper-secondary forms of elementary schools, and in lower socio-
economic urban schools rather than upper socio-economic or rural
schools. Teachers who look at their work realistically do recognise the general failure to Educate: what we must consider now
are some of the ways by which this failure is commonly accounted
for (not only by teachers) and how the common accounts mystify
and obscure the real situation.

THE RESORT TO PRACTICAL, IMMEDIATE FACTORS

If your car were to break down in the middle of a trip it is unlikely that your first thoughts would be directed either to the
slackness of the quality control personnel in the Detroit factory
where the car was assembled twelve months ago, or to the wiles
of capitalist producers maximising profits by using sub-standard
materials. And even if your thoughts were so directed, it is unlikely that your first action would be to sit by the roadside and
either write to the Consumer Affairs Bureau or else begin to
plan out a strategy for social revolution. It is more likely the
case that you would lift the bonnet and look for the immediate
cause of the failure, or call for an expert automobile organisation
to find and rectify the immediate cause. And since rectifying the
immediate cause is, after all, the only way of getting the car
running again, then seeking the immediate cause is an eminently
sensible thing to do.
Given this, it would seem anything but unusual for teachers,
when difficulties and frustrations mount, and things aren't running well, to seek about for immediate causes and even to call in
experts to rectify the problems identified.
Potential immediate factors exist in abundance for teachers to
call on. Often the lecturers at universities and other teacher-
training institutions end up bearing the blame for teacher-failure
because they, ostensibly being 'naive', 'academic', 'idealist',
'out of touch', etc., failed to prepare the teachers adequately
for the realities of the classroom situation. Or the problem might
be located in the actual physical conditions of the school itself,
such as run-down depressing buildings, poor equipment, over-
crowded classes, lack of facilities, etc. Teachers have also been
known to turn upon themselves, seeing problems arising out of
the actions and policies of power figures like principals and de-
puties, or as being brought about (for example) by a large proportion of inexperienced teachers (or female teachers!) in a
particular school, or by the effects of 'soft', 'progressive', or
'weak' teachers within their ranks.
The pupils within the school are an obvious and common target,
and are frequently charged with not wanting to learn, or with
engaging in wilful destruction and resistance, overt disruption,
and open antagonism to any effort on the part of the teacher. On
the other hand, problems are often seen as arising from beyond
the school itself. It might be the general policies of the Depart-

ment of Education or the Local Authority which are held to blame,
or the irrelevant curricula which have been imposed on the school
and the teachers, or the attitudes of the pupils' parents, or
general aspects of the prevailing local culture or sub-culture:
teachers often bemoan the fact that they have neither the time
nor the influence to combat and counteract parental and/or
local cultural attitudes. And if all else fails, there is always the
resort to vaguely metaphysical factors presumably fermenting
somewhere beyond the school walls, like 'the collapse of modern
society', 'the breakdown of moral values', or 'the signs of our
times'.

Now it can hardly be denied that these 'immediate factors', or
at least the most serious of them (and the list is hardly exhaustive), really do exist and really do bring about problems, just as
faulty fuel pumps and corroded spark-plugs cause cars to break
down. There are, of course, incompetent, over-idealistic, and
out-of-touch university and teachers' college lecturers, just as
there are kids who are resistant and antagonistic to teachers'
efforts.[15] There are principals and administrators who are adept
at making their staff's job harder rather than easier; and one
does not have to travel far to find continued instances of schools
wherein the actual physical conditions constitute a hindrance and
a frustration for teachers. Imposed departmental policies, examination board requirements and board of studies curricula do not
always sit easily on specific schools; and in certain physical
areas the value system of the school and its teachers is in sharp
contrast to the dominant value system surrounding it, such that
teachers, in their relatively brief contact with the children, are
hardly able to have much of a counter-balancing effect. The
mistake, however, and it is a serious mistake, is to regard any
of these things, or any combination of them as strictly autonomous
or isolated issues: while they do, of course, have a measure of
relative autonomy, they cannot be understood or investigated
properly in isolation from the overall context of which they are a
part.

Before developing that most crucial of points, however, we
should recognise that teachers, like our motorist, expend a great
deal of effort in trying to rectify immediate problems; and again
like our motorist (although usually more indirectly) they often
call in experts to study and rectify those problems. Since teaching does not have a well-developed internal feedback system, this
latter action provides employment for professional educational
psychologists, sociologists, and technicians, among others; and
not only does this contribute to an overall lack of control within
teaching itself, but it also tends to set up a cyclic, self-fulfilling,
and self-perpetuating context for identifying the problems that
need to be overcome. The factors, as identified, tend to be
immediate, practical, and overt; and it is on these matters that
research and study tends to be concentrated. Thus, during this
century educational research has trained its efforts on the
psychology of the child, the methodology of teacher training,

classroom procedures and interaction, teaching styles, testing and evaluation of teaching and learning, the production of teaching aids and equipment, social-class values, and so on. The cycle becomes a vicious one in that a large proportion of available time, money, and effort tends to be directed at investigating and curing clearly identified 'ills' within a given context such that those 'ills' gain further prominence as the things which have to be overcome, while the context itself tends to be accepted without serious question. Further to this, the 'ills' remain as the focus for further investigation when future problems arise. As a very elementary example, consider the vast amount of research (virtually constituting an industry) that has been done over the past fifty years and is still being done, on intelligence testing or classroom interaction analyses (even if with the intention of assisting the Education of children) compared with the paucity of research directed at the very functioning of compulsory schooling under capitalism. To take the analogy of the car a little further, the trends have been to repair faulty fuel pumps (and train others to repair them) without questioning why fuel pumps tend to be faulty; and to develop more efficient fuel pumps without questioning either the 'place' of the fuel pump as a subsystem of the internal combustion engine or, at a much broader level, the very place of the automobile within a specific set of social relations. The process has, in general, been one of focusing on relatively autonomous parts, or sub-systems, rather than developing scientific theories of the contexts in which those sub-systems or parts are instrumental pieces.

The strategy to be adopted in this book will be that of attempting to develop an overall theory to explain and account for teacher-failure within capitalist social relations; but we can, at this stage, quickly demonstrate that the immediate factors previously pointed to regarding failure to Educate could hardly be regarded seriously as isolated or autonomous ones. Let us proceed on two fronts.

First, if we assume that the immediate factors identified above are the actual fundamental causes of teacher failure, it would then follow that, in overcoming or curing them we would overcome or solve the general problem. Put concretely, if we staff teacher-training institutions properly, motivate children adequately, employ relevant curricula, equip schools better, reduce class sizes, and so on, then teachers would succeed in Educating children. This, however, would leave us with a different and far greater problem on our hands: how could we possibly integrate whole new generations of Educated people into a system of social relations which requires the vast majority of its participants not only to spend the greater portion of their lives engaging in alienating, routine, dull, mindless and meaningless labour (or, given present circumstances, no labour at all) but also to accept the lack of social privilege presently attendant on performers of such labour (or on the unemployed)? How could we induce these Educated people to sweep the streets, work on production lines,

and operate the check-outs at supermarkets let alone clean floors
and toilets in office blocks, especially while these jobs are given
low social status and relatively low financial remuneration? Put
simply, our existing system of social relations could not handle
new generations of universally Educated people: and if we were
to overcome all the immediate problems we would also have to
restructure our entire social system as well. Or, conversely,
only through major radical social restructuring in the first place
would we be in a position seriously to attack those immediate
problems which are now clearly manifested.

Second - and again assuming that the factors identified are the
actual fundamental factors underlying teacher-failure - we might
ask why, having identified them, and why, given the continually
outspoken concern for Education, they are not being overcome?
The answer, at its simplest level, is that they cannot be overcome independently and in isolation from much larger issues.
Cleaning up the teacher-training problem requires far more than
swapping one set of lecturers for another; it raises fundamental
questions (and practical issues) regarding why certain types of
people are employed in the first place whereas others are not.
Equipping schools better and reducing class sizes requires a vast
redistribution of money by ruling authorities: why are they re-
luctant to make such a redistribution, and why in the face of the
problems identified is spending on education generally being
slashed at present? Eliminating or reducing the bad effects of
departments, local authorities, boards of studies, and principals
requires in effect vast changes in social relations, not just a
little bit of internal reorganisation. And getting children to
cooperate with, rather than be antagonistic to, their teachers'
endeavours requires far more than clever motivation steps, good
learning and teaching theory, and the establishment of warm
classroom climates: this, too, would require vast changes in
overall social relations - not the least of which would be the
creation of conditions whereby schooling really did overcome the
differential social privileges which now accompany children at
birth and tend to remain with them right throughout their lives.

What is being suggested, then, is that there is far more to the
problem than simply identifying and overcoming immediate
'isolated' factors. On the one hand these immediate factors cannot
simply be overcome: rather than being discrete isolated factors
they are intricately tied up with much larger and far more basic
issues; they cannot be attended to in isolation, and any serious
attention to them must have ramifications reaching right into the
very core of our basic social (and economic) relations. On the
other hand, if we were somehow able to solve all the immediate
problems (without affecting basic social relations) we would be
likely to be more than embarrassed by the large number of
Educated people around who would not have the opportunity to
live and function in harmony with their Educated nature. And
being Educated, that is one thing they would quickly become
aware of. They could thus represent a threat to social stability.[16]

One final point. A commonly proposed factor for the failure to Educate universally is that a significant proportion of any population is simply too dumb to be Educated in the first place. Now it is not being denied that there are rare cases of biological malformation which seriously impair the ability of some people to learn and develop; and in this case such people might be described as being inEducable. But the similarly undeniable facts that some children learn some things more slowly than other children at certain times in their lives, that some are less motivated than others to learn certain things at certain times or in certain places like schools, and that some perform lower than others on 'general ability' tests administered at specific times – which are the grounds on which most of the 'dumb' are so declared – in no way tell against the Educability of such people. This being the case, the proposition (which represents structural features as personal faults) will not be entertained further here, for the mere act of paying continued attention to it could bestow it with more dignity and credibility than it is worth.

THE PROBLEM OF 'INDIVIDUALISTIC LOGIC'

It was noted in the previous section that the immediate factors we were concerned with could not be attended to in isolation. From certain perspectives however, it often appears as though they could be. Teachers in a run down, poorly equipped school, could reasonably expect that a few hundred thousand dollars directed their way from the newly announced multi-million dollar education budget would not only solve at least some of their problems, but also that this action would be sufficiently isolated so as not to have large-scale, far-reaching ramifications. The grant would be a great benefit to them, without having serious effects elsewhere.

Now this is to a certain extent correct. It is also an application of what I shall be calling 'individualistic logic'; that is, a form of thinking and arguing which focuses on the individual instance in isolation from, and without proper consideration of, the influence and effects which the larger overall context imposes upon the particular instance in question. The purpose of this section is to indicate how 'individualistic logic' can lead us into mistaken theories and conclusions, and thus erroneous conceptions regarding teacher-success in Educating.

The expectations of the teachers in the above example are, as has been suggested, reasonable. They become less reasonable, however, when made simultaneously by 20,000 schools, or when it is realised that half of the budget has been set aside for teachers' salaries, a further third for new building projects, and a fixed amount for curriculum development. What has to be recognised here is that, although any one school might be allocated, say, half a million dollars, not every school can be allocated half a million dollars; and that allocations in one area interfere with allocations in other areas even to the point of possible elimination of some allocations. This recognition opens up to us the two major problems of 'individualistic logic'; the 'anyone can, therefore everyone can' fallacy, and the 'interference-elimination principle'. Each of these requires detailed discussion, and this especially so when we realise that, despite failure in general, some teachers (if not all teachers) are, to a greater or lesser extent, instrumental in Educating some pupils.

(a)   *The 'anyone can, therefore everyone can' fallacy*
There is a basic rule in logic which indicates that if every A is B then any A is B. If it were the case that every person had red hair, then it would necessarily follow that any person we bumped into would have to have red hair. The reverse, however, does not hold: if any A is B it need not follow that every A is B. If any person has red hair we cannot deduce from this that every person has red hair. Now this is a law which seems to be well understood and, in most cases, properly applied. People don't go round claiming that if anybody is rich then everybody is rich, or that if anybody is a lawyer then everybody is a lawyer.

They do, however, go round making extremely similar claims; such as 'if anybody can become rich then everybody can become rich', or 'if anybody can become a lawyer then everybody can become a lawyer'. The difference, of course, is that these claims point to what can be rather than what is, and are thus much more tentative and conditional, but they are instances of the very same fallacy. In these instances the issue is compounded, however, by an ambiguity in 'every', and also by the introduction of empirical considerations, and thus the matter needs to be explored a little further.

'Every' is ambiguous between its disjunctive sense, referring to each instance taken separately (in this case being equivalent to 'any'), and its conjunctive sense referring to all instances taken together. Now the statement 'if any A can be B then every A can be B' can only be true in general if 'every' is used disjunctively, in which case the statement is only trivially true or tautologous. However, if 'every' is used conjunctively, then the statement 'if any A can be B then every A can be B' is false in general, and it can only be true in particular if it is empirically possible for every A, taken together, to be predicated with B. For instance, the statement 'if any man can dye his hair red then every man can dye his hair red' could only be true if all men were capable of dying their hair (which would be very difficult for those in comas, totally paralysed, or bald) and if there were sufficient red dye in the world to go round. Similarly the statement 'if any person can become President of the United States every person can' could be true only if it were possible for everyone simultaneously to be President, or if the Presidency carried a term sufficiently short enough to give everybody a go, and since these options are not on, then the statement is either tautologous or false, just as the statement 'if anybody can become a lawyer then every-

body can become a lawyer' is also either tautologous or false outside of societies where everybody practises law.

The committing of this particular fallacy is not always expressed
in the classical 'if any, then every' form, which often makes it
both harder to detect but easier to pin down. It has been commonly suggested that if Abraham Lincoln could go from log cabin
to White House then everyone can, or if a grocer's daughter can
become Prime Minister of Britain then everyone can. Here we
have two shining examples of the fallacy in operation, purporting
conclusions which are clearly false and which, because of their
specificity, cannot even be excused as tautologies. Similar
examples are the claims that, 'If, given my background, I could
become a doctor, everybody can'; and 'Since I (or some teachers)
can succeed in Educating pupils, every teacher can.' These
fallacious arguments (or examples of 'individualistic logic') impute
to everybody, as discrete individuals themselves, things which
not all of those discrete individuals could achieve when put together in the same situation. All subjects and all instances are
individualised out of the context in which they occur or act, and
thus the real situation is badly misrepresented. This will become
even more evident in the following sub-section.

(b)   *The 'interference-elimination' principle*
The 'interference-elimination' principle has already been touched
on when we considered the issue of the empirical possibility of
every person, taken together, being able to be predicated with
the same outcome. Let us approach it this time, however, through
detailed consideration of a further practical example.

It could be argued, and often is argued, that people living in
a capitalist society are not mere victims of the system. After all,
no one these days is forced at gun-point to sell his or her labour
power to the capitalists; and anyone (it might be suggested) can
go on the dole, or join a rural commune, or go in for subsistence
farming, or start a small business.

This much is, of course, correct - up to a point; but as we
have seen in our previous section it could and probably would
be fallacious to infer from this that everyone can go on the dole
or become self-employed, and so on. What has to be recognised
now, however, is that while any individual person might adopt
one of these alternatives, very few people taken together can
adopt any one of them. This is simply because each individual
who adopts one of the alternatives interferes with everybody
else's opportunity to do the same and eventually when a certain
point is reached they eliminate the possibility of anyone else following suit.

For instance, it was once possible for an individual to withdraw
labour, claim that a suitable job was not available in a particular
area, and then draw unemployment benefits. But in doing so that
individual (unwittingly?) made it harder for the next person to
succeed with the same action, and the more who did succeed the
harder and harder it became for those next in line. As the num-

bers built up the regulations were changed, and eventually willingness to take any job offered anywhere became a condition for
getting the dole. Then, with the growth of structural unemployment, and the build-up of dole applicants for other reasons, the
regulations were once again tightened up – married women were
excluded from eligibility, de facto relationships became recognised
as marriages, people had to produce stronger evidence that they
were attempting to find employment, and finally indicate their
willingness to enter retraining programmes.[17] Paradoxically as
unemployment increased the dole became harder to get, such that
each successful candidate actually made it harder for the next
person to succeed, and the situation has now been reached where
people are being refused the dole basically because too many
others are receiving it (although that, of course, is not the
reason actually given).

An even better example is afforded by the idea of going off and
working for yourself or starting your own business. Undoubtedly
some people have done this, and are still continuing to do this.
But capitalist social relations require both a large work-force selling labour power to a small number of capitalists, and the accumulation of capital in fewer and fewer hands. There is thus a distinct limit to the number who can be self-employed; and it is a
reductio ad absurdum to envisage the continued proliferation of
small businesses, for a stage would have to be reached where
there would be no employees about to staff them. Clearly everyone cannot start up a small business; in fact few can, and each
one who is successful interferes with, and eventually eliminates,
the possibility of the next person doing so. Much the same
applies to the establishment of rural communes; and we have seen
recently as they have tended to proliferate and succeed that they
have also been faced with changing restrictive legislation, escalat-
ing rates and land prices, increased harassment, and so on; such
that those who originally 'showed the way' could in fact be seen
as having made it harder for others to follow.[18]

We see then, from these and preceding examples, that there are
situations wherein the notion that 'anyone can, therefore everyone can' simply does not hold at a practical level because the success of one or some interferes with and virtually ensures the
failure of others. Such situations exist where there are pragmatic
restrictions placed on the number who can benefit, and they are
clearly obvious in instances of things like races where there can
only be one winner, or allocations of funds when, at a certain
point the kitty must run dry. They are less obvious but just as
insistent, however, within the context of social relations where,
in order to maintain a particular form of social relations, there
has to be say, a limit on the number of unemployed or the self-
employed or the number of doctors or professors who can be
accommodated comfortably. And in such situations to claim that
anyone can become self-employed or reach professorial status, to
'strengthen' the claim by citing a number of individuals who have
succeeded, and then to generalise to the conclusion that every-

one could do the same, is to commit both a logical and a practical error. It is also, as previously suggested, to mystify and misrepresent the situation. To note all the individuals who, in varying ways, have succeeded in withdrawing their labour from capitalists in no way invalidates the fact that under capitalism the vast majority of people are forced to sell their labour power to capitalists in order to survive. To note all the individuals who have risen from adverse circumstances to high professional positions in no way invalidates the fact that, given a certain set of social relations, very few will ever be able to rise from adverse circumstances.

Such applications of 'individualistic logic' abstract the individual from the overall context of which he or she is part. In doing so they often result in the production of logically invalid conclusions and implications; but more importantly they fail to account for the interactive effects among individuals within social relations or the effects imposed on individuals by social relations, and thus result in the production of theoretically misconceived and empirically false conclusions. And they have one other important mystifying and misrepresentative effect as well – they attribute blame to the individual in situations where barriers to success are actually structural parts of the context in which the individual exists and seeks success. If, for instance it is claimed that 'anybody can find a job therefore everybody can find a job', and examples are then provided of certain individuals finding jobs, it becomes relatively simple to lay the blame for unemployment at the feet of the unemployed, maintaining that it is their fault that they do not have jobs, whereas in fact there may not be enough jobs available to employ everyone. In much the same way individuals come to bear the blame for not becoming rich in situations where available wealth is limited, or for not 'getting on' in social situations which place structural restrictions on the number who can 'get on'.

In concluding this section we can look briefly at how 'individualistic logic' can be applied to teachers with regard to their role as Educators. Given, as we have noted, that some teachers are instrumental in the Education of some pupils, it could be suggested that all teachers could Educate all pupils; and from within the ranks of teaching it would not be unusual to find a teacher claiming that if only others had the same dedication and expended the same effort they too could be successful.

Now Education (and schooling) are not practices or processes undertaken by isolated individuals in atomised contexts. Just as individual labour is undertaken in cooperation with other individual labour within the context of a mode of production, and cannot be understood or analysed properly, either in nature or form, without reference to that context, so too does Education take place in a 'cooperative' system within the context of a mode of production, and similarly cannot be analysed adequately in isolation from that context. Since the particular context we are concerned with here is that of contemporary capitalism the question which is really before us is not whether it is possible to Educate all (or even most) children in vacuo, but rather whether it is possible to Educate all (or most, or many) children within the context of contemporary capitalist social relations. It is necessary, therefore, that we give some consideration at this stage to certain aspects of social relations under capitalism which bear on the issue of Education. It must be noted, however that what follows is a sketch of surface factors and not an analysis of the dynamics of social relations.

CAPITALISM, EDUCATION AND THE 'INTERFERENCE-ELIMINATION' PRINCIPLE

A capitalist society can be characterised, very roughly, as being comprised of four layers. At the bottom, or base, is a labour force performing menial and largely unskilled work in return for weekly wages - here we find the factory workers, miners, production-line workers, shop assistants, members of the typing pool, bus conductors and so on. This labour force is economically exploited, oppressed, and relatively underprivileged; it is also politically and ideologically oppressed to the extent that the majority either fail to recognise the real nature of their situation or else more or less willingly accept the broad defining features of the status quo as being immutable and not subject to change through their own agency.

Above this group is a second very large group performing servicing and managerial functions, some in return for weekly wages and some as salaried labourers.[19] The work of this group tends to be more skilled, and is usually mental rather than manual. Included here are public servants, employees in banks and insurance offices, accountants, teachers, private secretaries, and low-level managers. This group is also economically exploited and oppressed, but has economic privilege over the former group, usually justified in terms of reward for attaining and making use of relatively expert and esoteric knowledge; and it bears (as well as being the object of) ideological representations which tend to distinguish it and elevate it from the former group in spite of the large number of commonly shared characteristics that exist.

Next comes a relatively small group of experts in complex, specialised fields. Here we find the doctors, lawyers, academics, economists, architects, engineers and computer programmers; some of whom work for fixed salaries but many of whom determine their own fees and income. This group is economically privileged and bestowed with high social status, and the justification for that privilege and status is once more usually given in terms of reward for attaining and making use of expert and esoteric knowledge.

Finally we have the capitalists themselves - a very small class characterised by its ownership and/or control of the means of production.

Now there are two things to note especially about the non-capitalist groups. First, they are hierarchical groups in terms of status, income, and formal (school type) knowledge. The 'top' group has higher status, earns more money and is deemed to have or require more expert knowledge (of the type provided by schooling) than the 'middle' group which in turn has higher status, earns more money, and is deemed to have or require more expert school-type and school-provided knowledge than the 'bottom' group.

Second, their membership is, in a very large sense, proportional. This is not meant to imply that the proportions remain static (the second group, for instance, has grown enormously over the last century), only that a sense of proportion must remain. There must, for example, be far more workers in factories than there are owners/controllers (and the number of workers will determine the number of overseers required) just as there have to be far more people building bridges, roads and cars than there are designing them. What this means is that, regardless of people's abilities or desires, the 'top' group must be kept proportionately small - which it is by means of continuous selection devices and quotas - such that many who have the capability to enter it (see below, pp. 104-10) are selected out and confined to lower places. The entry of any person to this privileged group is thus achieved at the deliberate exclusion of a large number of similarly capable others: things are so structured that there really is no room at the top - a 'top' which is reached formally by the acquisition of expert knowledge in schooling-type institutions and from which social status and economic privilege then flow.

Now if any mode of production (which includes social and productive relations) is to be maintained and reproduced this requires at least that each new generation be initiated into the prevailing culture, integrated into the dominant value, norm and belief systems, and formed so as to contribute to the stability and perpetuation of the mode of production in question. And this is precisely what (using Gintis and Kandel) we identified earlier as the function of schooling. This is not to say that schooling is the only place wherein this reproduction takes place, or that such reproduction is the only function of schooling. It certainly is, however, one function of schooling; and we are left with the question of where Education fits in with schooling under capitalism.

Schooling under capitalism is successful in its reproductive aspect only if the vast majority of the population which passes through it (that is, the entire population, given compulsory schooling) ends up in the two major groups identified above, which together, although in changing proportions, have always encompassed at least 80 per cent of the work-force under capitalism. In this way schools undertake what is euphemistically referred to as their selection function. But among the basic characteristics of people in these groups is their general acceptance of and compliance with the 'need' to spend the major part of their lives doing menial or boring work, their acceptance of the prevailing social relations which they themselves perpetuate (which includes acceptance of their own social oppression and exploitation), their acceptance of their own economic exploitation and oppression, and their acceptance of the selection devices and mechanisms which have placed them where they are. Basically, people in these groups accept things as they are (or better, as they are ideologically represented) and perpetuate the existing order of things largely unquestioningly as if that order were given, right and immutable; with the majority of them earning their living undertaking jobs which they recognise variously as alienating, dirty, menial, or boring – subordinating their labour to demands which have little if any correspondence to their special talents or the fulfilment of their inner needs.[20] Significantly absent are visions of greatness, the drive for cultural improvement, people who have been led as deep as philosophy and as high as art, manifestations of the achievement of the highest degree of individual development possible or the leading out of the true fulness of each person's nature, serious extended development of intellectual and critical powers, and most of the features which mark out the Peters prototype of the Educated person. The characteristics which do exist and mark out this group are in fact quite opposed to those which, according to liberal theorists, mark out Educated people – so much so that we can say that schools, in selecting these people, are socialising them to fit a certain set of social relations, but they are hardly Educating them!

Educated people are a threat to any oppressive or repressive social system, and no such system would deliberately or consciously subsidise its own demolition by producing an abundance of potentially subversive people. A small number can be tolerated, assimilated, and even put to very good use, and any society which espouses liberal-democratic ideals is committed at least to the appearance of producing some Educated people; but if the liberal-democratic facade is only a mask covering an exploiting and oppressive society, then the number has to be strictly limited.

None of this is meant to suggest, however, that Education is reserved for the people in the third, specialist category; or that we are gracing them with the title of being Educated. Our point is a strictly negative one; namely that under capitalism (or any repressive or exploitative system) Education is kept from rather than provided for the vast proportion of the population.

We see, therefore, that on two counts it is just not on to seriously contemplate the Education of all children, most children, or even many children, within the context of capitalist social relations. On the one hand, even if we were to accept an equation between the small specialist group and Educated people we would find the 'interference-elimination' principle in operation, such that the Education of some would have to be achieved at the expense of the non-Education of many. On the other hand, regardless of whether we accept this equation or not, it becomes obvious that Educated people are potentially subversive under capitalism, and that the production of too many of them could interfere with and possibly even eliminate capitalist social relations themselves. What capitalism requires for its continued reproduction is a series of well-socialised, new generations, or a continued production of well-schooled people. This much it has provided for, and it is of more than passing interest to consider why this much alone is generally spoken of and referred to as 'education'.

TEACHER ADAPTATIONS

If it is the case that, under capitalism, only a small proportion of each generation can become Educated, where does this leave our teachers?

Generally they are left in an invidious position: invidious because it is contradictory, and contradictory because it is destined for failure at the level of ideals and geared towards success at a level which few teachers would consciously aspire to or be totally satisfied by.

Schooling is basically a socialising agency, not an Educative one; and capitalist liberal democracies cannot afford to Educate very many people. The unkindest cut of all, however, is that a society espousing liberal ideals could not admit openly to those points, and so they are covered over – in fact inverted – by means of ideology. People are led to believe that schools, while having a socialising function, are for Education (even though there might be practical immediate problems mitigating against this, like lack of funds), and that the aim within a liberal democracy is to Educate as many people as possible. Thus R. S. Peters:[21]

> Most schools which are concerned with education have also to act as agencies for selection and training for careers. Such schools, under modern conditions, have taken over many functions of the home. . . . These *subsidiary tasks* of the school should not be lost sight of, though few would dispute that *its essence should be education.*

and:

> though *education is the essence of a school*, schools must also fulfil functions of a more instrumental nature . . . they must have regard to the needs of the community for citizens who are trained in specific ways.

Teachers, as suggested earlier, are charged by the educational theorists (including their lecturers) and by prevailing ideology in general with the noble ideal of Educating (it is actually an aristocratic ideal which sits as an uneasy contradiction within ostensibly egalitarian social formations); while at the same time they are placed in institutions invested with the central social

purpose of moulding new generations to fit an existing social
order, which under capitalism means denying Education to the
vast majority of the people. The invidiousness of this position
was extremely well grasped almost seventy years ago, when compulsory schooling was in its infancy, by D.H. Lawrence (who
failed to find a publisher for these words):[22]
> Jimmy Shepherd, aged twelve, and Nancy Shepherd, aged thir-
> teen, know very well that the eternal flame of the high ideal
> is all my-eye. It's all toffee, my dear sirs. . . She's got her
> thirteen-year-old eye on a laundry, and he's got his twelve-
> year-old eye on a bottle-factory. Headmaster and headmistress
> and all the teachers know perfectly well that the high goal of
> all *their* endeavours is the laundry and the bottle-factory. . . .
> The high idealists up in Whitehall may preserve some illu-
> sions around themselves. But there is absolutely no illusion
> for the elementary school-teachers. They know what the end
> will be. . . .
> The elementary school-teacher is in a vile and false position.
> Set up as a representative of an ideal which is all toffee. . .
> [h]e is caught between the upper and nether millstones of
> idealism and materialism. . . .
> The elementary school is where the two meet, like millstones.
> And teachers and scholars are ground between the two.

The adaptations which teachers make to this situation (usually
after a short period of teaching wherein the reality of their
experience is seen not to coincide with the ideals put forward by
lecturers, administrators and theorists, or with the ideals they
first carried forth and probably still treasure as ideals) generally
lead to one of two basic courses of action.

The first of these entails, to a large part, a playing down of
Educative ideals and the role of Educator; and this is often
accompanied by disillusionment and a negative attitude towards
teaching itself. Education might be pursued if and when possibilities present themselves, but the primary role of the school as
socialiser is recognised and accepted (even if with indifference
and joylessness) as is the idea of the relative ineffectualness of
the teacher to do much about the condition of Jimmy and Nancy
Shepherd. Teachers who make this adaptation often come to consider themselves as little more than integral parts of a system
which they can do virtually nothing about except serve, especially
if they want to retain their jobs. They tend to hold few practical
hopes about Educating; and survival, for them and their pupils,
becomes the name of the game. At the worst their careers are
measured out in years, the years in terms, the terms in weeks,
and the weeks in lessons put over and got through. This is not
to suggest, however, that such teachers necessarily turn into
inhuman agents, mechanically working away. Many, having penetrated the illusions of their context, perform admirable work in
mitigating some of the worst effects of schooling for their pupils,
doing what they can to make the socialising process as pleasant,
warm and human as it might be.

The second common adaptation is to cling to the ideal of Education, to seek success wherever it might come, and to use instances of success to substantiate the notions that Education as an ideal is on, and that Education as a practical outcome is possible. Teachers making this adaptation tend to become supremely individualistic in outlook. They work out criteria for measuring Education within the ambit of intellectual and moral parameters (exam results serve well here), they count up their successes, and they measure their personal effectiveness in terms of the number of their successes (often in proportion to the particular contingent factors militating against them). Their careers are measured in terms of the number of children they have Educated, and 'Educated' is often defined according to rather mundane criteria like getting third-graders through the third grade syllabus, teaching children basic literacy and/or numeracy, or the number of passes achieved in a particular exam. A teacher who has made this adaptation is very likely to apply 'individualistic logic' ('If I can Educate then every teacher can') and also to look very heavily to immediate practical causes (especially the presence of dumb and/or uncooperative kids 'whom you can't do much with') when Education fails to eventuate. The immediate result of this is self-exoneration from criticism or blame. Those common criticisms levelled at schooling and teachers in general are not regarded as applying personally, and any perceived personal failures are accounted for by referral to immediate contingent factors. This then often leads, in a circular fashion, to a defence of schooling in general as being Educative (or at the worst, potentially Educative) based solely on the fact that personally defined individual instances of success have been achieved. General social training can then be safely looked on with indifference while being practised under another name.

Now it should be obvious that both of these adaptations have very serious reactionary consequences, especially as far as Education is concerned. The first accepts the socialising aspect of schooling and at best tries to make the experience a little more pleasant and humane. The second assists in building ideological defences of aspects of schooling which do not really exist, while in its own way it too simply reinforces the socialisation process. In their separate ways each positively assists the socialisation of new generations into existing social relations or the reproduction of social relations under capitalism.

CONCLUSION

While it is quite likely that some teachers are attempting to undertake subversive roles in schools (and there are certainly many who declare that they would like to if such a thing were possible) most teachers operate within the framework of the general adaptations which we have just outlined, and thus basically undertake a socialising function. Problems of dissonance might lead to

differently rationalised expressions or perceptions of what is
being done or achieved, and given that teachers themselves are
successful products of schooling, it is highly likely that many
of them will see no basic faults or problems in what they are
doing. For instance, teachers commonly justify their actions in
terms of the need to prepare their charges for 'the real world
out there' rather than pursue ideals (regardless of whether these
ideals are revolutionary or not). But the question that really
confronts us at this stage is whether teachers could possibly do
anything fundamentally different from that which they are already
doing - namely assisting in the reproduction of social relations
under capitalism.

Now it might be suggested here that the adaptations we have
considered so far are hardly exhaustive, and even if the previous
sketch of capitalist social relations is accurate there is still a
third adaptation open to teachers - that of doing their level best
to Educate despite 'the system'. There is, after all, a world of
difference between teachers producing Educated people and the
ability of prevailing social relations to accommodate such people,
just as there is a similar difference between positing the requirements of social relations as calling for teacher-failure and positing
those same requirements as the cause of failure. On grounds such
as these the objection could be raised that identifying the need
for well-schooled but un-Educated people within capitalist social
relations does not, in itself, explain why teachers fail to Educate.

Such an objection is well-founded. Teachers are not the pathe-
tic passive victims of a 'system' which forces them openly to come
up with set proportions of socialised and Educated people, and
they could hardly be castigated if they were highly successful in
Educating. On the other hand, however, the adaptation suggested
above is not open to teachers. They can't just go ahead and Educate despite 'the system'. The basis of their failure, as we shall
show in our following chapters, lies not simply in a mechanistic
response to particular social relations but rather in the way that
the technical job of teaching has been structured within a set of
social relations, such that the very performance of the technical
job itself entails entering into, participating in, and perpetuating
situations, processes, and relations which themselves are anti-
thetical to Educating.

In order to demonstrate this adequately we must do at least
three things. First, we have to provide a detailed analysis of
capitalist social relations (in contrast to the sketch given above)
and the means by which they are reproduced. Second, we need a
detailed analysis of the function that schooling performs within
the total dynamics of the reproduction of social relations. And
third, we must focus very serious attention on the function of
teachers within the whole reproductive process. This last matter
stands in need of some explanation at this point.

Teaching is a form of work - a job. It is a job which has many
times been put under a microscope, analysed and dissected, such
that today we have a wealth of information about things like the

number and types of questions teachers ask, the forms of interaction they use, the types of explicit and implicit cues they put
out towards children, and which narrative techniques have been
found to be effective in particular situations. The job of teaching
has also been subjected to role-theory analysis, which has provided us with a similar wealth of information about the interpersonal roles teachers play, or are perceived as playing, as part
of the performance of their job. But what has rarely been recognised is that teachers (or anyone) are never in the position of
only doing a technical job: to perform a job is at the same time to
undertake an activity which has social significance or a social
function – not in the sense commonly ascribed to people like
teachers or social workers (as when we referred to teachers performing a socialising function) – but a social function which has
specific reference to production relations. This particular aspect
of the job of teaching, which has otherwise been treated with
near-to-universal neglect in previous research concerning
teachers, shall be the focus of this present study.

The analysis which follows will have less to do with exploring
capitalist social relations than perhaps it might, for that area has
already been well charted and needs only a summary here. The
major areas of concentration will be the role of schooling in the
reproduction of social relations, and the social function of
teachers with reference to overall production relations. The result of this will be that while we shall gain no insights into how
reading can be better taught or whether open classrooms are
more effective than traditional ones, we shall end up with a
detailed understanding of where it is that teachers stand, and
what it is that they actually do, within the total dynamic of a
social system. Such an understanding will also serve to reveal
where their actual objective interests lie, and what future actions
can reasonably be expected of them.

Chapter 2
Classes and class struggle

INTRODUCTION

All investigations and analyses are made from the perspective of some particular theory or theories: they are theory-dependent or theory-laden, and this is so regardless of whether or not the underlying theory is declared, admitted to, or spelt out. There can be no such thing as a neutral examination, or an examination which is objective either in the sense that it is a-theoretic or else sufficiently eclectic so as to encompass all theoretical perspectives.[1]

The theory-ladenness of investigation gives rise to a large number of methodological issues and problems, and it is hardly our purpose to discuss these here. On the other hand, it is our purpose to undertake an investigation, and this we shall do by following the broad features of a methodological device outlined by Imre Lakatos; that is, by casting our investigation into the context of a research programme (or problematic) wherein certain basic or 'hard core' hypotheses and propositions are accepted as being secure and inviolable for the purpose of operating or working with the research programme.[2] Under this schema, an astronomer investigating planetary motion would adopt a research programme, say Newtonian physics, and while working within this programme would necessarily, deliberately and unquestioningly accept the 'hard core' propositions of Newtonian physics (or the Newtonian problematic) as a working basis. Similarly, a psychologist studying aggression in middle-aged people from a psychoanalytic perspective or research programme would accept and work with aspects of the Freudian problematic such as defence mechanisms, object relations, and the id-ego-superego categorisation of the human psyche. Now this unquestioned acceptance of 'hard core' propositions does not, of course, mean that these propositions are necessarily correct or that they express 'necessary truths': what it provides is nothing more than a methodological device for allowing investigations to get under way untrammelled by many of the problems brought about by theory-ladenness (although we might hope that investigators would have good reasons for beginning with one set of propositions rather than another).

The investigation which follows here is carried out within the framework of Marxism or historical materialism, and thus certain 'hard core' propositions of that theory or research programme, propositions regarding the nature of the State,[3] the nature of

classes, and the role of class struggle, for example, will form
the basis for our investigation: that is, they themselves will not
be argued for here (they are being accepted as viable starting
points because a wealth of previous argument, along with practical outcomes, has established their value for investigations of
social relations). But whereas (given our approach) they do not
have to be argued for here, they do at least need to be introduced, explained, and where necessary contrasted with other
approaches to similar issues.

The purpose of this chapter, then, is to outline the Marxist
concept of 'class' and to distinguish it from the more common
bourgeois concept (with special consideration being given to the
social-class 'placement' of teachers); and to indicate the place of
class struggle in the process of historical transformation.

TEACHERS AND SOCIAL CLASS:
THE 'ORTHODOX' PROBLEMATIC

Over the past few decades there have been a large number of
studies undertaken regarding the social-class status of schoolteachers, most of which have been situated within the context of
an 'orthodox' empiricist sociological framework concerned mainly
with socio-economic definitions of 'class'. Within such a framework
classes are defined basically, although not totally, in terms of
relative income within a social formation; and social formations
are characterised, at least in one dimension, in terms of the co-
existence of groups of different economic privilege. Commonly
we find reference to the upper class (the richest group), the
middle class, and the lower class (the poorest group): the lower
class is also often referred to as the working class, and while
this might be intended as a euphemism it tends to have a sharp
cutting truth about it. At a higher level of sophistication this
trichotomy tends to be stretched out and we find talk of and
reference to not simply one middle class but rather an upper-
middle, a (middle?) middle, and a lower-middle class: there has
also been a tendency to recognise an upper echelon of the working class - a sort of upper-lower class.

Studies undertaken within this particular type of framework
have tended to focus on two issues; the social-class origins of
schoolteachers, and the social-class status of schoolteachers
(that is, the place teachers occupy, or are perceived as occupying, within the social hierarchy). The social-class status of
schoolteachers is fairly easily settled: in western capitalist
societies they drop neatly into the middle class, and somewhere
pretty close to the middle of the middle class. Social-class origins,
however, are just a little more complex. In the ancient Grecian
setting which is so often taken as the seat of our civilisation,
teaching, or at least elementary teaching of the common children,
was considered to be below the dignity of a free person, and
teachers were drawn from the lowest of the low, the slaves. Gain-

ing dignity, respect, and status has been a slow, long, and hard struggle for teachers. Teaching, after no longer being confined to slaves, became the province variously of the lower orders of the church, of refined but non-endowed ladies, of ordinary workers offering instruction in their spare time, and even of children themselves serving under a grand master within a monitorial system.

It was the growth of compulsory, elementary schooling in the nineteenth century that brought into being the 'professional' teacher; 'professional' in the sense of undertaking specific pre-service training, and then engaging in a full-time career of instructing children. The growth of secondary schooling, and then compulsory secondary schooling in the twentieth century called for and brought into being a far more refined product; one who had already mastered the more advanced content of secondary schooling and who was also considered sufficiently well trained (and of proper moral standing) to pass it on to others. Within a very short period of time the well-intentioned and largely self-styled dame-school mistress had become replaced by a specifically trained tertiary-educated product, not only in secondary schools but in primary schools and kindergartens as well. The modern schoolteacher, unlike the farmer, the miner, or the shoemaker, is a new phenomenon; and thus it is only to be expected that sociologists might want to identify from which part of the older order this phenomenon arose, and where it is settling in the present order.

The results of such studies have been more or less predictable. On the one hand, teaching has tended to recruit from the upwardly aspiring end of the lower/working class. For people in such a position teaching has always been more accessible on practical grounds than the traditional professions which, because of the longer periods of study involved, have imposed longer periods of delayed financial remuneration on their aspirants. Also, at the time of the mushrooming of elementary schooling, teaching had had little time to become 'respectable' enough to become an attractive lure for upper- or middle-class children seeking appropriate employment. Teaching also proved to be a better candidate than traditional professions in terms of aspirations for upward mobility: for upward mobility is generally (and realistically) seen as a gradual climb, whereby it is more likely the case that the daughter of a miner might become a teacher whose child in turn might enter the medical profession, rather than that a miner's child might aspire to, and move straight in to an 'upper-class profession' without first having been pedigreed in the middle regions. Teaching also offered far less 'cultural dislocation' for the lower/working-class child who, while almost certainly knowing nothing of the ways of law or medicine or engineering, had experienced schooling and thus knew, to a large extent, what teachers did and what was required of them. Teaching, being accessible (especially to women barred from most professions), realistic in terms of aspirations, and familiar to the working class,

while at the same time being beneath the aspirations of the middle
and upper classes, drew heavily in its initial 'professional' stage
from the working class – thus beginning the long-standing relation between teaching as a career and working-class aspiration,
and so introducing (or reintroducing, if we recall that slaves in
ancient Greece could attain freedom in return for successful teaching activities) the familiar figure of the teacher emerging and
emancipated from the lower class.

Two factors, however, were about to change the overwhelming
direction of this social drift. First, as teaching itself became more
respected and gained in occupational status – with longer, more
specialised pre-service training; with higher qualification requirements; through offering higher salaries; and through elevation in
status in periods of economic expansion – it tended to become
more attractive to the middle class. Added in with this was the
fact that teachers had clearly become bona fide middle-class practitioners themselves, no longer to be looked down on, or at least
far less to be looked down on. Teaching, comprised of new middle-
class performers, was no longer 'below' the aspirations of the
middle class. The second factor was the vast proliferation of
secondary schooling needing to be staffed by highly schooled
people capable of transmitting cultural elements at a fairly high
degree of sophistication. Teaching, or secondary-school teaching,
rather suddenly became a very respectable thing for an aspiring
middle-class university graduate to go into, especially a graduate
in the humanities: it tended, in time, to become *the* thing to go
in to. As the days of taking an Arts degree purely for self-
betterment quickly vanished, yet students continued to take Arts
degrees, teaching emerged as a very viable goal; and the phrase
'What else can you do with an Arts degree?' became a common
utterance, not always issuing out of despair. Overall, a new
pattern emerged: middle-class children (and even a few from the
upper class) aspired to succeed in school and university, undertake post-graduate training, and then become teachers.

For a time a sharp division existed between elementary-school
teaching (infants and primary) and secondary-school teaching.
Elementary teaching was regarded as requiring less schooling and
less pre-service training from its practitioners than secondary
teaching, and it also tended to pay considerably less. Thus the
two streams entering teaching tended to follow fairly distinct
courses. Elementary teaching, being more quickly accessible, drew
from the lower class; and, paying less, kept its practitioners
closer to their socio-economic origins. Secondary teaching, requiring longer periods of delayed remuneration, being more concerned in content with the corpus of middle-class ideals (the
study of fine literature, languages, etc., as well as aiming pupils
towards university entrance), drew from the middle class; and by
offering greater financial rewards again kept its practitioners
near to their socio-economic origins.

The division has been gradually broken down, yet has by no
means disappeared. The period of training for elementary teaching

has been increased and in places is equivalent to that required
for secondary teaching, yet it is still possible for an elementary-
school teacher to emerge from training up to two years earlier
than his or her secondary-school counterpart. The salary differential has also been broken down, except that where salary is
based on years of training, secondary teachers still tend to be
paid higher than elementary teachers. And the establishment of
scholarships has to some degree reduced the problems associated
with having to postpone earnings for several years where financial
assistance is not available from the home situation. The end result
of this is that the two streams now tend to follow less distinct
paths. Secondary teaching is now 'more available' to lower-class
aspirants, and elementary teaching has become more attractive
to the middle class. Added to this, the respective salaries now
paid to both groups establishes each of them clearly within the
'middle class' range.

In summary, 'orthodox' studies of teachers and social class
indicate to us that the teaching force is drawn both from the
middle class and the upper end of the lower class, with the trend
moving more towards recruitment from the middle class; and that
teachers settle fairly neatly into a middle class position in society.
Teaching today has become more markedly middle class, both in
origins and status; but still retains its long-standing connection
with the upwardly aspiring section of the lower or working class,
and still fails to draw 'even moderate numbers' from among the
children of upper professional groups.[4] Anderson summarises the
situation in England and Australia thus:[5]

> Students destined for teaching tend to come from families with
> lower incomes, the parents have had less education, and the
> father is less likely to be a self-employed professional or large-
> scale employer or manager. The majority of these students have
> been to state schools. . . . Teaching differs from engineering
> (and even more from medicine and law) in that both fathers and
> mothers have had less education and the proportion of fathers
> who are semi-skilled manual workers or farmers is the highest
> of any group. The mothers of girls in teaching have had more
> education than the mothers of men, but their average level is
> still well below the average of either parent of students of either
> sex in any other profession. The very low level of formal edu-
> cational attainment of the parents of male student teachers is
> particularly noteworthy: three-quarters of the fathers and four-
> fifths of the mothers had not completed secondary education.

TEACHERS AND THE 'ORTHODOX' PROBLEMATIC:
A CRITIQUE

People living within a social formation can be categorised into
whatever groups we might want to divide them into. We could, for
instance, speak of upper, middle, and lower classes based on
height; or study the respective life-styles of people with different

eye colours. What is important, of course, is not the means of categorisation per se, but what the particular categorisation can reveal to us about the workings and dynamics of the society in question and the place and function of the chosen groups within the overall dynamic. The 'orthodox' problematic, based largely on economic differentials, in fact tells us very little about such things; and although it focuses on empirically observable and measurable factors, it actually mystifies the real social relations operating within a social formation.

It is hardly possible to argue this fully here, but two central points need to be stressed.

In the first place, a characterisation of classes based on relative economic privilege is not well suited to reveal very much about the interactive effect of the groups it picks out within the total social formation, or the function of each in maintaining and repro-ducing the overall network of social relations. To recognise that teachers are 'middle class' or that production-line workers are 'lower class' might lead to further studies regarding their respec-tive reading habits, values, or child-rearing practices, but little of this throws any significant light on their place and function in maintaining and reproducing the social relations of which they (and their habits and values) are part, and by which they (and their habits and values) are formed. Studies based on such a definition tend to embody the worst of empiricist processes and methodologies; namely taking what is 'given' (in this case economic differentials), correlating other factors to the 'essential givens', and then presenting pictures of 'the way things are' as if all factors necessarily relate to the 'essential givens' as natural con-comitants of the order of things. From such studies we learn about facets related to things like 'middle-class values' or 'lower-class morality', but these are presented in such a way as to indi-cate both that the features in question actually do have an income-determinant, and that other determining features need not be sought after. Thus the clear facts that lower-class adolescents are far more likely to run foul of the law than their upper-class counterparts, or that middle-class children aspire to mental labour whereas lower-class children aspire generally to manual labour, are put down to issues of 'values' or 'morality' spawned in circum-stances of relative economic privilege, rather than to issues of structured oppression and repression, or the mechanics of systematic social reproduction.

The second point to stress is that the trichotomy of 'upper, middle and lower' classes is not merely empirically descriptive - the labelling is highly value-laden. 'Upper-class' membership de-notes, at least by implication, far more than economic privilege: it denotes a whole range of supposed superiority, especially when used in contrast to 'lower class' or 'working class'. Similarly, the very notion (or ideal) of 'upward mobility' refers to far more than simply getting more money; it suggests improvement or betterment over a wide spectrum of factors. Under the 'orthodox' schema to be 'lower class' is to be least economically privileged, and also to bear the relatively lowest general characteristics of the society: it is to be most in need of improvement, or furthest behind the norm, even to the extent that things such as speech and accent come to be looked on evaluatively, with 'inferior' lower-class speech patterns and accents emerging as candidates for 'correction' by institutions such as schooling. And as we have seen, 'lower class' and 'working class' tend to be used interchangeably: thus the notion of 'working class' comes to bear the stigma of relative inferiority, and all that which marks out the 'working class' tends to become a candidate for 'correction' if one is to rise in society. To get on, working-class children have to abandon not only long entrenched values, habits, beliefs and cultural forms, but also certain grammatical structures, pronunciations, postures and manners lest, as Henry Higgins observed, 'they give themselves away every time they open their mouths'.[6] And abandoning these things for the sake of upward mobility is at least implicit recognition and acceptance of their inherent inferiority.

The evaluative nature of the class labels, along with the equation of 'lower' and 'working' class, thus serve a very strong ideological purpose and function: that which is identifiable with the working class becomes equated with inferiority, such that it is not merely the income factor but also things like performing manual labour which serve to place people at the bottom of the heap. By implicit definition that which marks out the working class is inferior to that which marks out the middle and upper classes; and thus institutions upholding 'middle-class values' (among which the school is always cited) become charged ideologically with being both the guardians of 'proper' values and ideals, and with functioning as corrective agencies for the working class. As Grace (among others) has shown, teachers from earliest Victorian times were sent into a working class pictured as demoralised, disorganised, and with only itself to blame for its conditions, to exert an ameliorating and civilising effect; and the notions of the teacher-as-missionary and the social-pathology approach to the working class still loom large in teacher-training institutions.[7]

TEACHING: A WORKING-CLASS OCCUPATION?

Within the framework of the 'orthodox' problematic today's teachers are generally recognised as *not* belonging to the working class. Their level of economic privilege sees to this immediately, but there are a number of other factors involved as well, and it is important for us to consider just four of these here.

First, there is the apparently minor matter of how teachers are paid. Teachers receive a salary, either fortnightly or monthly, and usually by cheque or by means of an automatic bank deposit. The working class, however, tend to receive wages, and remuneration for labour comes in the form of weekly tangible cash payments stuffed into brown envelopes.

Second, teachers are regarded as 'white-collar workers', and though they might get pretty tired after a day's work, they don't work with their hands. They neither make things (as a carpenter does), nor does their work depend primarily on physical exertion in the sense that a miner's or a ditch-digger's work does. Now, even though it is doubtful that teachers expend less physical effort than some of those commonly regarded as manual workers (e.g. truck drivers or ticket sellers at railway stations), teachers (including those like woodwork and metalwork teachers who do work with their hands) are generally recognised as people who work with their heads, and within the overall context of the 'orthodox' problematic this too is significant in differentiating them from the working class.

Third, teachers are serviced by a small number of staff who clearly are members of the working class. Among these people we find typists, janitors and cleaners; and while it is usually only the principal or head who has control over non-teaching staff in schools, teachers do assume control power over these people in a de facto manner. Teachers direct the activities of some (e.g. typists) and they even judge the activities of those whom they do not direct. For instance, teachers often interfere in a cleaner's duties or complain about the standard of cleaning, whereas cleaners do not interfere in the teachers' duties or complain about the standard of science teaching in the school. This control is also reinforced by subtle forms of interaction, such as teachers referring to typists by their first name - a familiarity which typists don't commonly reciprocate - and by teachers openly directing the activity of other workers in the school; 'would you please not light the incinerator while my class is doing field work in the playground.' Teachers clearly exercise managerial functions over some members of the working class, which further serves to elevate them above that class.

Finally, teaching is rarely referred to as a job. Sometimes it sinks as low as an occupation, and occasionally it is honoured as a vocation,[8] but most commonly it is referred to as a profession. And professions are carried out by professional people whereas jobs are done by workers. Thus, while teaching continues to be regarded or merely spoken of as a profession, teachers (as viewed from within the 'orthodox' context) will continue to remain distinguished from workers and the working class.

A highly significant feature of teachers' activities over the last century has been the quest for professionalism through continuous attempts to emulate and bring about the conditions which mark out the traditional professions. To this end teachers have formed learned societies, published journals, and fought for continually rising entrance requirements; they have also sought to free themselves from the constraints of external controls (like inspectors and Curriculum Boards) in order to achieve more control for themselves over their own work. They have also, at various times and places, resisted compulsory unionism and have refused to take strike action on the grounds that these are distinctly unprofessional activities; and they have been careful to attend to the trivia ostensibly surrounding professions - for instance, most teachers' organisations publish a list of professional ethics. The rate of success in these areas has been varied, with least of all being achieved in the central area of gaining control of work conditions.

The issue of teacher-professionalism has generated a vast amount of literature, and little consensus. It is generally agreed that teachers don't match up to lawyers and doctors with regard to self-determination of the organisation and control of their practice; but whether teachers match up on that other most crucial of factors - the possession of a high standard of esoteric knowledge on which their actual practice is based - is far more debatable. Teachers certainly have tried to increase this body of knowledge, or have it increased (as with longer periods of training), but many would argue that the 'esoteric knowledge' required for teaching is nothing more than common sense; common sense which is now being dressed up in scientific jargon; and that on this ground teacher-professionalism is basically fraudulent.[9]

Whether teaching does or does not require the possession of highly developed esoteric skills and knowledge is a matter of some importance for us, and will be taken up again in Chapter 5. It is sufficient here to recognise that teachers, and trainers of teachers, have worked hard to establish the belief that it does; and have thus served to promote the professional image of teachers in this area as well. The overall state of play at the moment is that teaching is not generally considered to be a 'full' profession, either from within its ranks or without;[10] but it is generally considered to be more than an ordinary job, and teachers are accorded higher status than mere 'workers' for the work they perform.

We see then, that from within the framework of the 'orthodox' problematic teachers become distinguished from the working class through the application of the manual-work mental-work dichotomy, through perceptions of their power relations vis-à-vis other workers in schools, and through association with the notion of professionalism - not to mention, of course, their relatively privileged income as well as the actual means by which this is paid over. The divisions, as highlighted from this perspective, far outweigh any areas of communality which may be found.

THE MARXIST CONCEPT OF 'CLASS'

According to Marxist theory the first historical act of human existence is 'the production of material life itself'. What this means is simply that before we can 'live' our lives we must establish certain basic conditions for doing so; namely we have to produce our food and our protection from the elements. These actions lead out, of course, into a myriad of aspects like division of labour, exchange relations, and so on; which in turn lead out

to historical actions and transformations like invention of new
tools for production, exploration (to find new sites and resources),
colonisation, and even war; but 'in every day and every hour'
the basic condition for existence remains that of sustaining human
life, or the production of material life.[11]

Now the production of material life can, of course, be undertaken by any number of means. For instance, we could all grow
our own food, make our own clothes, and build our own shelters.
Or things could be ordered such that some grew food for all,
while in return others made clothes or shelters for all. And if
either of those proved too onerous and time-consuming, slaves
could be employed to do all the work so that the rest of us might
engage in pleasure. The possibilities are indeed numerous, but
what Marxist theory has traditionally insisted on is that the form
of the production process employed, or the mode of production,
is the basic determinant factor of all aspects of the resultant
social order, and of all social conditions, including consciousness
(although there are other determining relations). How we produce
determines how we live (in its widest sense) and how we think;
or, more technically, the productive network is the basic and predominant factor in determining the character of any social formation.

The productive network, or mode of production, consists of
productive forces brought together into a productive process:
that is, forces such as raw materials, machines, and people are
linked up in order to make products which have particular uses,
and this being the case the people within the process stand in
particular relationships to the overall process or mode of production. For instance, under slavery some people operated the
machines and raw materials (the means of production) in return
for basic subsistence, while other people made use of the products
without contributing any labour to their production; whereas
under capitalism some people operate the means of production to
make products in return for wages while the owners of the means
of production sell the products at a profit. It is these differences
in relationship to the mode of production which, in Marxist theory,
mark out the different classes in a society. Or, to put that round
the other way, in Marxist theory *classes are defined in terms of
their relation to the mode of production*. While slavery was the
dominant mode of production we could thus identify slaves and
masters as distinct classes; under feudalism there were serfs and
lords; while under capitalism there is a basic division between
those who own and/or control and those who do not own and/or
control the means of production. Those who do not own and/or
control the means of production exist by selling their labour power
to the owners/controllers, and are thus commonly characterised as
the working class (or proletariat); the owners/controllers exist
by expropriating surplus value from the workers, or by selling
commodities at a profit, and are referred to as the capitalists
(often also as the bourgeoisie or ruling class).

The picture as painted so far is, of course, extremely simplistic.

Two further things that have to be recognised at this stage are
that social formations rarely have one single mode of production,
and that modes of production (and thus class relationships to
them) always exist within a framework of dynamic socio-historical
change. From the first of these points we recognise that in any
social formation there may exist a larger number of classes than
focus on the dominant mode of production might suggest. For
instance, in a capitalist society, that is, a society where the
capitalist mode of production is dominant, there might also be
vestiges or pockets of other modes of production. Some people
might be totally self-subsistent, others might live in feudal or
even slave relations, while pockets of socialist production might,
and often do, exist. Not everybody in a capitalist society can be
neatly labelled either 'worker' or 'capitalist', and it is a misconceived exercise to attempt to squeeze all people into one or
other of these respective classes. All people can, however, be
identified not necessarily in terms of which of the two major
classes they belong to but in terms of which particular class's
interests they predominantly serve (or, in the terminology to be
employed later, in terms of which particular function they perform).

From the second of the points noted above we must realise that,
since social formations are continually undergoing historic transformation or change, then the classes of which they are comprised
must also be undergoing continual transformation and change.
This change occurs in three main areas: we find changes in the
'balance' of classes within the total social formation; there are
changes in the form of their relation to the mode of production
itself; and there is change in the overt demonstrable ways in
which classes interrelate with each other. These are extremely
important matters, and thus require further discussion - discussion which, because of our immediate purpose, will be specific to
the capitalist mode of production.

The capitalist mode of production did not come into effect or
dominance overnight, nor has it remained unchanged since its
ascendancy. In the earliest days of capitalism feudal relationships
were still very strong, and the feudal classes that existed have
since passed through a long period of transformation. One particular outcome of this process has been the existence, at particular
historical periods, of transitional classes of varying sizes and
significance. The petit bourgeoisie, for instance, can be recognised as such a transitional class - its members remaining in conjunction with vestiges of the production relations based on serfdom, but tending to become fewer in number as capitalist production relations are extended. The petit bourgeoisie has always
existed under capitalism, but what was a rising class-force at the
beginning of the eighteenth century is now a rapidly declining
force facing possible extinction in the very near future. On the
other hand, capitalism has always incorporated a group of people
who are not strictly capitalists in that they do not own and/or
control the means of production but who are also not strictly

workers in that they do not engage directly in the production of
commodities; and this group, comprised of people such as public
servants, accountants, bank tellers, nurses, and insurance
brokers or consultants, has grown enormously over the last century. From being virtually unknown in the earliest days of capitalism it has come to represent something like 40 per cent of the
present day work-force,[12] and any analysis of contemporary capitalism which neglected this group would do so at considerable
peril. The message lurking within these examples should be clear:
the class balance within capitalism is not a constant thing, and
thus the outcomes of any analyses of class composition are relevant only to the particular historical periods actually under analysis. It is no criticism of Marxist theory to point out that things
have changed over the years, or since Marx wrote: certain
changes at least are expected and accounted for within the theory.

When we consider the capitalist mode of production itself we
find that there have also been vast changes in its operation, and
consequently in the sorts of tasks performed by both workers and
capitalists. Basically, there has been a transformation from entrepreneurist capitalism (often regarded as the classical or paradig-
matic model) to monopoly or corporate[13] capitalism. Under entrepreneurist capitalism it was relatively easy to identify the capitalists and the workers. The capitalists owned the means of production both legally and economically, and controlled labour quite
directly. Individual capitalists were the actual legal owners of
their factories and mills, they personally bought the raw materials,
and they were physically present to supervise the labour and to
sell the finished products. Under monopoly or corporate capitalism,
however, it is commonly the case that there is no single owner of
a factory: ownership and control tend to lie with corporations,
and some of the 'owners' (in the form of shareholders) might have
no connection whatsoever with the factory other than being in
possession of share scrips (possibly not even knowing where the
factory is nor having much idea of what it produces). Economic
control tends to be centred among the senior management and
directors of the corporation, while worker control has become the
province of junior management and fore people closer to the point
of production. Under corporate monopoly capitalism the function
of capital is no longer performed individually; it is performed
collectively or globally, and thus identification of capitalists requires, in the first place, detailed consideration of those who
undertake the global function of capital, either through various
forms of control and surveillance of the production process, or
through economic (or legal) ownership, or both. It should be
noted here, as a prelude for later discussion, that all work of
control and surveillance (e.g. keeping up production rates, ensuring machinery is properly used, discipline of workers, and
even producing in workers the 'proper' attitudes to their work)
is part of the performance of the global function of capital.

As far as the workers are concerned, it is also obvious that the
tasks they now perform with regard to the production of commodi-

ties differ greatly from the tasks performed under earlier models of capitalism. There was a time when individual workers made individual products: a shoe-maker made a shoe from start to finish, just as a tailor made a garment from start to finish. Under corporate capitalism, and with the introduction and proliferation of division of labour, this is no longer the case. The tailor who once made a garment, and who could be identified as the specific producer of that product, has now been replaced by designers, cutters, seamstresses and button-holers, who in turn use machines serviced by technicians, greasers, and so on. All of these people contribute to the final product, yet not one of them could lay claim to having made it or be identified specifically with it. We see then that labour too is now performed collectively, such that workers, who could once be identified as direct producers (and who, as direct producers consequently had greater control of the production process) are now to be identified in terms of their performance of the function of the collective labourer: that is, in terms of whether they take part in the complex organised labour process contributing labour power to the production of commodities. Thus, among the workers in a clothing factory we would find not only the cutters and seamstresses, as well as those who keep their machines functional, but also those who are involved with coordinating and organising the fragmented labour process, like foremen and foreladies, quality-control personnel, time and motion consultants, and even those who teach the labourers their specific skills. Identification of workers, then, is no longer a matter of pointing out 'people who make products'; or 'people who work with their hands'; it is, rather, a matter of identifying those who perform the function of the collective labourer. This, however, raises a very large complication, for many of those who perform the function of the collective labourer do so unproductively in the loose sense that they don't actually make anything; e.g. quality controllers - and the class identification of these unproductive labourers will be discussed more fully at a later stage.

One final point to note here is that the capitalist/worker dichotomy is no longer properly applicable to individual people in a totally embracing or exclusively definitive sense. It often puzzles people when first confronted with the Marxist schema that many people own the means of production yet also work productively in their own factories, or that even the lowliest worker today can own shares in a major corporation. These people, it would appear, are both capitalists and workers, so what happened to the dichotomy? The answer is that it was applied either wrongly or oversimply in the attempt to pin discrete labels on people without detailed consideration of the class-interests they predominantly serve and/or the functions they perform. The same person can perform both the global function of capital *and* the function of the collective labourer. Where such a person comes out in terms of class identification is, however, often a complex matter, and this too will be considered more fully later.

The third area in which social classes undergo change is that of their overt and demonstrable interrelations with each other within the overall social context. The factory worker today, for instance, no longer doffs his cap to the owner, and the owner is no longer able to direct physical violence (in the form of beatings) upon the worker within the factory. But it is outside of the actual work situation that the clearest changes have emerged, in that owners and workers now share many of the things which once served to differentiate them. For instance, with regard to consumer items, both are likely to have television sets and cars, and it is not only the owners who are installing back-yard swimming pools (although the methods of payment for these things might be different). And at the level of social mobility, divisions have broken down such that the worker now has access to many of the cultural outlets that were once the province only of the ruling class. In a general sense there is interaction and communality between the classes to the extent that outside of the workplace it may be difficult at times to tell who belongs to which - a situation which certainly did not exist a century ago. This phenomenon, along with the fact that many workers and many owners belong together within the 'orthodox' economically defined middle class, has led some to speak of a general levelling-out process occurring and a movement already existing under capitalism towards the establishment of a classless society. This is an interpretation which Marxists regard as mystifying, for whereas various surface features certainly have changed for some (there is no general levelling-out process, however: the rich *are* getting richer and the poor *are* getting poorer) what has not changed is the basic nature of the relationship: owners still expropriate surplus value from the workers, just as they have always done under capitalism. A Marxist identification of class location, concerned basically with relationships to the mode of production, must attend to changing behaviour interrelationships, but these are recognised as part of the overall complexity of class struggle (to be discussed in the next section) rather than as determining features of class location.

We can now summarise the two central points of this section. First, within the Marxist problematic, classes are defined in terms of their relationship to the dominant mode of production. Second, the continuous process of historical transformation will result in changing balances of classes within a social formation, in changes in the nature of the production process, and in changes in the outward manifestations of class location and inter-class relationships. It is thus a serious error to posit a fixed classical model of production and to conduct investigations within the context of such a proposed fixed model. We see, then, that identification of class location turns out to be a far more complex matter than focusing on relationships to the mode of production might at first suggest: it requires at least a fairly detailed understanding and analysis of the actual current operation of the mode of production in question, which in turn cannot be divorced from an historical account of the development of the particular mode of production.

Three things can now be said about the Marxist categorisation

of classes. First, although it may appear so on first sight,
it is not an empiricist categorisation; and class identification
(given the complexities we have touched on) is more than an
empirical matter of counting up those who fit a given definition.
What is required, eventually, is a historically oriented analysis of
the basic determinants of the social relations which constitute a
particular social formation. Second, the Marxist position is 'objective' or 'scientific', especially in comparison to the ideologically
ridden 'orthodox' schema. Marxist theory is relatively value-free
concerning ascriptions to class location; 'working class' for
instance, carries with it no connotations of contingent inferiority
as it does in the 'orthodox' schema, and even though Marxists
tend not to take kindly to capitalists both the definition of 'capitalist' and the word itself (unlike upper class) are non-evaluative.
Third, the Marxist categorisation, again unlike the 'orthodox'
problematic, is able to reveal the dynamics of the functioning of
social formations, and is further able to account for historical
transformation (which includes the maintaining and reproduction
of, as well as bringing about changes in, social relations). It is
to this aspect that we now turn.

CLASS STRUGGLE

When Plato conceived of his Republic, he envisaged that the
classes within it would work together harmoniously for the common
good of the State. Whether this could have eventuated or not we
shall, of course, never know, for Plato was speaking of an ideal
that had no material basis in history. Marxist theory has no place
for ideals. Its analyses derive from material circumstances; and
through analysis of such material circumstances it has been recognised that, throughout recorded history, all class societies that
have ever existed have had at their base a mode of production
incorporating exploitative relations among people. Classes, in fact,
are the product of any mode of production based on relations of
exploitation; such that to speak of a class society is in reality to
speak of a social formation wherein such relations exist. And
classes, defined in relation to the mode of production, thus stand
in an antagonistic relationship towards each other since they are
comprised respectively of the exploiting and exploited groups
within the social formation. Under slavery masters exploited slaves,
under feudalism lords exploited serfs, under capitalism owners
exploit workers.

Now in any antagonistic situation it is to be expected that each
group would strive to serve its own interests, which in turn
means lessening the interests of the opposing group. Thus,
masters attempted to extract as much work as possible from their
slaves, while the slaves, wherever it was possible, sought to subvert their masters' interest and serve their own by means of
sabotage, escape, or even revolt. Lurking at the heart, then, of
what appeared to be a cohesive slave society (or feudal or capi-

talist society) was basic antagonism manifesting itself in constant struggle between two opposed classes. This struggle, for Marx, was the characteristic feature of exploitative social relations; it was also the motive force of history.

Social formations, Marx recognised, were dialectical in nature, consisting of contradictory elements or classes, and the nature of a social formation at any particular time could be characterised in terms of the state (or current resolution) of class struggle at that particular time, whereas social change (that fundamental mystery which had baffled earlier metaphysicians and social philosophers) was brought about by nothing more than shifts or the achievement of new syntheses in the dialectic process of class struggle. Thus it was class struggle which brought about social change and historical transformation; and human history, properly written, would be a record of past class struggles.

Class struggle is generally recognised as taking place on three closely interrelated levels:[14] the economic, the political, and the ideological. Let us consider each of these in turn.

Central to all forms of exploitative relations is economic exploitation: the attempt by the exploiters to procure the labour power of the exploited while offering the minimum in return. (This need not, of course, involve money; the slave owner provided only food and shelter for the slaves, and that in quantity and quality commensurable with extracting maximum labour power.) Class struggle at the economic level occurs when the exploited engage collectively against the exploiters in order to seek a better deal for the 'sale' of their labour power, or when the exploiters engage collectively to extract further surplus value from the labourers (and as such it differs from the individual entrepreneurist action exemplified in an individual employee threatening to join an opposing firm unless a substantial raise is forthcoming). At this level, class struggle commonly takes the form of strikes, shut-downs, proposing awards which represent a loss in terms of real income, and appeals (from either side) to arbitration.

Class struggle at the political level is a struggle for power, or to be more precise, a struggle for State power. The State, in Marxist theory, is not (as liberal bourgeois theory would have it) a neutral body or an impartial umpire arbitrating fairly and disinterestedly over the interests of all of the people; just as the Government neither represents nor promotes in any near-to-equal sense the interests of all citizens, regardless of the way political leaders express their functions in addresses to the nation, and other apologies. The State, in a class society, is class-interest serving; serving the interests of the ruling (or exploiting) class. These interests are served through State institutions such as the legal and education systems, and through control (and even repressive force) exercised by people like the police (and as we shall see, teachers) who implement the terms of power-reference. Class struggle at the political level is manifested in attempts by the exploiting and exploited classes to gain or further State power for their own particular ends. At its most extreme, this would

result in the overthrow of the government and the seizure of all
power by the exploited, but most political class struggle falls far
short of that. Historical examples of victories for the exploited
class under capitalism would include forcing the State to legalise
trade unions and repeal laws permitting strikers to be gaoled;
whereas recent ruling-class victories include introduction of the
Summary Offences Act in Australia (which gives police virtually
unlimited power), instigation of legislation permitting the government to deregister unions, and on a much broader level, the
establishment of compulsory State (or State-approved) schooling
for all children.[15]

It should be noted that class struggle at the political level when
practised by the exploited is always 'anti-establishment': it is
reaction to that which already has been, or is about to be, instituted, and thus can easily be interpreted, promoted or misrepresented as an attack on 'the people', 'the nation', or even on 'our
way of life'; that is, as an attack on the whole of the people by a
group of dissidents rather than as part of the continuing struggle
for power between two distinct, conflicting and antagonistic sections of 'the people'. Headlines such as 'Grasping Unionists
Threaten Nation' reinforce the former attitude; they also lead us
towards the third level of class struggle, the ideological level.

An understanding of class struggle at the ideological level requires, of course, an understanding of the operation of ideology
within a social formation - and this is an extremely complex (and
controversial) issue. The account which follows is little more than
a sketch, and is itself controversial. (For further reading see
Select Bibliography, Section F.)

To begin with, 'ideology' has to be seen in two senses. On the
one hand it can be seen as a level of any social formation. In this
sense it is a 'system' or 'network', comprised of ideas, representations, attitudes, customs and adaptations concerned with political,
legal, moral, religious, aesthetic and philosophic ideas and institutions within a society, along with people's habits, customs and
tendencies to act and react in certain ways to 'given' situations.
This 'system' or 'network' serves to reinforce existing social
relations, to present them as if they were 'naturally given', and
to adapt individuals (especially new generations) as bearers of
the general qualities required for overall social reproduction to
take place. Ideology, in this sense, is descriptive of an objective
social process which has definite theoretic, practical, and institutional forms. The practical aspect consists in the rituals, customs,
conventionalised patterns of social behaviour, and so on which
are inculcated in people according to their location in a society.
The theoretical aspect consists in the theoretical expressions
which arise from these practices, and which also serve to rationalise them. The institutional aspect is made up of the institutions
which embody, concretise and express the rituals, customs and
theories, and which also produce, maintain, and reproduce ideol-
ogies. As a quick example here we can recognise that a boy growing up in a western capitalist society would have inculcated into

him rituals, customs, and patterns of behaviour appropriate to his future place in a monogamous marriage relationship (a girl would have different things inculcated; her place in the same relationship being different from the boy's). Along with this would come theoretical expressions and rationalisations ('men must build careers for themselves', 'a woman's place is in the home') and finally institutions (the church, the legal system, housing suited only for nuclear families) embody and concretise the rituals and theories, and maintain and reproduce the objective social process. (Schooling, as we shall come to recognise later, is an example of the operation and interrelation of a practical-theoretical-institutional ideological network.)

The power of ideology at this level cannot be overestimated. No State could muster the repressive forces necessary to stop the workers seizing control of the means of production if, collectively, they really set their minds to it (just as no teacher could stop a class taking over if it really wanted to). But workers can be kept from seizing control if the law forbids such action; if the workers, by and large, acquiesce to the laws of the land; and if repressive agents such as the police and the army side with the law rather than with the workers. Writing the law (political control) and producing the required attitudes to it (ideological control) has a far stronger effect than the use of overt repressive force, and also goes far towards eliminating the need for such repressive action. Control in schools, as we shall see, is achieved in much the same way.

The second sense of ideology that requires attention is the notion of ideology as a distortion of reality - a distortion which, in any class society, serves the interests of the ruling class. Ideology, in this sense, arises out of two factors. First, the actual class division within the society itself 'places' people in particular relations to the economic structure such that their perceptions are determined by their location to the extent that it becomes extremely difficult to see the whole of the picture and/or correct these perceptions in terms of what the state of affairs really is. For instance, few workers and possibly fewer capitalists see the capitalist mode of production as basically exploitative. Those workers who can live fairly comfortably on their wages tend to regard those wages as a just return for the sort of work they do (and the sort of work they do as commensurable with their general ability and capacity), while capitalists-in-general continually express their role in terms of their willingness to offer 'a fair day's pay for a fair day's work'. Second, there is the promulgation of ruling-class ideology which reinforces and legitimates the already distorted perceptions. As Marx and Engels pointed out in 'The German Ideology', the ruling ideas in any age are those of the ruling class; and it is these ideas, or this ideology which is reflected, concretised, institutionalised, and generally legitimated as the right way of seeing the world, and also as representing the common interests of all members of a society.[16] For example, laws designed to protect private property are instigated

by the ruling class which has both the political power to instigate
the laws and most of the private property in need of protection.
The laws are then represented as being equally in the interests
of all since we all have some private property, and through promulgation of the theory that social cohesion in general would
necessarily be threatened if everybody's claim on their own private property was not protected. Ruling-class ideology presents
a way of perceiving the world which, while favouring the interests
of the ruling class, claims (and appears) to favour the interests
of all, and/or to present an objective account of the world as it
really is. People living within a class location, and dominated by
ideological representations, not surprisingly find it difficult to
recognise either their own viewpoint, or ruling-class ideology, as
a distortion or misrepresentation of the actual state of affairs.

Given this context we are now in a position to understand class
struggle at the ideological level (and also to recognise that it
must be a largely one-sided struggle at those times when the ruling class is politically secure). On the one hand we find the ruling class serving its own interests by promulgating ideology
dressed up as objective accounts of the way things are and as
accounts of what is in everybody's interests ('Grasping Unionists
Threaten Nation'); while on the other hand there are attempts,
usually by the few, to counter both the promulgation and the ideas
themselves, and also to develop a framework and a means for
proposing alternative accounts. The struggle against ruling-class
ideology takes forms such as discussions and meetings with and
among workers, publication of 'alternative' literature, and attempts
to adopt lived practices contrary to dominant ideological social
formations (such as forming food cooperatives, or establishing
urban communes rather than living in isolated nuclear family-
type housing arrangements). Such struggle is fraught with
double difficulties. First the difficulty in countering dominant
ideology is directly proportionate to the power of the dominant
class in a society: groups of activists with duplicating machines
might be highly effective in some social situations, yet they provide only the tiniest of threats to vast media networks, both in
terms of volume and of 'respectability' - people are more likely to
accept what is printed in 'The Times' than what they read on a
hand-bill pushed in their direction by a scruffily dressed person
on the streets, and this especially so when the (respectable,
legitimate, unbiased, carefully-researched-by-professional-
journalists) 'Times' report corresponds in a very large manner to
what is being said in other respectable papers as well as on radio
and TV. Second, the struggle to establish resistant or counter
ideology has to take place largely within the structures and constraints of the ruling ideology, using many of its means, its con-
cepts, and its more general elements. For instance, the struggle
against sexism has to take place in a sexist society, within sexist
institutions, and through an inherently sexist language; and the
struggle against ruling-class educational ideology has to take
place largely within State-educational institutions and within a

This full-page advertisement, placed in major Australian newspapers by the Australian Government in July 1979, illustrates many aspects of ideological struggle.

ruling paradigm of educational orthodoxy covering both content
and method. (Anyone who has ever attempted to establish a
counter-ideological course in universities, or teach by counter-
ideological means in schools, will be well aware of the difficulties
involved.)

Three further things need to be said about class struggle. The
first is the obvious point that economic, political and ideological
struggle do not go on independently of each other. They are, in
fact, intricately intertwined and interrelated. For instance, the
struggle to secure equal pay and equal job opportunities for
women carries with it vast political and ideological overtones,
ramifications and social outcomes. Similarly, ideological struggle
against nuclear energy is (and must be) thoroughly interrelated
with economic and political issues, just as political struggle for
the establishment of legalised trade unionism is inextricably
caught up with economic and ideological issues. Although class
struggle takes place at three levels, which we have in abstraction
considered separately, it never takes place at any one of these
levels in isolation. The theorist arguing against nuclear energy
is engaging in political and economic struggle as well, even if this
is unintentional or counter-intentional (history is full of examples
of theorists attempting to absolve themselves from the political/
economic outcomes of what they proposed 'only as theory') just
as the person on the picket-line is involved also in economic and
ideological struggle in the very act of picketing.

Second, it must be stressed that class struggle on the part of
the ruling class, especially at the political and ideological levels,
should not be viewed simply as a conscious conspiracy perpe-
trated by those in power to put down and delude the working
class. Elements of conspiracy are, of course, present; but when
we recognise that politics and ideology exist as levels of the
social formation it becomes clear that what we really have are
rationalisations for existing social relations and practices as
being 'natural' and right which are generated from representations
of actual lived experience rather than from evil conspiring minds.

The third and final thing to note is that struggle does not take
place only between classes; it takes place within classes as well.
Classes, defined in terms of their relationship to the mode of production, each have a central common interest, but this neither
means that all members of a class will observe that common
interest, nor that there are not areas of conflict within the
bounds of that common interest. For instance, by no means do all
members of the working class recognise their exploitation, or
even their actual class location, and many may not see it as in
their interests to bring about a radical change in social relations.
And within the working class itself we find women struggling
against male domination, races struggling against each other,
unionists in struggle with non-unionists, conflict between religious
groups, and even very serious overt struggle between the supporters of different football teams. Such internal struggle is not
confined to the working class (although, for reasons which we

shall see later, it is more prevalent there): within the bourgeoisie
we also find conflict and struggle between, for instance, industrial
and financial factions or mining and agricultural interests.

One further important factor must be attended to before this
section is brought to a close. So far we have been speaking almost exclusively about class location, which, in technical terms is
an objective determination of the location of agents of production
processes within a class structure on the basis of their real
(economic, political and ideological) relations in that process. This
is not to be confused with class position, which is the alignment
taken up by these agents at particular stages of the class
struggle; and it is important to recognise that the class location
and class position of particular agents need not necessarily coincide. At times some sections of the working class take up capitalist
class positions, just as capitalists on occasions ally with the working class. It would be a serious error to presume that once the
class location of groups is identified for any historical period,
then a corresponding class position will automatically or necessarily
be taken up. While it would appear that a realistic understanding
of class location is necessary for serious adoption of the correctly-
corresponding class position, this much alone is not sufficient;
and as we shall see later there are many other factors which influence the form and position of alignment in the class struggle.

IMPEDIMENTS TO WORKING-CLASS GAINS

It is fairly easy to recognise why slaves so rarely rose up against
their masters. Even though they must have been aware of their
exploitation and oppression they had no political power, and
extremely little physical power, especially when they were
literally chained to their place. With serfs, however, the matter
was somewhat different. Again they had no political power, but
they had a greater degree of freedom, and in times of external
threat they were actually armed by their lords. Why, then, did
they not turn these arms against their lords and overthrow the
feudal system? The reasons, of course, are highly complex and
would vary for different socio-historical situations, but central
among them is that feudalism developed under the aegis of the
notion that this particular mode of production, and the relation
of people to it, was divinely ordained. To be an exploited serf
was to do God's bidding; to overthrow feudalism would be to
act against God's plan. While the slavery mode of production was
maintained and reproduced almost entirely by political power and
force, much of this power and force had been transferred to the
ideological realm for the maintenance and reproduction of feudalism. And with the growth of capitalism, and the attendant free-
doms and reforms that have been won resulting in ostensibly
democratic societies governed by the people for the people, we
have witnessed an ever increasing growth of ideological means for
keeping people in their places within a context where 'all men are

equal' and there are no politically or divinely ordained places to be kept in.

The call for workers of the world to unite was first put forward formally over a hundred years ago. But the workers of the world have not, as yet, united; and there appears to be little evidence to suggest that they might unite in the immediate future. If such a thing were to happen then there would have to be at least two preliminary antecedents. On the one hand there would have to exist a predisposition towards uniting, or achieving and maintaining solidarity. On the other hand the workers would have to recognise themselves, in class terms, as workers, and also recognise the other workers whom they are to unite with. A highly significant role of bourgeois ideology (considering its operation in assisting the maintenance and reproduction of capitalist social formations) is to prevent such unity occurring, and two of the most common and pervasive means by which this is achieved are the promotion of individualism, and the disguise or masking of class lines.

The promotion of individualism concentrates on two aspects; independence and individuality. Each aspect stresses the role and importance of individual action in determining the nature of a person's life; and both can be seen highly stressed in the motto of one of Australia's most prestigious State schools - 'Every man is the maker of his own fortune.'[17]

As far as independence is concerned, bourgeois ideology urges us to make our own way in the world, to be autonomous, to make decisions for ourselves, to act out of conscience, and so on. And a whole host of practices embody this theoretical conception. Students at school study individually, and sit their exams as individual centres isolated from and in competition with other students. Independent actions are praised and rewarded (when they are not anti-social) and within the context of 'free enterprise in the market-place' people are lauded for 'pulling themselves up by their own boot-straps' and for taking independent action (starting that business, or pressing on where all others have failed). The hallmarks for a successful person are the ability to stand on one's own feet, to be able to make it alone, to be self-sufficient and to climb one rung higher than the rest. The rather nasty corollary of this, however, is that people tend to become selfish, distrustful of others, and unwilling to share or work cooperatively. Students tend to guard zealously that individual knowledge which might give them an edge at assessment time, commercial researchers patent discoveries so that others can't use them, practitioners are loath to share their esoteric skills with the public, and none of us who at this moment crave some Kentucky Fried Chicken can make it for ourselves because the Colonel's internationally famous recipe is still a secret.

Individuality is the other prized aspect of individualism, whereby what is stressed about people is their particular uniqueness or what they do *not* have in common with other people. The progressive education movement has tended to concentrate heavily on this aspect, and its literature refers continually to the development of the inherent special individual qualities of each particular child as opposed to the more traditional approach of teaching class groupings en masse. The following, taken from the prospectus of one progressive school, is not uncommon (although the final sentence is particularly enlightening):

as there is individual growth, so there must be individual learning. The school is concerned with individual differences, and there has to be individual preparation of work, programming and progress, with each child working at tasks where he can have success proportionate to his effort and so be able to achieve inner security and confidence . . . All learning is individual, progress and performance are assessed on the ability of the child and the next step in his learning is planned to build on what has gone before, but concern for individuals is more than this. It is helping the child to find himself, catering for him as though he, alone, were the group.

Now people are, of course, unique individuals, but they also share a great deal in common with all other people. Bourgeois ideology, in focusing on individuality, tends to make more out of unique features than those features actually bear on life-situations and thus places the stress on the irrelevant, while at the same time masking or underplaying the features which people have in common. And even where individual qualities are required to be brought together in collective efforts it is the uniqueness of individuals which still tends to be stressed, as newspaper reports of sporting contests will generally attest to. The exploits of the great batsmen, scrum halves and centre forwards are highlighted rather than the performances of the teams they played for (how many who remember Bradman scoring 452 n.o. recall how many his team scored that day, who else was in it, or who bowled out the opposition without which there would have been no victory?), just as it is the Generals rather than their units who are usually given the limelight.

The ideological stress on individualism clearly militates against people taking collective action and it also produces negative attitudes towards collective action by representing it as the negation of individual freedom (many people, in the same breath, praise the endeavours of socialist activity - 'I really admire what the Chinese have done' - yet declare their preference for maintaining their own freedom and individual independence). It is thus a powerful weapon, and deterrent, against collective action, and consequently against effective class struggle. Workers, steeped in their individual independence, and aware mainly of their individual uniqueness, are less likely to unite in what is their basic historical struggle.

And they are of course, even less likely to unite if they see no communality with each other; if they see either no common struggle, or else fail to recognise who their fellow class members are. A predominant aspect of bourgeois ideology serves precisely this end, through breaking up class consciousness and solidarity by uniting people *across* class lines. We have already noted, in passing, the most common form of theoretical representation in this area: the 'orthodox' division of people into upper, middle, and lower socio-economic classes, to which we can add the popular definition of 'workers' in terms related mainly if not only to manual productive labour. Within the context of such representations many who really do belong to the working class, or whose interests lie in common with the working class, perceive themselves as middle-class members and/or as 'white-collar' workers, and thus do not align themselves or even recognise the need to align themselves with working-class movements and struggles. And it is reasonable to expect that while they continue not to recognise their communality with that class they will continually fail to align themselves with the working class. In this respect ideology strikes a double blow. It obscures, for certain people, their class location (that is, their objective place in the class struggle), just as it also confuses what their class position (the place to be taken in the class struggle) is, or ought to be.

This mystification is further enhanced by building up the allegiance of people to fetishised centres of unity; to centres such as the family, the school, the church, the team, and most importantly the nation or State - centres which really do unite people (thus the use of 'fetishised'), but which unite people across class lines, and thus serve three distinct yet closely interrelated purposes. First, such unity disguises and conceals class lines by bringing workers and capitalists together on the same side of the fence: they can belong to the same church, go to the same schools, support the same charities etc., as if it were the case that their objective interests were common. Second, this unity both provides and encourages the search for common interests and goals; in times of impending 'moral breakdown' both workers and capitalists are urged by the clergy to maintain the notion of the sanctity of the family, and in times of crisis both workers and capitalists are expected to subordinate any sectional interests in favour of the 'national interest' (what is rarely noticed is that the 'common' interests - here the family and the nation - are instituted and defined to the capitalists' advantage). Third, such unity manages to divide the working class against itself: allegiance to fetishised centres of unity can pit men against women, race against race, protestant against catholic, school against school: at a pitiful extreme it results in the workers of one city engaging in violence with the workers of another city when their respective football teams meet (not to mention the workers of one State killing workers of another State to protect their national interests in times of war). The ever increasing unity and struggle across fetishised centres, and the corresponding failure of workers to unite successfully as workers pay great tribute in practice to the pervasiveness and effectiveness of ideology in protecting and maintaining capitalist social relations. In effect the ruling class is actually succeeding in the class struggle in this respect by confusing its opponents with regard to where the real battle ground is.

CONCLUSION

It was stated at the end of the first chapter that what we were
seeking was a detailed understanding of where teachers stand
and what they actually do within the total dynamic of a social
system, or an understanding of the social function of teachers
with reference to production relations. If we now take the Marxist
leads – that classes are groups of people bearing particular relations to the mode of production, that the nature of any social
formation can be characterised in terms of the state of play of
contemporary class struggle, and that it is class struggle which
brings about social change and historical transformation, it follows that what we are really seeking is an understanding of 'where
teachers stand' with regard to contemporary and future class
struggle.

To achieve such an understanding we must accomplish two
things. First, we must identify the class location of teachers: that
is, the location (within the contemporary class structure) of
teachers (as agents within an ongoing production process) on the
basis of their real (economic, political and ideological) relations in
that process. Second, we have to examine the interrelationship
of class location with the technical job of teaching itself, with
special reference to those very basic contradictions previously
identified as being inherent within the technical job under the
conditions of capitalism. This latter examination will assist in
throwing further light on the issue of the class position of
teachers as it now stands, and as it might stand in the future.

The two tasks will not be undertaken in complete separation:
they will be integrated at least to the extent that the second of
them will be undertaken within the overall context of identification
of the class location of teachers; and it is to this matter that we
now turn.

Chapter 3
The economic identification of teachers

INTRODUCTION

Just as class struggle takes place on three completely interrelated levels - economic, political, and ideological - so too must class location be identified on the basis of the interconnection of economic, political and ideological relations to a production process. These relations are, in practice, inseparable as far as the final picture is concerned, but the sheer logistics of writing demand, at least in the first place, that they be dealt with separately and thus to some extent in abstraction from the real situation. This chapter, therefore, will be concerned with economic identification or the economic relation of teachers to the contemporary capitalist situation, while political and ideological relations will be explored in the chapters to follow: with all three examined an attempt will then be made to build up a composite (and less abstract) picture.

If we were dealing with the economic identification of a production-line worker or a coal miner the question might be easily settled, and this chapter could end in a matter of sentences. Teaching, however, raises more problems regarding economic identification than most occupational groups, and so we are in for a long, hard, and ultimately inconclusive slog. Teachers obviously do not own or control the means of production and thus cannot be identified exclusively in terms of performing the global function of capital. But on the other hand teachers neither make products directly, nor are they connected with actual production even to the extent that quality control personnel or forepeople are, and thus it would appear, at least on the face of it, that they cannot be identified simply in terms of performing the function of the collective labourer. Just how they are, in fact, to be identified depends eventually on how certain theoretic and practical issues are resolved, which means entering into some initial forays, the first of which concerns the nature and economic implications of productive and unproductive labour.

PRODUCTIVE AND UNPRODUCTIVE LABOUR

If we held fast to our initial (simplistic) definition of classes we would find that close to 90 per cent of the contemporary labour force could be characterised as working class in that they do not own and/or control the means of production and in that they gain their livelihood by selling their labour power either directly or

indirectly to capitalists. But two complications immediately arise.
First, some of these people exchange their labour power against
capital (being paid directly by the capitalists) while some exchange
their labour power against revenue (being paid, for instance, out
of taxes), and so we already have one difference in economic
relations within this group. Second, some of these people engage
in the production of commodities such that their labour valorises
or increases the value of capital (the workers on the General
Motors production line produce cars and other commodities which
the capitalist sells at a profit and thus increases the value of
capital), while some people do not produce commodities and therefore provide the capitalist with no surplus value by means of
their labour (the bank teller, for instance, makes nothing which
can be sold, and so does not contribute to the valorisation
process). Thus we have a second difference in economic relations
within the overall group. But the two issues are not mutually
exclusive. Someone who exchanges labour power against capital
might or might not contribute directly to the valorisation process
(the panel-beater does whereas the tea-lady doesn't) just as
someone who exchanges labour power against revenue might or
might not contribute to the valorisation process (in this case the
miner in a nationalised industry within capitalism does, whereas
the ordinary bank teller doesn't). It would appear, then, that
four different economic relations actually exist within the initial
group.

They can, however, be reduced in number to two by the application of a more objective form of categorisation, and here we turn
to Marx's distinction between productive and unproductive labour.

Marx is perfectly clear and consistent with regard to this distinction. The concept of productive labour in Marx's formulation
is a historically specific concept; that is, there is a distinction to
be made between productive labour in general and productive
labour under the capitalist mode of production. Now the concept
of productive labour under the capitalist mode of production has
nothing to do with the determinate content of the labour itself
nor has it anything to do with the use value of that which is
produced. The very same kind of labour may be productive or
unproductive (the rider 'under the capitalist mode of production'
is implied from here on). The crux of the productive/unproductive
distinction lies in the area of exchange. Productive labour is
exchanged with capital to produce surplus value; unproductive
labour is exchanged with revenue.

Productive labour (which, we recall, is now performed collectively) is also not to be equated necessarily with direct engage-
ment in the production of use values. As Carchedi notes: 'The
technician engaged in quality control work, for example, takes
part in the labour process just as much as the worker who directly
produces the commodities whose quality must be controlled';[1] and
in the words of Marx himself:[2]

> The product ceases to be the direct product of the individual,
> and becomes a social product, produced in common by a col-

lective labourer, i.e. by a certain combination of workmen, each
of whom takes only a part, greater or less, in the manipulation
of the subject of their labour. As the cooperative character of
the labour-process becomes more and more marked, so, as a
necessary consequence, does our notion of productive labour,
and of its agent the productive labourer, become extended. In
order to labour productively, it is no longer necessary for you
to do manual work yourself; enough if you are an organ of the
collective labourer, and perform one of its subordinate functions.
The notion of the productive labourer thus extends over all who
take part in the process of production of surplus value, whether
this be done manually or mentally, and whether the labourer is
engaged directly in the production of use values or not. Similarly
the notion of the unproductive labourer extends over all, mental
and manual workers alike, whose labour is exchanged with revenue; and these unproductive labourers can be divided into three
categories: (a) those employed by capital to control, account for,
channel and sell the use values or commodities, e.g. managers,
accountants, bank employees; (b) those employed to provide personal service to their employer, e.g. chauffeurs, tax agents,
domestic servants; and (c) those employed by the State to maintain the overall conditions of capitalist production, e.g. public
servants and certain transport workers.

Now, where does this leave teachers?

As far as Marx was concerned teachers were productive labourers
producing surplus value for capital. As he noted:[3]

a school master is a productive labourer, when, in addition to
belabouring the heads of his scholars, he works like a horse
to enrich the school proprietors, That the latter has laid out
his capital in a teaching factory, instead of a sausage factory,
does not alter the relation.

But conditions, of course, have changed since Marx wrote, and
now within the capitalist mode of production the vast majority of
teachers (especially the ones we are concerned with in this book)
are no longer employed by individual capitalist proprietors. They
are employed by the State and they are paid out of revenue –
they are therefore unproductive labourers who fall clearly into
category (c) above. Thus we reach our first definitive point concerning the economic identification of teachers – but only to find
ourselves poised on the brink of a highly controversial area.

When we move further into the implications of productive and
unproductive labour we find that two possible positions can be
held: (1) that productive labourers, and only productive labourers,
are to be identified with the working class; and (2) that there is
no theoretical or practical basis for identifying only productive
labourers with the working class. As Gough has demonstrated[4]
both positions, while contradictory, can lay claim to supporting
evidence in Marx's writings; and not surprisingly we find that
contemporary Marxists are divided over this issue. And as far as
our particular investigation is concerned, it is clear that if we
adopt position (1) then teachers must be excluded from the work-

ing class, whereas if we adopt position (2) then the possibility remains open of including teachers within the working class.

A second complication now arises. There are similarities between some productive labourers and some unproductive labourers. A characteristic which most unproductive labourers have in common with productive labourers is that they are expropriated of surplus labour. With productive labourers this occurs indirectly through the production of surplus value (and here we speak of economic exploitation) whereas with unproductive labourers it occurs directly (and thus we speak of economic oppression). Could we therefore place those unproductive labourers who are economically oppressed in the same alignment with productive labourers - a move which might open up the possibility of including teachers in with the working class? Another characteristic held in common among productive and unproductive labourers is that some in each category produce use values. Could we use this characteristic to determine a similar alignment among those productive and unproductive labourers sharing this feature (which again might place teachers back with the proletariat since teachers today can be considered as producers of use value)?

Further complications arise when we recognise that unproductive labourers are not a homogeneous group, and thus the possibility emerges of subdividing them in terms of certain characteristics, into differently aligned groupings. One of the most ingenious attempts to do this has been provided by Paul Baran.[5]

Baran initially breaks the nexus between productive labour and the production of surplus value, and re-defines unproductive labour as:

all labour resulting in the output of goods and services the demand for which is attributable to the specific conditions and relationships of the capitalist system, and which would be absent in a rationally ordered society.

He is thus able to distinguish a particular group of people who are supported by surplus but the demand for whose labour would be magnified rather than nihilated in a rationally ordered (non-capitalist) society:

Scientists, physicians, artists, teachers, and similarly occupied people live off the economic surplus but engage in labour the demand for which in a rationally ordered society, far from disappearing, would become multiplied and intensified to an unprecedented degree...

and Baran suggests the advisability of considering these people separately especially as far as class identification is concerned, in terms of the context of rational social reconstruction.

Now there is much to argue with regarding Baran's basic re-definition, but he does raise a particularly important point regarding the function of teachers, and one which is echoed by other major theorists in the area. Mandel, for instance, without similarly redefining unproductive labour, includes teachers (along with scientists and technologists) among those who 'enhance the impact of the working class and revolutionary organisation'[6] because of

their capacity to pass on indispensable knowledge; and teachers
are again distinguished from certain other unproductive labourers
on the grounds that teaching is not demanded specifically by
capitalism (as company law, conveyancing and advertising are)
and would actually expand in a socialist system. Put more technically, teachers are differentiated from certain other unproductive labourers in that their objective interests are neither tied to
nor limited by the continuation of capitalism. This is a point which
will assume greater importance as this overall investigation proceeds.

Having now introduced the major issues and controversies which
bear on the particular problem at hand our purpose from here on
(considering the nature of this work) will be merely to attend to
them rather than engage in lengthy and technical discussions aimed
at resolutions. We can conclude this section, therefore, by reiterating that teachers are unproductive labourers employed by the
State to maintain the overall conditions of capitalism; but also by
recognising that our further exploration into identification of
class location would do well to consider the specific conditions of
the economic oppression of teachers - to what extent does this
approximate the economic exploitation of productive labourers? -
as well as the historically specific circumstances surrounding
teachers (who have already changed, under capitalism, from productive to unproductive labourers, yet whose future interests
are not objectively linked either to maintaining that position or to
maintaining capitalism itself).

One final point. For the purpose of the following discussion I
am adopting the position labelled (1) above; namely that only
productive labourers are to be identified with the working class.
This manoeuvre, which entails a prima facie exclusion of teachers
from the working class, is being employed not because of any con-
viction in its rightness (actually I am by no means convinced that
the general issue concerned can be satisfactorily resolved) but
rather as a precaution against avoiding complexities and being
lured too easily into nice conclusions.

THE 'NEW MIDDLE CLASS'

We noted in our previous chapter that modes of production undergo historical transformation, and we recognised there that capitalism has developed from an entrepreneurial form into a corporate
form. This development has carried with it a large number of
changes, three of which are particularly relevant to this present
investigation. First, the function of labour is now performed
collectively, and this in turn has led to a large proliferation of
unproductive labour concerned mainly with coordination of a now
much-divided labour process. Second, the function of capital is
now performed collectively or globally, which in turn has led to
a similar proliferation of people now concerned with control and
surveillance of the divided labour process. Third, and in large

part but not entirely related to the first two points, a high proportion of the present day work-force is not engaged in the production of commodities. The overall result of these changes indicates that, with regard to relations to the mode of production under contemporary corporate capitalism, we appear now to have three rather than the two traditional classes commonly associated with the capitalist mode of production. A new middle class has emerged.

This new middle class is not, of course, being identified in terms of social stratification picked out by such factors as income or status, but rather in terms of the position it occupies within the capitalist production process as determined by the social division of labour. We are not talking, therefore, about a vertical structure with the capitalists on top, the workers on the bottom, and this class somewhere in between; but rather of a class within the capitalist mode of production which performs an economic function not identifiable strictly with either the function of the collective labourer nor with the global function of capital, and in this sense positioned 'somewhere in between' the proletariat and the bourgeoisie.

There have been many attempts to account for and analyse this class, and to identify its economic location; and it is hardly our intention here to enter into the controversy and debate which has been generated. (For detailed references see Select Bibliography; Section B.) What we shall do instead is follow one particular line which we consider to be promising, and then consider what implications it throws up regarding teachers. To begin with, therefore, we will lay out, in slightly amended form, the position put forward by Guglielmo Carchedi.[7]

Carchedi defines the working and capitalist classes in terms of four fundamental dichotomies. The working class are:

A   the producers (in the sense of producers of surplus value) and thus the exploited.
B   the non-owners of the means of production.
C   the labourers.
D   those agents whose income (i) is determined by the value of their labour power; (ii) is produced by themselves; and (iii) is thus paid back to them by the capitalists.

The capitalist class is the exact opposite, and is defined as:

A_1 the non-producers (and thus the exploiters).
B_1 the owners of the means of production.
C_1 the non-labourers.
D_1 those whose income (i) is derived from surplus value; (ii) is limited by the extent of that surplus value (and by the needs of capital accumulation); and (iii) is not produced by them, yet is produced in their own enterprise, by 'their own' workers.

The four fundamental dichotomies then, are those of producer/non-producer, exploited/exploiter, labourer/non-labourer, and owner/non-owner; and these in turn lead to two sets of equivalences:

E_1 labourer = non-owner = exploited or oppressed = producer.
E_2 non-labourer = owner = exploiter or oppressor = non-
producer.

Now Carchedi suggests that these equivalences (the inclusion
here, and at other places in this section, of 'oppressed' and
'oppressor' is ours, not Carchedi's) are concise ways of defining
the working and capitalist classes respectively, on the level of
the pure capitalist structure, and considering only the production relations upon which the surplus-value-producing process
rests.

There are, however, two central problems to be overcome. First,
the 'pure capitalist structure' is an abstraction; and second, the
changes from entrepreneurial to corporate capitalism – with the
attendant loss of control of the labour process by the direct producers, and the proliferation of people in positions of coordination,
control and surveillance – demand that reconsideration be given
to contemporary production relations wherein unproductive labour
has become a major element 'within' the overall surplus-value-
producing process, and wherein the functions of labour and capital are now performed collectively (these two particular matters
obviously being closely interrelated).

Carchedi thus enters into detailed analysis of how the function
of the collective labourer and the global function of capital are
performed within contemporary production relations; and it is
from the latter that the most important insights (as far as this
particular investigation is concerned) emerge.

The global function of capital, according to Carchedi, is performed by a tripartite structure. There is one part which performs only the function of capital and has real ownership of
capital (the 'pure' capitalists). A second part performs the global
function of capital without having the real ownership of capital
(e.g. directors and senior management). And there is a third
part which does not have economic ownership of capital and which
performs both the function of the collective labourer and the
global function of capital in a variable balance. The global function of capital, then, is not the province only of the 'pure' capitalist. It is performed also by a class which:

1   does not own, either legally or economically, the means of
    production.
2   performs both the global function of capital and the function
    of the collective labourer.
3   is therefore both the labourer (productive or unproductive)
    and the non-labourer.
4   is both exploiter (or oppressor) and exploited (or oppressed).

It is this class which Carchedi terms the 'new middle class'; and
its key features are the first two listed above: it performs the
global function of capital without owning the means of production,
and it performs this function in conjunction with the function of
the collective labourer.

We see, then, that neither of the equivalences previously drawn
out holds for this class. Since its members do not own the means

of production, E_2 does not hold together, and thus the elements
of non-labourer, non-producer, and exploiter are not always
dominant in this class. And since this class performs both the
global function of capital and the function of the collective labourer
combined in a variable balance, there are sectors of it where the
function of the collective labourer, and thus the elements of E_1
are dominant. The lesson to be taken here is that, when investigating particular members of this class, specific attention has to
be given to each element in the equivalences. Not very much is
gained by identifying (say) both accountants and teachers as
members of the new middle class. The task still remains of determining the balance in which each performs the function of labour
and the function of capital, and the extent to which each is owner
or non-owner, exploited (or oppressed) or exploiter (or oppressor), and producer (either productively or unproductively) or
non-producer. It may turn out, for instance, that one is far more
closely related to the working class (or the capitalist class) than
the other.

In summary, we can state that the new middle class does not
own, either legally or economically, the means of production, yet
part of their labour time is devoted to performing the function of
capital; i.e. the (unproductive) work of control and surveillance.
Part of their time, however, is also devoted to performing the
function of the collective worker, either through performing the
(unproductive) work of coordination and organisation of the
labour process, or through productive labour directly related to
the process of production of surplus value, or both. And we can
now appreciate why they usually have economic privilege over the
working class; for there are, in fact, two components making up
their income. There is a wage component connected with performing the function of the collective labourer, and a revenue component connected with performing the global function of capital.
Income is thus only partly determined by the value of labour
power. For instance, a forelady on a job is paid more than the
labourers not because her labour power is 'worth more' in exchange terms, but because she receives a wage component for
her direct labour and/or work of coordination, as well as a
revenue component for the work of control and surveillance,
which requires specialised knowledge which the labourers do not
have.

TEACHERS, AND THE 'NEW MIDDLE CLASS'

Before approaching Carchedi we had established two apparently
contradictory things about the economic identification of teachers.
On the one hand they are unproductive labourers (belonging to
the category employed by the State to maintain the overall conditions of capitalist production) who do not produce surplus value:
on that count we excluded them from the working class. On the
other hand they do not own the means of production (and although

they derive their income from the surplus value produced by others, they derive this indirectly through taxes, and not directly): on both counts they must be excluded from the capitalist class. If nothing else Carchedi's analysis should provide us with the confidence not to be deterred by this contradictory state of affairs, but it provides us with more than this - namely with particular reference points for making a more positive identification. It might be well, then, to see how teachers match up with the categorisation of the new middle class which we have adopted.[8]

Teachers, as State employees (or as we shall see later, as employees of the State-as-representative-of-capital-in-general) automatically perform the global function of capital. In the most general of terms they perform this function by maintaining and legitimating the overall conditions of capitalist production. More specifically, they exercise control and surveillance over the new generations (and thus the future work-force) in the actual performance of their technical job through the part they play in character moulding, in the development of attitudes, through assisting in the hierarchic selection process through which school children are inserted into the labour force, and through their role as legitimators in all these areas. Eventually we have to be far more specific than this, but such specificity must wait until the following chapters dealing with political and ideological identification when we examine what teachers actually do in terms of their technical job. But at a fairly wide level of generalisation we can equate performing the global function of capital and thus the exercise of control, mainly, but not only with that part of the teacher's labour which is directed towards socialisation through transmitting the hidden curriculum of schooling.

Teachers also perform the function of the collective labourer (unproductively) through their part in instruction and coordination of the (future) work force; by transmitting to the new generation, in unequal fashion, those general (and at times specific) skills and knowledge which will enable the individual members of that generation to take up, collectively, all the respective places in the divided labour process. At the same wide level of generalisation we can equate performing the function of the collective labourer, and thus the exercise of instruction, mainly, but not only, with that part of the teacher's labour which is directed to transmitting the overt curriculum of schooling (and it is here that Education must come in, if it is to come in at all). Part of the reason for these generalisations being so wide (and qualified) lies in the fact that not only are transmission of the hidden and overt curricula inextricably intertwined processes, but also (as we shall see in Chapters 4 and 5) in that control is similarly caught up with instruction in schools as they now stand. It is far less of a generalisation or abstraction to state that, in the technical job of simultaneously transmitting the hidden and overt curricula, teachers are simultaneously controlling and instructing, and simultaneously performing the global function of capital and the function of the collective labourer. Another way of putting the

generalisations, and one which will be made more of later, is to
suggest that teachers, in performing those technical aspects
related to socialisation (which include control and some instruction) are performing the global function of capital, while in performing those technical aspects related to Educating (which are
concerned only with instruction, although not all instruction is
related to Educating) they are performing the function of the
collective labourer (remembering always that these aspects are
performed simultaneously as the technical job is now structured).
If this generalisation is seen to hold then it becomes obvious that
teachers, on two counts, can never be concerned exclusively
with Educating within a context where they perform, in part, the
global function of capital. In the first place performance of the
global function of capital is, as we have already seen, directed
mainly if not entirely towards socialisation and control. And in
the second place performing the global function of capital entails
serving capital; and as we have also seen, capital (or capitalist
social relations) are properly served only if large numbers of
the population remain unEducated. If teachers were to be solely
concerned with Educating, and if they were able to direct their
activities towards the Education of all pupils, they would at least
have to cease performing the global function of capital. Educating
related as it is to instruction (even though not all instruction is
Educative) brings into play only the function of the collective
labourer; and, conversely, teachers can begin to direct their
efforts solely towards Educating only when they perform a single
economic function – that of the collective labourer – which in turn
means engaging in instructional activities in a context radically
different from the one presently experienced. (Such a context
would not, of course, somehow magically cast off any attachment
to a hidden curriculum, but with the function of control gone the
hidden curriculum would also change radically.)

Certain more obvious and elementary points can also be made
regarding the economic identification of teachers. Teachers
clearly perform the function of the collective labourer in that they
are salaried, contract workers. Also teachers, while not being
economically exploited since they do not produce surplus value
directly, are nevertheless economically oppressed in that they
are expropriated of surplus labour. Their actual affinities on
these elements with the working class cannot be determined, however, without a far more detailed examination of their actual conditions of work, and this will be considered at a later stage. Next,
since teachers perform both economic functions their income is
made up of a wage or salary component and a revenue component,
which gives them a small economic privilege over the working
class. Finally, teachers neither own nor control the means of production, and as teachers can never own or control the means of
production: they are thus forever separated from the 'pure' capitalists, and at the most can function only as agents of capital.

We can conclude, therefore, that in terms of economic identification teachers can be recognised as being located in neither the

working nor the capitalist classes, but rather as bearing features common to both. They perform both the function of the collective labourer and the global function of capital. In terms of the fundamental dichotomies set up earlier they are identifiable as being: labourer (unproductive)/non-owner/oppressed (economically)/non-producer (of surplus value). This relationship fits neither of the basic equivalences. It is completely distinguished from the capitalist equivalence (E_2) because of the element of non-ownership; but it could be brought in line with the working-class equivalence (E_1) if non-producers of surplus value (in the form of unproductive labourers) were included there, in which case it would fall into line to the extent that the economic oppression of teachers approximates in form the economic exploitation of productive labourers. To this we can add that teachers are at present 'tied' to capitalism since they are employed by the representative of capital-in-general, and thus have an immediate interest in the continuation of capitalism; but since their job does not depend on the continued operation of the capitalist mode of production their long-term objective interests are not necessarily linked to the preservation and survival of capitalism.

PROLETARIANISATION

While the 'orthodox' problematic seems preoccupied with the issue of upward mobility within social formations, the Marxist problematic is particularly incisive with regard to the process of 'downward mobility' or proletarianisation within capitalist production relations.

To understand proletarianisation we need to grasp only two fundamental points. First, the continuation of the capitalist mode of production requires a continued contraction in the number of agents involved in the global function of capital as pure capitalists: or, to put that more simply, capital must pass into fewer and fewer hands. This, in consequence, means the increasing exclusion of people from the global function of capital, or a continuing push towards the function of the collective labourer. Second, if the capitalist mode of production is to continue, then the accumulation process must continue. This requires that there be an ever-rising rate of surplus value which, in the long term, can be brought about only by the progressive devaluation of labour power. But this cannot be done universally, for the point would soon be reached where many labourers would not be able to consume sufficiently to reproduce their own labour power. What happens, then, is that the devaluation is directed primarily at skilled labour power, which is progressively devalued to the level of average labour power. This, it must be realised, is a continuing (virtually cyclic) process. It is not a matter of present skilled labour power being devalued to average labour power, and that is that. The case is rather that the actual devaluation of skilled labour power brings about increases in the social division of

labour, which in turn calls for new skilled labourers to perform
new functions, which in turn establishes new skilled labour
power, which in turn must be devalued, and so on. What we find,
then, is 'the constant creation of new skilled functions and, at
the same time. . . the constant need of capital to devalue, to
down-grade those functions to simpler and simpler ones.'[9] What
is linear rather than cyclic about the process, however, is that
the number of bearers of skilled labour power gradually diminishes
in the process. Let us consider a practical example.

In the early days of the motion-picture industry, theatres
were, in general, independently owned, and often the owner was
also the projectionist, which was a highly valued skill at the time.
With the contraction of capital, the independent theatre owner
was either bought out or squeezed out, and many joined the ranks
of the collective labourer, some as projectionists along with the
other highly valued projectionists. But then projectionism began
to become less valued. On the one hand, technical colleges trained
an abundance of projectionists (at minimal cost to capital), such
that the skilled labour power became less rare, and thus of less
value. On the other hand, new skilled functionaries developed
projectors that were self-threading and self-focusing, such that
projectionism became de-skilled as labour, and thus further devalued as labour power. The next step, performed by newer
skilled functionaries, was the development of computer-linked
automatic projectors, such that today one operator of a computer
keyboard can control projection simultaneously in a large number
of theatres without a projectionist to be seen anywhere. Thus the
once highly valued skills of projectionism, and then also of
developing self-threading projectors, have become greatly devalued, as will the skill of operating the computer keyboard in
turn become devalued as a new skilled functionary develops some
means whereby many keyboards can be operated by a silicon chip.
That, under capitalism, is progress! For the people suffering it
at the time however, it is proletarianisation - basically to be
understood as a process of devaluation of labour power from skilled to average labour power, but bringing with it very obvious
manifestations: namely lowered living conditions and real wages,
loss of control and independence along with growing alienation in
the work situation, movement from prestige employment to un-
qualified employment or unemployment; and overall, vulnerability
to further exploitation and/or oppression accompanied by a need
to acquiesce in whatever might still be going. And no one is
immune from the proletarianisation process: while it might be nice
to be among the newly skilled bearers of highly valued labour
power, that labour power itself must inevitably become devalued
under capitalism. While the writing might not be on the wall for
individuals, who might fail to outlive the devaluation process or
who might re-train, it certainly is on the wall for skill-groups.
In terms of our immediate concern today's living teachers might
not become proletarianised in their life-times (and even this is
very doubtful) but teaching will become progressively de-skilled

and devalued as labour power. In fact the process is already
under way.

Proletarianisation has a special significance for the new middle
class; and seeing that we followed Carchedi into this area let us
now follow him further.[10]

Carchedi argues that the new middle class is vulnerable to proletarianisation on a double front. As performer of the function of
collective labourer it will find its labour power progressively devalued. But since the accumulation needs of capital require a constant decrease in the area devoted to the performance of the
global function of capital, and thus a tendency to decrease the
number, and the real wages, of those performing the function of
control and surveillance, the new middle class can expect an
erosion also of the time it spends performing the global function
of capital, and eventually the complete loss of this function. Proletarianisation, for this class, means a return to the function of
the collective labourer along with devaluation of its labour power
to an average or unskilled level. (To be more technically correct,
proletarianisation is the actual limit of this process.) The most
vulnerable members of the new middle class are those at the lower
end of it; but it might be worth the while of all those occupying
this middle position to reflect on the fact that, with very few
exceptions, there is only one direction they can go in.

This is a depressing picture. It might appear, however, that
for teachers in particular rays of hope shine out of the gloom,
given our previous recognition that loss of the global function of
capital and a return to the function of the collective labourer are
the very things required if teachers are to have any chance of
engaging solely, or primarily, in Educating. Unfortunately this is
not so, for Carchedi's overall picture must be modified in small
yet highly significant ways when relating it specifically to
teachers. We shall indicate shortly that the proletarianisation process for teachers involves progressive devaluation of labour
power accompanied by an increased yet de-skilled performance of
the function of control and surveillance, as teachers become
alienated agents of the proletarianisation of others.

THE ECONOMIC FUNCTION OF TEACHERS

In order to understand the economic function of teachers two
initial (and extremely obvious) points must be recognised. First,
almost all the expenditure on schooling comes from taxes; that is,
from surplus value generated by productive labour and from
exchange against revenue from unproductive labour. Second, as
we have continually noted, there is a growing proportion of unproductive labourers (constituting virtually the whole of the new
middle class, plus some others) being employed within societies
based on corporate-capitalist production relations. Now what
this simply means is that more and more of those who pass through
schooling (under the present circumstances) will end up in un-

productive labour, not generating surplus value (directly) for the capitalists; and thus a growing proportion of educational expenditure is presently being consumed unproductively by capital. Schooling, as it now stands, therefore represents a drain on surplus value for capitalism which is, of course, an intolerable situation (for capital). And since capitalism is firmly stuck with its ideological commitment to and political need of compulsory schooling, and possibly with lengthening the average period of schooling, the only possibility open is to turn some aspects of educational expenditure towards counteracting the drain on surplus value.

There are two related ways by which this can be achieved. The first is to direct educational expenditure towards enhancing the basic training of future productive labourers such that they require less training elsewhere, and such that their increased future productivity offsets both the increased cost of their reproduction and the drain in surplus value, actually resulting in an increase in surplus value. The second is to reduce the drain brought about through the production of future unproductive labourers either by producing less of them, or by directing them back into the area of productive labour. To put all of that more simply, capitalism, in order to offset its growing educational expenditure on unproductive labour, has to get a lot more back out of its educational expenditure on productive labour as well as making present unproductive labour more productive in the future. And to put that even more simply, capitalism has to direct its educational expenditure towards the increased proletarianisation of the future productive and unproductive labourers.[11]

It is rarely put in those ways, however. What we tend to hear instead are calls for more emphasis in schools on the 'basics', and expression of the need for a closer relationship between schooling and future employment (this latter often being put forward as a panacea for structural unemployment). And what we are tending to find in schools is precisely this – increasing concern with the 'basics' (rationalised as a necessary balancing reaction either to recent progressive tendencies or to the perennial myth of declining standards); increased job orientation and concern with future employment; and increasing expenditure directed at productive labour coupled with decreasing expenditure directed at unproductive labour, as the recent and continuing cuts in areas like Arts and teacher education alongside the growing allocations to technical education within schools and varied advanced colleges bear witness to. As O'Connor noted almost a decade ago:[12]

> In the last analysis, the only way to ameliorate the fiscal crisis in the schools and colleges is to place the production and distribution of education on a more 'efficient' basis. This includes abandoning traditional liberal arts programs (except in upper-class schools) and substituting 'career education'. At the secondary level this 'reform' is well under way. . . . The essence of the 'reform' is to reorder and modernise school curricula to ensure that every youth has a 'marketable skill' no matter when he or she leaves school.

The situation, then, is that educational expenditure is being re-
directed towards enhancing productivity, while educational
ideology is pushing the line of making pupils more employable.
And teachers, as the agents caught in the process, are actively
(if unconsciously) promoting the proletarianisation of the new
generation of labourers. This whole issue now requires further
and more methodical consideration.

There can be little doubt that the actual emphasis in schooling-
in-general has shifted away from ideals associated with Education
(like 'enlightenment', 'liberation from ignorance', 'development of
the full capabilities of each child', 'initiation into forms of knowledge' etc.) and towards enhancing the basic training of productive workers. Now teachers-in-general are faced with two groups
of children in their classrooms; those who will become productive
labourers and those who will become unproductive labourers (and
on a State-wide basis these groups are near to equal, although
they might not be in any particular classroom).

With regard to the future productive labourers teachers, regardless of how they might see or rationalise their role, are engaged
in little more than raising the future productivity and exploitation of this group. But what of the future unproductive labourers?

Teachers will, of course, continue to assist in the reproduction
of children of engineers, architects and lawyers into future
engineers, architects and lawyers; and they will continue to elevate some children of the production line or the factory floor to
the level of unproductive labourer (and even to the level of professional). But success in this area (which could be loosely linked
with 'Educating') is directly connected with the unproductive educational expenditure of capital which cannot be consumed indefin-
itely, and which when consumed must be recouped by capital in
the form of surplus value. Two obvious conclusions follow, on
strictly economic grounds.

First, there must be a limit to the number of unproductive
labourers which schools can produce. It is an economic absurdity
to suggest that teachers could elevate (or Educate) all to the
various levels of unproductive labourers: the interference-
elimination principle is thus seen to apply not merely at a theoretical level but at the practical bedrock level of economics. It can
also be added here that the number of unproductive labourers
produced must begin to decline, and that, while a small (decreasing) number of highly skilled functionaries must continue to be
produced, the skill-level in general of unproductive labour must
continue to decrease and be devalued. Thus teachers in the future
will be faced not only with a quantitative limit steadily on the decline, but also with a necessary decline in the qualitative limits
required of all but the very highest among their top graduands.
Or to put that another way, teachers will be required to train
(and perhaps Educate) a decreasing number of people more highly,
but overall to Educate less people, less well.

Second, the cruel fact has to be faced that the production of
unproductive labourers must at least be counterbalanced by the

production (at minimal cost) of productive labourers equipped for increased productivity. Teachers cannot escape this, nor can they escape the ironic paradox underlying the economic function of their work; namely that whatever success they have in turning children into unproductive labourers must be at least balanced by the production of more, and more exploitable, productive workers: the production (or Education) of unproductive labourers impels the production of exploitable workers. Again this holds at the hard bedrock level of economics, rather than just at the theoretical and practical level of recognising that not everybody can become a doctor. The situation as it actually stands is that those children 'elevated' or directed by teachers into unproductive levels (and as we shall see, they are not necessarily the brightest, most able, or 'best suited' children) are so elevated and directed at the expense of others who must not only be 'kept down' but be kept further down. Thus if teacher-success is defined in any way related to the production of unproductive labourers (which it usually is, as is the rhetoric surrounding the notions of 'Education' or 'Educated people'), then teacher-success entails teacher-failure. Of course, any individual teacher might succeed with any individual child or group of children, but in doing so then the more that teacher, or others, have to serve the function of capital with the rest. And teachers taken globally clearly serve the interests of capital: ironically, through their very efforts to better the conditions of all they become (largely) unwitting agents in worsening the conditions of the majority of their charges.

THE PROLETARIANISATION OF TEACHERS

Teachers already resemble the proletariat in a large number of ways. Although salaried, they work for the wage form, and are contracted to perform agreed-on activities in return for agreed-on remuneration. They cannot select their clientele, and despite fairly intense struggle and some gains they have little occupational independence, little control over their labour process, and little access to the means of production – things which become clearly evident when teachers are compared with lawyers, doctors, or even university lecturers. Their differences from the proletariat lie in the areas of the exchange relation of their labour (teachers are unproductive labourers exchanging labour against revenue), along with their marginal economic privilege based on their possession of (disputably) specialised esoteric knowledge and skills required for the performance of their job. In all of these areas they are highly vulnerable to proletarianisation.

Let us consider first that area central to the notion of proletarianisation; namely devaluation of skilled labour power to average labour power.

Teachers, as we have seen earlier, have resolutely hung on to and perpetuated the notion that they are bearers of highly skilled

labour power, and it would appear from the continued lengthening
of teacher-training courses and the attendant injections of further
pre-service theoretic studies concerning both content and method
that they are becoming more highly skilled labourers. This, however, is not borne out in the classroom where, in fact, teachers
are now finding themselves facing both de-skilling and devaluation
of labour power.[13]

This is most obvious in the areas of curriculum packages and
technical innovations. The production of curriculum packages has
developed into a very large industry, and in many cases the
existence of such packages has already de-skilled some teachers'
work to the level of distributing pre-chosen material, checking
pre-set tests, and general filing duties. While it is almost certainly the case that such materials are employed (by teachers)
with the pupils' benefits in mind, teachers should be aware that
the more they rely on SRA or National Geographic or other
packages the more they are making themselves substitutable by
less skilled people, and the less their particular labour power
becomes valued (they are also, of course, assisting the capitalist
producers of the packages to increase profits). The same holds
for the use of new technical innovations like video-recorders,
computer terminals, and the like. Many lessons now require of
the teacher little more than the turning on and off of a switch -
the rest is done by the video-tape or computer print-out. Now
there is obviously the opportunity here for vast rationalisation,
whereby classroom teachers could end up as not-so-glorified
child minders and filing clerks while a few newly highly skilled
experts select kits and programme the day's activities for the
whole school. The trend is very much under way already.

The second area of vulnerability to proletarianisation is that
of production relations. Although we have accepted that unproductive labourers are outside the valorisation process it is
possible, under certain conditions, for their exchange relations
to very closely approximate that of production of surplus value.
This occurs when increasingly capitalist methods of organisation
and criteria of accountability are introduced into the labour process which bring about the necessity of reducing socially necessary
labour time to a minimum. And this is precisely what has happened
to teachers. The calls for a return to the 'basics' and to make
schooling job-oriented have also been accompanied by calls for
teacher-accountability, elimination of 'wastage', and increased
efficiency. The pressure is now on teachers to come up with
tangible results and to cut out the frills, in much the same way
as the pressure is on a piece worker or a production-line attendant, and there is a very clear drift back to an unofficial 'payment
by results' system. Actually it is more like a 'payment for results'
system, wherein the teacher loses autonomy and independence
and simply turns out products, and whereby exchange relations
fall more into line with those of productive labourers. Here, as
with the rationalisations pointed to above, we find the capitalist
mode of production increasingly impinging on, invading, and

restructuring the technical job of teaching.

One further and obvious area of impending proletarianisation is revealed by the recognition that teachers-in-general will be progressively required to Educate less people, less well. Under such circumstances a large number of teachers (most especially those who now teach both junior and senior secondary forms) will not require their present level of expert content knowledge, and the possibility looms of the reintroduction of an old-time division among teachers – namely the existence of a few highly trained people teaching the 'bright' children, with a far less skilled labour force looking after the masses. The move has already been suggested in many countries, especially so in terms of introducing or reintroducing selective secondary schools (or special upper levels of secondary schools like Sixth Form Colleges) for 'brighter' children. Clearly in any move away from the teacher-as-Educator towards the teacher-as-socialiser (or even trainer in basic skills) the teachers involved must themselves become proletarianised in the process.

As far as the teacher's marginal economic privilege goes, this too becomes highly vulnerable in the wake of de-skilling and devaluing the teacher's labour power. It is not, however, likely to be lost, for reasons to be seen shortly. But a third way of counteracting the drain on surplus value brought about by schooling is to extract more surplus value back from the teachers by making them more productive, and this is what we are likely to see happen. Teachers are going to become more economically oppressed, and more and more accountable in cost/benefit terms in the future: they will maintain some economic privilege, but they will have to work harder, and at different tasks, to hold on to it. If this seems too chilling, or too personal a flight of fancy, then consider also the following extract from the 'Guardian' leader of 5 August 1980 (my italics):

> Two separated but inter-related policies are going to make the present worries of the teaching profession look like flea bites later in the decade. The first . . . was the instruction to the teacher training colleges to carry on preparing students for teaching in the primary schools even though the Department of Education believes there will be no jobs for them until the late 1980s. The second is the edict from 10 Downing Street that, like other public sector workers, teachers should only be paid what we can afford. But as no arbitrator has been able to determine what this level is, we must presume that the Government means market forces. With the surplus of teachers produced by the training colleges *it is going to be a buyers' market.* Pay levels in the profession could drop to even below the level they had reached when the Houghton committee on teachers' pay came to the rescue in 1974.

Whether pay levels will actually drop is another matter. What certainly does seem to be the case (and the situation is not applicable only to Britain) is that the economic oppression of teachers is well on the way to approximating in form the economic exploi-

tation of productive labourers, and that this approximation will
continue and accelerate in the foreseeable future.

Two final points have to be considered before bringing this
section to a close. First, we suggested earlier that Carchedi's
notion – that of the proletarianisation of the new middle class
implying a loss of the global function of capital – did not apply
to teachers; and this certainly needs to be explained. Teachers
have a dual role, which we can divide (abstractly) into that of
instruction and that of control. The instruction component corresponds (although not in its entirety) to performing the function
of the collective labourer, and this will be de-skilled, devalued
as labour power (and in all likelihood, decreased). The control
component corresponds to performing the global function of capital; but in this particular area teachers are largely unique in that
their function of control is not exercised over fellow labourers
and thus does not have to be rationalised away by capital. It
could be, of course; but in doing so capital would destroy a large
part of its own capacity to reproduce bearers of labour power at
minimum cost. Teachers function so well in this regard (as we
shall see in the following chapters) that the most likely outcome
would be that their work of control and surveillance will remain,
and actually increase, albeit with the relevant associated skills
in this area also devalued as labour power. The proletarianised
teacher will control children more and instruct them less (and
with the global function of capital retained the marginal economic
privilege will remain on the basis of that control and its ultimate
value to the State).

The second and last point is much briefer. Our entire discussions of proletarianisation have been limited to a process within the economic sphere, and proletarianisation as such is not to
be confused with 'becoming a member of the proletariat'. Before
the latter can happen the economic process must be completed,
and along with that certain political and ideological conditions have
to be met.

CONCLUSION

As far as economic identification goes, teachers can be seen to be
located within a complex set of contradictions. They belong neither
to the working class nor the capitalist class, but rather share
functions with both. In terms of production relations and ownership of the means of production they are much closer to the proletariat than they are to the capitalists. They can never, as
teachers, become pure capitalists, and on many fronts they are
highly vulnerable to proletarianisation. They can perform the
technical job of Educating through performing only the function
of the collective worker; and the performance of this job is inter-
fered with by performance of the global function of capital. As
teachers (rather than employees of the capitalist State) they have
no objective interests in the continuance of the capitalist mode of

production. And yet all the indications suggest quite strongly that while capitalism remains dominant teachers will act as agents of capital, and will perform the function of capital in ever increasing proportion.

This, of course, is only part - and a very incomplete part - of the story. In order to fill in another major section we must now turn to the political identification of teachers.

Chapter 4
The political identification of teachers

INTRODUCTION

When we consider the political identification of people we usually think in terms of whose side they are on in the political-party struggle of the time: are they Republicans or Democrats, Conservative Party supporters or Labour or Liberal supporters, and so on? To a lesser extent we also think in terms of how politically active people are, either individually or in groups. Some people, because they go to meetings, or work for unions, or even because they are always stirring, are regarded as being political, in contrast to those (the silent majority) who simply go along with things; whereas some groups who regularly seem to be in the thick of some confrontation or another, such as waterside workers, are commonly regarded as being political in contrast to other groups, like lawyers for instance, who 'just get on with their job'.

Within the context of a Marxist analysis, however, these issues are regarded as being very largely tangential, although not completely irrelevant. The major struggle in Marxist theory is a class struggle, not a party struggle (although party struggle could be part of class struggle); and people, through their very function in the social division of labour, are recognisable as serving the interests of one of the major classes regardless of the nature or degree of their overt political activity.

Politics is a matter of power, and dominance and subordination. Under capitalism the major political struggle takes place between capitalists and workers, and it is a struggle for power - eventually State power. It is also a struggle for dominance, and while capitalism remains as the dominant mode of production then obviously the capitalists exist in a dominant relation over the workers. This relation, however, is never static, since it is continually influenced by the ongoing actions of people, few of whom are neutral in the matter. Lack of action or involvement, for instance, is anything but neutrality: it is implicit support for the status quo which, in the present circumstances, is support for capitalist domination of workers. But neutrality is particularly out of the question for any member of the work-force, since the very performance of a technical job within the social division of labour itself entails a political function in that it is either assisting capitalists to maintain or increase domination over the workers, or in that it is assisting workers to achieve dominance over the capitalists. An analysis of the political identification of teachers, therefore, is an attempt to determine their location in the class struggle;

it is an attempt to identify not who they vote for or how much clout they have as a pressure group (although this latter issue will be considered later), but rather whose class-interests they serve in the actual performance of their technical job, and how these interests are served.

Teachers work in schools, and schools are either provided by the State or else operate by licence of the State. For the purpose of our discussion here we shall draw no distinction between State and private schools, and we shall consider all teachers as being employees of the State. In examining the political identification of teachers, then, it is essential that first we consider the political role of the State, and also the political function of schooling.

THE ROLE OF THE STATE

As we have noted earlier, there is a vast difference between the bourgeois or 'orthodox' view of the State and the Marxist view. According to the 'orthodox' view the State is a neutral body, an honest broker, a 'Supreme Other' which, through its institutions, serves the people and the nation, looking after common interests impartially, and bending to the will of the people (often as expressed through the ballot box). And just as the State is represented as impartial and neutral, so too are its institutions. The law, for instance, is represented as favouring no person or group particularly; and the education system, as concretised in schools, is represented as offering equal opportunity for all, and as being neutral with respect to conflicts occurring elsewhere in society. Thus the Director General of Education in New South Wales, in a recent circular to school principals entitled 'Controversial Issues in Secondary Schools' could declare:

> Schools are neutral grounds for rational discourse and objective study and should not become arenas for opposing political, or other, ideologies.

According to Marxist theory, however, the State governs in the narrow interests of one class, the ruling class, and exists to ensure the continued dominance by the ruling class. Engels, in 'The Origin of the Family, Private Property and the State',[1] indicates that the very existence of a State is based on antagonisms generated between classes by the organisation of the production process, and that the State comes into being to hold a class society together by maintaining and protecting the interests of the ruling class in the face of opposition and antagonism by the dominated class. The State, however, maintains a form of relative autonomy from the ruling class, and in this way it is able to preserve common rather than factional interests within that class, while also giving the appearance of representing national concerns and unity. Thus while the State is often seen to act against the short-term interests of the ruling class, or sections of it, its basic function is protecting the long-term interests of that class in general. And under capitalism, of course, this means protect-

ing the long-term interests of capitalists, which entails establishing the best position for securing the promotion of capital accumulation while at the same time maintaining a stable social order.

In seeking to achieve this the State has to carry out certain
quite specific functions. For instance, with regard to securing
the promotion of capital accumulation it has to:

(a) mobilise counter-tendencies in the face of declining rates
    of profit. Thus it intervenes in the production-distribution-
    exchange circuit to either increase the productivity of a
    given amount of labour power (e.g. by subsidising the
    cost of machinery through offering tax and tariff conces-
    sions) or by lowering the reproductive costs of labour
    power to increase the rate of exploitation (e.g. introducing
    universal compulsory schooling).

(b) ensure that workers are adequate to capital's requirements
    in terms of training, work attitudes, and consumer atti-
    tudes.

(c) ensure that factors exist which force workers in to, and
    keep them in, commodity relations.

(d) attempt to keep the cost of reproduction of labour power
    as low as possible.

(e) politically disorganise the dominated classes and maintain
    them in a position which safeguards the extraction of sur-
    plus value: and

(f) introduce social policies to preserve capitalist relations
    against the interests of the working class.

With regard to maintaining a stable social order, however, the
State also has the crucial function of responding to demands put
forward by the working class through class struggle. But responding to such demands could easily conflict with (f) above:
and so it is central to the successful functioning of the State that
it adapts policies originally won by the working class to serve
the needs of capital. The hard-won forty-hour week, for example,
leaves workers with considerable leisure time which they are now
encouraged to occupy through consumption rather than, say,
following political or cultural interests and activities. Production
of consumer items to fill these leisure hours - cars, TVs, boats
etc. - now serves capital far better than if workers worked longer
hours and had less time and energy for particular forms of consumption. Similarly, labour days - days won as a concession
whereby workers could down tools, organise, and meet with employers to discuss working conditions - have been turned into
'long weekends' or mini-holidays geared to extraordinary spending
and consumption.[2]

This particular view of the State is not a commonly held one,
and it is particularly rejected by those who point to the modern
Welfare State as a clear counter-instance. For this, as well as
other reasons, it is important here to give brief attention to the
notion and development of the Welfare State under capitalism.

Over the last century there has been massive expansion of
State activities under capitalism, whereby the State itself has be-

come a major employer of labour as well as the provider of many
services, especially in areas such as education, health, and
general social welfare. This latter has come about partly through
granting concessions to the working class as a result of class
struggle, but the central thing to recognise is that these concessions and services have been adapted to meet the needs of the
bourgeoisie rather than the workers, and thus basically serve
the needs of capital and function in order to preserve capitalist
relations. In this regard five points should be emphasised.

First, all State welfare (and administrative) services are funded
from taxation, which is mainly a portion of the surplus value
produced by the workers themselves. Thus, while a real measure
of health, schooling, social security etc. is provided, it comes
as no benevolence for the working class since they have in fact
paid quite heavily for it.

Second, the distribution of welfare services and the forms in
which they are supplied have been steadily tailored to meet the
needs of capital. For instance, most health and social-security
funding is aimed at the employable and is directed towards getting people back into the work-force as quickly as possible. Getting the dole, for example, is contingent upon one's continued
willingness to seek a job; and the totally disabled or chronically
ill come off at the worse end of health benefits. And with schooling the situation is even more obvious. The costs of schooling a
child increase sharply in the latter years of high school, and
especially in tertiary institutions, yet it is here that we find a
massive disproportion of working-class children. The situation,
then, is that the working class (which collectively pays more
although individuals pay less) is actually subsidising the further
schooling not of its own members but of the bourgeoisie, such
that the welfare this class pays for through producing surplus
value is mainly distributed elsewhere.

Third, the massive State expenditure on infrastructure services
like roads, airports, water supplies, housing projects and so on,
can be recognised as being directed mainly towards capital accumulation rather than social welfare. International airports (in
Australia used by less than 1 in 500 of the population) and super-
highways provide little direct benefit to the working class, while
the provision of things like water supply and housing allow capital to maintain propitious conditions of production and also to
control where, geographically, that production is to take place.
And this sort of State provision is anything but a burden on the
capitalist sector; rather it is becoming increasingly more necessary
as a precondition for private capital accumulation.

Fourth, welfare services have tended to develop into forms of
political and ideological domination of the working class itself.
This, as we shall see in our following discussion, is especially so
with regard to schooling. But at a more general level we can recognise the increasing State control over services (which is occurring
in most western capitalist countries at the moment, under titles
like 'centralisation' or 'federalism') as further capitalist control,

and thus as a continued breaking down of local and/or working-class control. For instance, under 'nationalised' health schemes, doctors and nurses are subject to greater control (by the capitalist State) and consequently have less control over their own work conditions (just as workers have less control as employees of multi-national companies); and similarly local governments are becoming more controlled and consequently have less power of their own under contemporary centralising tendencies.

Finally, we have to recognise that the State itself has become the employer of millions of workers. The vast majority of these are wage or salaried labourers suffering economic, political and ideological domination and oppression, yet they are dependent for their employment on the State. They are thus in a paradoxical position in having to serve the State if they wish to remain employed, while at the same time contributing to their own oppression and domination. Their immediate interests must, of course, lie with the preservation of their own jobs, and thus in carrying out the work of administration and welfare they actually support the State in preserving capitalist relations while working against their own interests and the interests of those (the workers and future workers) whom they have control over. And the vast State-employed work-force also serves to maintain social stability: being basically dependent on the State for its livelihood, it is hardly likely to engage in revolutionary politics designed to overthrow the State.

We see, then, that the modern Welfare State continues, under capitalism, to protect and maintain capitalist social relations; and this of course also applies to its various institutions. We are now in a position to consider in some detail the particular State institution which is both the focus of our concern and (arguably) the major political arm of the State - namely schooling.

THE POLITICAL FUNCTION OF SCHOOLING

A continuing feature of the capitalist mode of production has been the increased collectivisation and socialisation of the work process; and this in turn has resulted in the increased expulsion of the family unit from the production process (although not, of course, from the internal network of social relations). The family unit, which was once adequate (through its possession and transmission across generations of specialised skills) to the task of reproduction of specific labour power, consequently became increasingly less adequate to the overall task of reproduction of labour power in general. Further, with the expulsion of the family unit from commodity production there followed a de-legitimation of its informal educational processes. By the early nineteenth century there had arisen a three-fold need:
   (i)   to provide an arena for passing on the skills and knowledge required by workers in general - skills and knowledge the family alone could not provide

(ii)   to rationalise the reproduction of labour power in general
(iii) to provide a now-necessary link between, or better, an
       institutionalised transition from family relations to work
       relations.

It is no accident that the emergence of free, compulsory, universal
elementary schooling paralleled this development. Schooling, as
we know it, arose not out of a vacuum, not as a response to well-
meaning educational theorists, and certainly not as a manifestation of a working-class victory in the class struggle (even
though theorists such as Matthew Arnold and Kay Shuttleworth,
along with working-class movements, were not without their
influence). It was brought into being to meet a contingency, or
set of contingencies, within the historical development of capitalism; and it stands now much as it stood in the beginning - as
the intermediate institution between the family and the labour
market; as the key institution in the process of reproduction of
labour power, operated by the State (as the representative of
capital in general) for the reproduction of bearers of labour
power in general for capital in general.

The provision of free, compulsory, universal schooling was
seen from the beginning as a potentially two-edged sword, and
the original debates surrounding the issue in the first half of
the nineteenth century consistently called attention to both edges.
On the one hand it was argued that schooling would provide better trained and more acquiescent workers; and as Homer Bartlett
attested:[3]

> I have uniformly found the better educated as a class possessing
> a higher and better state of morals, more orderly and respectful
> in their deportment, and more ready to comply with the whole-
> some and necessary regulations of an establishment. And in
> times of agitation, on account of some change in regulations or
> wages, I have always looked to the most intelligent, best edu-
> cated, and the most moral for support and have seldom been
> disappointed . . . they will generally acquiesce and exert a
> salutory influence upon their associates. But the ignorant and
> uneducated I have generally found most turbulent and trouble-
> some.

On the other hand it was feared that schooling might rebound on
its providers: pupils, having learned to read good works, would
also be able to read and be influenced by seditious material; and
could become rebellious and fractious. The interests of capital
demanded that the chance be taken. And to ensure, as far as
possible, that only the desired outcomes would result, special
emphasis was placed on the new teaching force which was very
carefully chosen and very carefully trained. With regard to the
situation in Britain, Grace reports that:[4]

> In the initial selection of students heavy emphasis was placed
> upon the moral and religious qualities of the candidates, esti-
> mations of their 'character' and knowledge that they originated
> from the 'respectable' section of the working class. Goodness
> and steadiness were much to be preferred to cleverness. . . .

Intellect without a moral and religious commitment was a potentially dangerous force.

And as for teacher-training:[5]

The regime of the colleges was designed to produce an occupational group characterised by hard work, informed by religion and respectability, committed to the ideas of rescue and improvement, who could act as the cohesive agents for an industrialised and urban society. It was desirable that these agents themselves should be apolitical and ideologically bland.

Grace concludes that teachers were originally selected for and cast in the role of social and cultural missionaries - 'a kind of secular priesthood dedicated to the work of "civilisation"'; and that this notion dominated teacher-training throughout the nineteenth century and beyond.[6]

Much the same thing happened in America. Merle Borrowman, writing in 'The Encyclopedia of Education', notes that the founding fathers of teacher-training (e.g. James G. Carter, Horace Mann, Henry Barnard and Calvin Stowe) were statesmen and ministers rather than teachers, and that:[7]

Their concern as ministers and statesmen was to ensure an orderly society by creating a stable, conservative corps of dedicated and self-effacing people who would, in turn, inculcate habits of obedience, loyalty, morality, and economic efficiency in the young.

Similar sentiments were expressed throughout the capitalist nations; and in the initial mushrooming of universal schooling the responsibility for the direction it would take and the products it would produce was placed squarely on the shoulders of the teachers, who themselves were never too far from supervision from above.

The purpose and point of compulsory universal elementary schooling was not in the least ambiguous, right from the very beginning; and beneath the rhetoric of the time, expressed as it was in moral and religious tones, there lurked one constant theme - schooling was to be the new institution charged with the reproduction of bearers of labour power. And as it was instituted, so it has become.

Before proceeding further it is important that we recognise exactly what is entailed in the reproduction of bearers of labour power. On the one hand the bearers must have certain skills and knowledge which may vary from job to job (they might also require certificates licensing them to perform certain jobs). But these alone are not sufficient. The bearers must also be willing to enter into certain social relations of production, and so they must also be bearers of particular norms, values and attitudes which are not specific to particular jobs, but which are conducive to the reproduction of the social relations in question. Reproduction of bearers of labour power, therefore, involves the passing on of skills and knowledge, at times the issuing of certificates or licences (legitimation) and necessarily the inculcation of the norms, values, habits etc., essential for the reproduction of social relations. With that said we can now turn to examine the political function of schooling in some detail.

According to 'The Encyclopedia of Education':[8]

Teaching is a social function, its aim being to guide desirable growth in others. It involves a social relationship, the interaction of teacher and pupil. A school is an organised community of learners and teachers, ordered to facilitate their communication.

Such a definition, distinguished by imprecision, tells us very little about schools; and even what it does tell us is very much open to question. What we need, to begin with, is a far more objective definition and characterisation of schools; and a particularly useful one is provided by Illich and Reimer.

Illich and Reimer define schools as institutions requiring full-time attendance by pupils studying obligatory curricula in age-specific teacher-supervised relationships.[9] The four criteria, taken together, are adequate to mark out schools in general, and so there might be benefit in beginning this discussion with a consideration of each of these aspects.

In modern capitalist societies attendance at school is compulsory for approximately ten years, roughly from ages five to fifteen or six to sixteen, and such attendance is monitored by the State which can invoke legal penalties in the case of truancy. And for those pupils wishing to take out certain certificates this legal compulsion is extended by further de facto compulsion. It would be fair to say, then, that in virtually all cases full-time attendance at schooling is synonymous with compulsory full-time attendance of one sort or another. Now there are two sides to compulsory schooling. On the one hand it is provision, for all, of a set of experiences deemed to be desirable (by the State). But on the other hand it is a very powerful constraint; first on experience, in that it effectively keeps children away from a whole range of situations which they might otherwise encounter; and second, on freedom. Compulsory schooling is notice served on all children that they must do what has been ordained for them, that they must be where they have been told to be, and that they have no choice in the matter. A substantial part of a major period of life has already been subjected to the determination of others: a situation has been set up over which the child has no choice (or no real choice) and over which the child has no control. Compulsory schooling, then, is the child's first lesson that a considerable portion of living must be given over to doing what others have decreed, whether one likes it or not. It is the child's first experience of being legally controlled, and it is an experience which lasts for a long period spanning particularly formative years of a person's life.

Once in attendance at school the child then comes up against the obligatory curriculum. This is fixed for the child, usually from somewhere far above in the structural hierarchy; and again the pupil has no choice or control (or at the best, very little)

over how the pre-empted schooling time shall be spent, or what
shall be learnt or studied. Thus not only is schooling prescribed,
but so too is its content, and the child learns (or suffers through)
what others decree ought to be learnt. And since all 'official'
learning is done in teacher-supervised relationships the child
loses further control over the learning situation, which usually
develops to the point where, if the teacher is not present, then
no learning takes place. Pupils quickly abandon any notions
that they can control and organise their own learning experiences
(which they have managed to do extremely well in their pre-
school years) and internalise the notion that someone else knows
best what they should learn - a someone else who must be physically present if anything 'worthwhile' is to take place. Alternative
content - things pupils work out for themselves - is not given
the same status that the obligatory curriculum has, and the situation quickly develops where the absence of a teacher in a classroom results in a muck-up period. These attitudes are so tragically
entrenched that even advanced university students almost always
disperse if their lecturer or tutor fails to turn up, as if it were
the case that there was neither point nor worth in carrying out
discussion in the absence of the official teacher.

Age-specificity also has its impact in schooling. It is a divisive
form of categorisation which places age as the key criterion of
what a pupil may or may not do. Regardless of ability or interests,
pupils usually cannot undertake activities which are not prescribed
for their particular ages, let alone sit for certificates they are
'too young' to obtain. The child learns to give deference to those
who are older, both pupils and teachers alike; and also to recognise the need for timing and pacing - things are done, promotions
are gained, certificates are acquired when the *time* is right, not
when the pupil is right - with the crucial time-factor once more
being determined by external decree.

It should already be clear from this initial and elementary discussion that success at school requires acquiescence to a 'given'
situation wherein the pupil basically does what others decide
when they decide it. It should also be clear that, regardless of
what content makes up the obligatory curriculum, all pupils come
to learn through at least ten years of experience certain basic
'facts of life' concerning their position in the 'order of things':
for most this is little more than an idea of their relative worth-
lessness and powerlessness, and their need to follow the dictates
laid down by those with more worth and rightful power. It is in
this sense that schooling serves the political function of promoting
the governability and control of the population, and of *restricting*
the ability of most people to develop the skills and understanding
required to govern and control their own lives. Here, especially,
schooling is counter-Educational. Or as D.H. Lawrence put it,
schooling is 'a very elaborate railway system' where people are
so well 'broken in' to running on lines that they 'stay on the lines
and rust there.'[10]

It must also be remembered that a very large part of schooling has little if anything to do with transmitting the overt curriculum: much of what goes on would be better described as being oriented towards the administration of a large and complex institution rather than as facilitating learner-teacher communication. What we tend to find is a proliferation of rules, rituals and procedures basically related to administration, organisation and control. Bells determine when lessons start and finish, and when lunch shall be eaten: and regardless of motivation or hunger it is the bell which must be obeyed and the timetable which must be followed. Pupils assemble in pre-marked places in the playground, movement is confined to particular sides of corridors, there really are 'Up' and 'Down' staircases, pupils stand and sit according to parti- cular cues, certain ball games are prohibited at lunch time, restric- tions (often very severe ones) are placed on dress, permission has to be sought to go to the toilet, maths cannot be done in history lessons, eating (and often chewing gum) is prohibited in lessons, there are specific, correct ways of addressing teachers, certain areas (like science laboratories) are out of bounds at certain times, books must be covered in a certain way, red pens may not be used for note-taking, pupils must be punctual at all times, and so on almost ad infinitum. Now experience of schooling encompasses experience of all these things as well as lesson con- tent; so much so that 'rule conformity' emerges as one of the major facets of schooling, with breaches of the rules (when detec- ted) accompanied by some form of punishment or expression of disapproval. And it is not only the rules which the child comes to learn: what is also learnt is that the rules are made by others, that regardless of their rationality they have to be obeyed, that they cannot be changed by pupils, that breaches lead to punish- ment or reprimand, and that rule conformity is a highly praised and highly valued characteristic.

We see, then, that the very structure and functioning of school- ing (under capitalism) parallels the social relations of production under capitalism. There are controllers and the controlled. The controlled have no power over the production process and have to accept it, and the rules which come with it, as given. They must, in order to succeed, acquiesce in their lack of control, in the overall fragmentation of the process, in the alienation which arises from work unrelated to interests or capacity, in accepting a large degree of role differentiation, and in accepting the overall rule-orientation of the institution. We would expect people who have spent a minimum of ten years of their lives in such a situa- tion to be well formed to enter a work place which requires basic- ally a continuation of the same ways of thinking and behaving. Schooling transmits to future workers the behaviours, attitudes, norms and values required by the existing relations of production; and it produces people who are bearers of those norms, values, habits, etc., which are essential for the reproduction of social relations. Schooling can thus be recognised as a major force in the reproduction of bearers of labour power.

One highly significant qualification must, however, be entered here. There has been a marked tendency by some, especially those who have been largely influenced by the work of Althusser and Bourdieu, to present this situation in an over-deterministic fashion as if there were a perfectly neat and unchallengeable fit between the work of the school and the requirements of capitalist society; as if it were the case that the school undertook its reproductive function rather smoothly - so smoothly in fact that schooling virtually secured endless reproduction and virtually nullified any possibility of change being brought about through class struggle. This is simply not the case. The situation within schooling, just as it is within society at large, is a contested one; and it is much to the credit of those working at the University of Birmingham Centre for Contemporary Cultural Studies (among others) that they have focused their attention on the contest and conflict, as a much needed correction to the simplistic and therefore misleading type of picture which some (myself included) have tended to paint recently.[11] Reproduction of capitalist social relations is a continually contested process, and schooling is one of the sites of the ongoing contest. We must continue to remain aware of this; and provided that we are there is no contradiction or major error involved in still recognising the schooling process in general, or the institution of schooling, as a major force in the reproduction of bearers of labour power. The present discussion, and that which follows in the next two chapters, is more concerned with reproductive aspects than contested ones, and so the matters of contest and conflict will remain implicit at this stage, although they will become explicit in the final chapter. With our qualification now brought out into the open, we can return to the issue of reproduction of bearers of labour power.

Bearers of labour power, as we have seen, must also have skills and knowledge, and licences or certificates. Schooling again is highly instrumental in providing both.

On the matter of skills and knowledge very little need be said, for schooling is well recognised as the major institutionalised arena for passing on skills and knowledge within a society. But not just any old skills and knowledge of course - what is passed on is that which is relevant to perpetuating the capitalist mode of production. This does not mean, however, that the skills and knowledge in question are directly related to future employment in the form of actual job preparation (although, as noted earlier, we are now hearing the call more and more that they should be). In elementary and junior secondary schooling (which is all the schooling most children get)[12] basic skills are acquired like reading, writing, numeracy, and particular information about the natural and social world relevant to maintaining the production process. Much more will be said about this in the following chapter, but two things have to be noted here. First, the transmission of skills and knowledge is carried out in a differentiated way such that some children get more than others. This obviously occurs in the very act of some children staying at school longer than others, but it also occurs during the compulsory period of schooling as

**NEW SOUTH WALES
DEPARTMENT OF EDUCATION**

END OF YEAR ACTIVITIES YEAR 12 STUDENTS

As the 1979 Higher School Certificate Examination draws closer, students in many schools will be organising activities intended to be enjoyable and harmonious.

Last year, it was pleasing to note that a responsible approach to end of year activities was generally evident. The great majority of schools organised activities which reflected the significance of the occasion and set a good example for junior students.

Unfortunately, however, there were still a few reported cases of unseemly conduct involving unauthorised visits to other schools, trespassing, offensive behaviour and the dangerous use of motor vehicles.

It is timely therefore to reflect on the fact that the award of the Higher School Certificate and School Certificate not only attests to academic performance but is dependent also upon the Principal's certification as to satisfactory conduct.

Parents are requested to maintain close liaison with the School Principal in order to ascertain the standing of farewell functions. Not all have the Principal's agreement.

Principals have discussed with students the guidelines within which school activities can be organised. I am certain that within these guidelines memorable and appropriate school functions will gain the support of parents and the community. Education endeavours to develop a responsible, caring and responsive society. I trust students will continue to reflect its intent in the manner in which end of year activities are undertaken.

D. a. Swan

**D. Swan
Director-General of Education**

The notice above was placed in all major NSW newspapers in October 1979. Note especially the fourth paragraph.

well, with schools divided into streams or tracks, and offering
basic and advanced courses. The differences in skills and knowledge gained become a crucial factor regarding the nature of
the certificates the child can obtain, and this, as we shall see
shortly, is directly related to social selection and job opportunity.
The second point to note is that the school has a virtual monopoly over the transmission of skills and knowledge. While it is
possible to gain the same skills and knowledge elsewhere it is,
at the very least, extremely difficult to do so. On the one hand,
compulsory schooling keeps people at school and thus away from
other resources; on the other hand, the mammoth economic out-
lay on schooling by the State results in a lack of similar resources
(especially the teachers) being available elsewhere. The overall
result of this is a marked tendency towards legitimation of those
things learned at school as being the most important and worthwhile things to learn; and one result of this is the measurement
of people's worth (especially on the labour market) in terms of
the number of years of schooling they have had. And an obviously
vicious circle is set up here: measuring people's worth in terms
of their schooling itself serves to legitimise schooling as a determining agent of people's worth, and thus schooling continually
reproduces the propensity to legitimise itself. With very few
exceptions you *do* have to do well in school to get on in this world.

It is not perfectly correct, however, to claim that people's
worth is measured in terms of the number of years of schooling
they have had: worth is usually measured in terms of the certificates people have gained; and these are, of course, graded in
proportion to the years spent at school. We thus arrive at another
major political function of schooling - certification.

Within modern capitalist societies the capitalists' control of
employment, and selection for employment, is almost universally
mediated by certificates. Only a certain range of jobs are open to
those without any certificate, a further range opens up for holders
of junior secondary certificates, yet a further range opens up for
those with higher school certificates, while tertiary certificates
are required for what R.S. Peters innocently calls the 'more prized
jobs'.[13] Now there are certain things we have to note about these
certificates.

In the first place, they can usually only be obtained by full-time
attendance at schooling (and where the provision is open for obtaining them in other ways the practical possibility of so doing is
virtually nil). Thus in order to gain a particular certificate one
has to be subjected to the schooling process for the requisite
number of years (and it is often the case that a certificate awarded
on the same examination criteria but to non-school attenders is
named differently to distinguish the way in which it was obtained).[14]

Second, the certificates in question are ostensibly cognitive
certificates, or certificates of cognitive attainment; and rarely is
it ever admitted that they might have other than a cognitive
basis. Certainly official admissions to this effect (as in the one
opposite) are exceedingly scarce. School certificates are repre-

sented as fair rewards for intellectual merit; fair because all are given equal opportunity to attain them, and based on intellectual merit in that they are graded (as is school work) such that pupils are gradually weeded out, with only the more intellectually capable being able to stay on, master the harder content, and gain the higher certificates. Now we will have a great deal to say in the following chapter about this representation, and its implementation; but without opening up full discussion here we can still note the extremely important point that, while it certainly is the case that only those who stay at school longest get the highest certificates, it is by no means the case that it is the brightest and most able students who stay at school longest. Staying on at school (and thus confronting the more advanced content, and getting the better certificates and the most prized jobs) has been shown to be related tenuously, if at all, with measures of cognitive ability which are independent of school performance; and what seems to be required are certain endowed economic factors, along with personality characteristics closely related with the ability to 'stick it out'. School grades have been shown to be closely correlated with personality characteristics, and different personality characteristics at different levels of schooling. Further, it has been shown that the personality characteristics rewarded in lower-secondary schooling are the same as those rewarded in jobs requiring only lower-secondary schooling, while the particular personality characteristics rewarded in upper-secondary schooling or tertiary institutions are the same as those rewarded in jobs requiring upper secondary or tertiary schooling.[15] It would thus appear that school certificates embody a very clear affective factor, and so indicate not merely the level of cognitive attainment of the pupil (measured in terms of content mastery) but also what sort of person that pupil is. To gain a particular certificate, then, the pupil must not only master the necessary cognitive material but must also bear and display the appropriate sorts of character traits that (unofficially) 'go with' the certificate. But there is even more to it than this. It is now thoroughly documented that working-class children with high cognitive ability have a far smaller chance of completing secondary schooling and entering tertiary institutions than their middle- or upper-class counterparts have; and consequently that success in schooling correlates highly with socio-economic background factors.[16]

We see, then, that there are three factors involved in staying on at school and gaining higher certificates. First there is socio-economic background, and with regard to this factor it is clear that school certification largely reproduces class membership across generations, such that children of controllers become controllers, while children of the controlled become controlled. In this way schools serve the political function of maintaining, reinforcing, and reproducing existing class relations; or, more technically, they perform the task of reproducing the relations of production. As Rist notes:[17]

It appears that the public school system not only mirrors the

configurations of the larger society, but also significantly contributes to maintaining them. Thus the system of public education in reality perpetuates what it is ideologically committed to
eradicate – class barriers which result in inequality in the social
and economic life of the citizenry.

Second, there are personality factors involved, such that bearers
of particular certificates are also generally bearers of particular
personality traits. And since 'sticking it out' at school involves
at least those acquiescent attitudes discussed above, we see that
certification also serves the political function of attesting to the
values, habits, norms, etc., which have been internalised by the
pupils; and possibly of attesting to the degree of internalisation
as well. Finally, there is the cognitive or intellectual factor, which
turns out to be the most tenuously related of the three to certification, at least in the sense that large numbers with either equal
or greater cognitive ability are disqualified from gaining certain
certificates on non-cognitive grounds.

We can conclude from this discussion that schooling serves the
political function of reproduction of bearers of labour power
through certification in that certification: (i) reproduces class
membership across generations, and (ii) attests to the values,
attitudes, etc., of pupils as well as to their possession of requisite
skills and knowledge.

Given that we have seen how schooling functions in inculcating
the norms, values and attitudes, essential for the reproduction
of social relations; how it passes on requisite and relevant skills
and knowledge; and how it attests to and legitimates both of the
above through certification; the picture of the technical political
function of schooling in reproducing bearers of labour power in
general for capital in general is now complete (which is not to
say that the day-to-day functioning goes on uncontested). What
needs to be considered now is a further and closely related political function of schooling; namely that of lowering the overall
costs to capital of reproduction of bearers of labour power. While
this is, of course, largely achieved through the very performance
of the technical functions discussed above, it is also achieved in
further part through what is commonly known as the school's
selection function.

We have seen earlier that entry to employment is mediated by
school certificates which are accepted by capital as legitimate
(possibly the only legitimate) forms of licensing. What we find,
then, is that schooling delivers up to the job market pre-sorted
stratified people, ready by means of the length and content of
their schooling to enter either factory work or clerical work or
managerial work or professional work. Now given that the skills
and knowledge gained at school are not necessarily related to
specific jobs, this does not save the employers from having to
provide on-the-job training. What it does save the employers
from, however, is training in basic skills (for instance, reading
and writing) and in attitude and value formation: it also saves
the employers the time and expense of having to do the sorting

themselves.[18] Thus reproduction costs are dramatically lowered; and since schooling systematically ensures that most children will finish up in much the same places as their parents, reproduction of the relations of production is also neatly controlled. That schooling rather than employers does the sorting and controlling is also a matter of great ideological significance, and as such will be dealt with in the following chapter.

We can conclude this section by reiterating that schooling is a direct form of political control over children, and as such also contributes to their future governability; that through attitude formation, transmission of skills and knowledge, and certification schooling is highly instrumental in the reproduction of bearers of labour power in general for capital in general; and that schooling serves capital further by reducing the cost of this reproduction. What remains to be seen now is how teachers fit in with these functions.

THE POLITICAL FUNCTION OF TEACHERS

Teachers are the effective agents in schools. They are the people who transmit knowledge and skills, form values and attitudes, and prepare children for and subject them to the certification and selection processes. Their political function qua teachers, then, parallels the political function of schooling as set out in the previous section; and just as schooling is a direct form of political control over children, teaching is a direct political struggle with children, especially working-class children. That in itself could be the end of the matter; but it would be an unsatisfactory end for a great deal more can be gleaned about teachers through examining the detail of their technical job in the context of political criteria.

Politics, as we noted earlier, is concerned with power, dominance and subordination. Now even if we accept that teachers, as the effective agents in schooling, serve the interests of capital in the domination of the working class, there is still a lot to be said and filled in concerning the nature of the dominance/subordination relations (and the aspects of political struggle) that occur in (and make up) the teachers' actual work situation.

Positions of dominance and subordination are rarely fixed and universal. Most people are located in the middle rather than at the extremes of dominance/subordination relations in that they are dominant over some people while also being subordinate to other groups or individuals; and these relations themselves change as daily living situations change (the political party leader, for instance, might be totally dominant in the House yet be completely dominated in the home) and also as historical conditions become transformed. Now if we consider teachers only within their work-place and under contemporary conditions we quickly realise that they, like most, occupy a middle position. On the one hand, teachers are subordinate to their employer (the State) and to their controllers (principals, inspectors, Examination Boards, School Boards) - and it is in this sense that we can say that they have little, if any, control over the production process. On the other hand, teachers are dominant to a small extent (usually in a de facto fashion) over a few workers (the cleaners, aides and typists within a school) and to a very large extent in a legal as well as a de facto fashion over the pupils they teach. Teachers are thus seen to be in an extremely unusual political location. As employees of the State they are totally subordinate members of the work-force. Within the work-force, however, they exercise little domin-ance and have minimal real control over other members of the work-force (in contrast, for instance, to forepeople and man-agers). But within the work-place they are completely dominant over those people on the receiving end of their services, and this, because of compulsory schooling, to an extent unparalleled by any other occupational group whose work is not concerned primarily with overt control and repression.

Now the dominance relation of teachers over pupils is not, as we shall see, accidental: given certain circumstances it is, in fact, integral to the technical job of teaching; and within the context of such circumstances we can identify teacher-pupil relations as being extremely similar to the general political relations between controllers and workers - similar enough for us to be able to identify teachers as carrying out the task of control and surveil-lance, and functioning as bearers of political relations of domin-ance and agents of capitalist domination. That teachers control and are dominant over their pupils rather than workers is largely irrelevant: for it is the relations rather than the victims which mark out the basic political function.

Bearing relations of political dominance is not inherent in teaching per se; and teachers would not bear such relations if all they did was teach, and teach in conducive conditions. The poli-tical domination of teachers over pupils is related to two factors: the conditions under which they teach; and the non-teaching activities they are forced to perform as teachers (under certain conditions). Let us consider each of these in turn, focusing to begin with on teachers' instructional activities.

We noted earlier that teaching does not take place in a vacuum, but rather within a context or a determining set of conditions. The teachers we are concerned with teach under the capitalist mode of production, and they also teach in schools which are structured by that mode of production. We can now add in what at first will seem an extremely obvious point; namely that teachers also teach class groups. Although it might seem almost inconceiv-able that school teaching could ever have been done differently, the practice of teaching class groups, that is, of teaching all the children in a class the same thing at the same time, is a relatively modern innovation attributable to Pestalozzi who first proposed the idea, in opposition to monitorial and individual recitative teaching, in the earliest years of the nineteenth century, just when compulsory universal elementary schooling was about to take off. Pestalozzi's ideas, being compatible with the purpose and point of universal compulsory schooling (although being expressed in a far different language), spread widely and quickly, and the new (capitalist) State schools were designed around the concept of 'class teaching' - a method which remains dominant and near to universal today.

Teachers teach in schools: that is, they engage in the simultaneous instruction of class-groupings of children within institutions which we have previously characterised as requiring full-time attendance by pupils studying obligatory curricula in age-specific, teacher-supervised relationships.

Now full-time compulsory attendance must mean that, in any classroom at any particular time, there are likely to be some children who would rather be elsewhere or whose immediate concerns lie elsewhere, such that these children could be antagonistic to or uninterested in the particular instructional matter at hand. Obligatory curricula, followed according to timetable dictates, make it very likely that only a small proportion of any class would be intrinsically interested in the material presented at any particular time; they also raise the likelihood that the material presented could appear to have no relevance to the pupils' needs, which in turn brings about legitimacy problems for the teacher: 'Why do we have to learn this, sir?' Age-specific class grouping also increases the likelihood that the whole class might not be interested in the material at hand; and teacher-supervision immediately sets up a polarity between the two sides of the learning exchange which can easily result in antagonism - especially in the case of pupils (who have no choice over their teachers) being stuck with teachers whom, for good reasons or ill, they do not get on with.

The overall result of schools being organised in the way that they are is that teachers generally cannot simply walk into classrooms and present material which will be perceived as relevant, interesting and important to receptive, eager, positively motivated classes. There is just no way that thirty or more heterogeneous twelve-year-olds are all going to be positively inclined to learn about isosceles triangles at 2.10 p.m. on the third Tuesday of term! What we tend to find instead are problems of discipline and control (or perhaps just passive resignation on the part of some pupils); and teachers resorting to various positive and negative motivational techniques in order to press those pupils who are unwilling or unmotivated through a pre-ordained schedule. Instruction and control thus become integrated: teachers strive to maintain control in order to instruct, and instruct by means which facilitate maintaining control. In this way political struggle and relations of political domination (and, as we shall see, ideological struggle and ideological domination) enter the teaching-learning situation, and become an integral part of the very act of instruction itself. Thus, even if all classroom activity were confined to instruction, transmission of knowledge, or teaching lessons, we would (under present conditions) still find relations of political dominance prevalent.

But not all of class or lesson time is, of course, taken up with instructional activities; although just how much of class and lesson time is devoted to such activities is, unfortunately and significantly, an unknown factor. There have been innumerable studies of how teachers spend their lesson time, but these have tended to focus on things like how many questions teachers ask, and on what types of questions, rather than on instructional as against non-instructional use of lesson time. Now there are obviously large definitional problems involved here, but even despite that the paucity of research in this area is alarming. For instance, the AERA publication, 'The Second Handbook Of Research On Teaching' (1973)[19] runs to over 1400 double-column pages, in which 42 chapters review the findings of almost 5000 researchers, yet only twice is mention made of proportions of lesson time taken up with non-instructional activities. What information we have in this area is cloudy and imprecise.

Reimer notes that: 'Time studies conducted in Puerto Rico by Anthony Lauria show that less than 20 per cent of a teacher's time is available for instructional activities';[20] but how instructional activities are defined, where the studies are published, and even who Anthony Lauria is remain as mysteries. Deutsch, in a 1960 study that is available and well respected, found in a random sampling of New York City Public Schools that teachers spent between 50 and 80 per cent of class time in discipline, organisation, and attempting to maintain order.[21] Gump, in a largely unknown 1967 study, found that the teachers observed spent, on an average, only 51 per cent of their time in instructional activities, with 23 per cent structuring and organising behaviour, 14 per cent admonishing, giving permission, and dealing with deviant behaviour, and 12 per cent in other activities dealing with individual problems.[22] So much for the research. Now an accurate figure would, of course, be hard to obtain, and great differences would have to be expected in different schooling situations. But every practising teacher knows that only a part of any lesson is given over to teaching content, and that individual pupils in a class spend only a small part of most lessons learning their content. Time is lost getting the lesson going, in disciplining, making announcements, attending to personal problems, revising for a small minority while the rest mark time, checking attendance, answering irrelevant questions, and so on. Most informed guesses, and they have to be guesses, suggest that we spend six to eight times longer than necessary in covering primary and secondary curricula, and that given better conditions twelve years' work could be covered in two.[23] The suggestion at least is clear that instruction in schools is somewhat inefficient, and that teachers spend a significant proportion of class or lesson time undertaking activities more closely related to control and surveillance (e.g. disciplinary and administrative activities) than they are to instruction in curricular content. One thing at least is certain: teachers do more than just instruct (or transmit knowledge) in their classrooms.

And they do far more than just instruct, of course, in the totality of activities that make up the technical job of teaching: and it is here especially that we find teachers acting in relations of political dominance over pupils. Before examining these non-instructional activities, however, let us quickly sketch the power relations that exist between teachers and pupils in schooling.

To begin with, teachers are placed by the State in loco parentis over pupils, and are thus invested with certain legal powers. Teachers also have institutional *de facto power,* in that they make some of the rules while also enforcing the rest of the rules made by those higher up; they determine what will be taught and when; they prescribe the norms of acceptable behaviour; and so on. Added to this, teachers have reward power in so far as they are the judges of pupils' grades (and of pupils' behaviour); and finally teachers also have recourse to coercive power in many forms to gain pupil compliance. Thus, although it is the case that teachers have little, if any, control over the process of schooling, they do have virtually all the control and all the power within the operation of schooling; and often this extends far beyond its legal and humanitarian limits - teachers have been commonly known to extend their power to govern pupils' emotions ('wipe that smile off your face!') and pupils' bowels ('no, you can't go to the toilet; you've already been once this lesson!'). And in all cases the power relations are reinforced by the age differential between pupils and teachers. Thus, in virtually every way imaginable, relations of political dominance enter (or rather, are built into) the whole of the schooling process, of which the teaching-learning or instruction process is but a part.

With that background behind us this is now a good time to look a little more closely at the distinctly non-teaching activities which teachers perform within the present structuring of their technical job. These can be put together into two broad categories; namely police-type activities and bureaucrat-type activities; and each can be found in operation both inside and outside the classroom.

It appears as though pupils take classroom police-type activity on the part of the teacher for granted and actually expect and test out its operation. As Morrison and McIntyre note:[24]

> One expectation of teachers which appears to be shared by many British pupils is that among their primary functions are those of policeman and judge in the classroom. While it is assumed that every teacher will attempt to carry out these functions, what is not known about a new teacher is how efficient a policeman he will be, or how severe a judge. And since these aspects of the teacher's role can only achieve primacy when much of the class's uncurbed behaviour is considered to be unlawful, the question commonly asked about a new teacher is, 'How far, in out lawless behaviour, can we go with him?' A teacher entering this sort of situation who behaves as though these were not important functions, but as if his task were

simply to instruct or as if he will be accepted as a friend, coun-
sellor and stimulator of ideas . . . will rather be categorised
by pupils as 'soft' and incompetent, and be given little respect.
Similarly, the research of Marsh, Rosser and Harré shows that:[25]

> Each new teacher is put through a period of what we can call
> social apprenticeship by the pupils in order to ascertain what
> sort of a person and disciplinarian (s)he is going to be. . . .
> Being a soft teacher was seen to be one of the worst categories
> of offence. The pupils are insulted by weakness on the part of
> those in authority who they expect to be strong.

These are hardly uncommon findings and conclusions. The brute
fact of the matter is that classroom police-type activity is expected, required, and respected by pupils: it is perceived as an
integral part of the teacher's role; and it must be practised by
teachers if respect (and conditions conducive to instruction) are
to be gained. Teachers cannot limit their classroom behaviour to
instructional activities and expect to get away with it.

The work of police-type control within the classroom revolves
round such things as maintaining order and administering punish-
ments for varied misdemeanours; and activities like stopping
pupils talking, finding out who threw the ruler, calling for attention, removing privileges and putting pupils on detention, clearly
have more in common with the field of law enforcement than they
do with curriculum instruction. Teachers do have such powers
(they actually function as police, judge, jury, and correction
officer all embodied in one person) and pupils acquiesce to this.
And the power and the acquiescence to it are present even in
idyllic situations where order and discipline are not a problem,
as long as it is recognised by both parties that the person at the
blackboard talking about the rivers of Africa can also step in to
control any classroom situation which may arise. Police do not
necessarily have to make arrests in order to function efficiently
as police.

Out-of-class police-type activity commonly takes the form of
playground duty, bus duty, assembly supervision (the teacher
striding slowly, hands behind back, down the aisles watching
for errant behaviour), canteen duty, and marching children to
sport, excursions, etc.; actions far more closely allied to the
work of the police force and prison wardens than they are to
instruction in curriculum content. And the comparison is not
strained; rather it is all too apt. Teachers supervising children
at play, over meals, in assemblies, and in corridor movement
have only one parallel in our society - that of wardens in prisons
watching over the exercise yard, the mess hall, parades, and
corridor processions to and from cells. And teachers acting over
behavioural transgressions (or simply giving orders) in the
playground, in bus queues or canteen queues, and in extra-
school activities, also have only one parallel - that of the police.
Now it is something of a moot point as to whether teachers actually do have police-type power in such situations; it is less of a
moot point that they tend to act as if they have such power; but

what is of most importance is that pupils, in their very deference
to teachers in such situations, both accept that teachers do have
that power and also confer it on them in a de facto fashion. This
takes place countless times every day: each time a pupil obeys
an order to pick up an apple core, get into line, stop smoking,
stand up straight, or adjust a tie - or each time a pupil does such
things in advance of orders knowing that not to do them will
court at least a reprimand - then each time the pupil both accepts
and confers, or acquiesces in, a particular power relation vis-à-
vis teachers. Pupils perceive teachers as agents of police-type
control (sometimes as benevolent agents), which is perfectly
understandable given that within certain situations teachers are
agents of police-type control over pupils.

The bureaucratic activities of the teacher are very much like
the police-type activities in that some are concerned with establishing conditions conducive to instruction while many are related only to the complex organisation of institutionalised schooling; and they are identifiable in such situations as issuing and
reclaiming text books, issuing bus and train passes, keeping
rolls, attending to equipment registers, checking sports equipment and similar administrative minutiae. These, it should be recognised, are not common varieties of office work like typing and
operating duplicating machines. Schools generally employ non-
teaching staff in those areas. The jobs teachers do sit at a low
level of executive functioning, whereby the teachers mediate personally between the pupils and the 'system'. The pupil, to be
marked present, must report in to the teacher each day; text
books are signed over by a teacher and are returned to that
teacher; to get a bus pass the pupil must give particulars to a
teacher, and it is then the teacher who does what is necessary
to make that pass materialise for the pupil. What is important
here are not the particular duties (some of which are carried out
by assistants in some schools) but the pattern or structure,
whereby the teacher functions in a manner similar to those at
the counters of Social Security offices, banks, Health Funds, and
so on; as the person whom things must go through - as the person without whom pupils are powerless to achieve certain things,
most of which they could probably do on their own anyway, if
they were shown how. And as such a person the teacher again
carries out the work of control, and is perceived as carrying out
the work of control.

The figure of the teacher-as-bureaucrat within the classroom
is a well-known one. It is the teacher who makes the administrative decisions such as what shall be taught, when the TV is to
be turned on, and what the seating arrangements shall be. It is
the teacher who marks the roll, reads the announcements, and
conveys the school's administrative business to the class. It is
the teacher who must be applied to for permission to go to the
toilet, leave the room, or borrow a compass. It is the teacher
who checks uniforms, margins, covers on books, and notes for
absences. It is the teacher who brings round the forms to be

filled in, and who collects them again. Once more the teacher-as-
bureaucrat acts in what is accepted to be a necessary mediating
position; and from that position controls the whole show, through
undertaking activities as far removed from instruction in curriculum matters as the police-type activities are.

Now the crucial point to recognise here is that police-type
activities and bureaucrat-type activities are not external appendages tacked on to the technical job of teaching: they are part of
the technical job as determined by the conditions and context of
schooling: and teachers, even if they do not like performing
these activities, cannot escape them as schooling now stands.
They are as much a part of being a teacher as transmitting
science or history in the classroom is. In teaching, the person
who tells about the periodic table of the elements is the same person who breaks up fights in the playground, punishes offenders
at assembly, oversees the canteen queues, and issues and collects the science equipment: the person who devotes time and
effort to preparing and delivering lessons also devotes time and
effort, both in class and out of it, to performing duties which
have little, if any, direct connection with transmitting curricular
content and much to do with exercising the function of control
and surveillance.

Socrates was able to sit under a tree and teach willing pupils
without bearing relations of political dominance over them. Our
contemporary schoolteacher, however, is faced with conditions
demanding control (young Thrasymachus can't be allowed to
storm out, never to return) and is also instituted with certain
powers which, in sum, amount to the total power in the school
(as far as teacher-pupil relations are concerned). Thus control,
and with it the establishment and maintenance of relations of
political dominance, is completely integrated with teaching first
(as we have seen) in the very act of transmitting knowledge
within the schooling situation; and second, through the total
integration of the three major roles which the teacher performs
whereby the transmitter of knowledge is also, at one and the
same time, police officer and bureaucrat.

One final (and intriguing) point should be noted before this
section is brought to a close. Teachers are employed by the State
and given the right to control only after they have demonstrated
their ability to instruct; yet it is frequently if not generally the
case in schools that pupils 'give teachers the right to instruct'
or acquiesce to the teaching-learning situation only after the
teacher has demonstrated the capacity to control (even if some
pupils are less testing of teachers than others). For new teachers
who expect control to follow from their instructing ability and
capacities only to find that in order to instruct they must first
exercise and establish conditions of control (or as one of my ex-
students put it, 'fight for the right to teach') the experience
of schooling is often disillusioning, confusing, and even incom-
prehensible. This is hardly surprising, for the confusion is certainly there, although it is comprehensible. Control power (as we

shall demonstrate more fully in our following chapter) is derivative from the ability to instruct; but in school this relationship
tends to become inverted, and the inversion has serious implications as far as Education is concerned.

CONCLUSION

Teachers are employed by the State; that is, by the representative of capital in general. They work in schools, which are institutions provided by the (capitalist) State to play a major part in:
(i) ensuring that future workers are adequate to capital's requirements in terms of training, work attitudes, and consumer attitudes; (ii) the reproduction of bearers of labour power – which
entails the willingness to acquiesce to existing social relations;
and (iii) keeping the cost of reproduction of labour power to a
minimum (which is achieved, in part, through employment-related
selection functions). In so far as teachers assist in or are the
agents of these processes, then to that degree they are agents
of capital serving the political function of capital by contributing
to the controlability and domination of the (future) working class.
They also serve capital by assisting in the reproduction of social
relations wherein it is virtually assured that children of controllers will themselves become controllers, and by instilling in those
children, at the higher levels of schooling, those qualities and
skills related to the function of control. Thus, in performing
their technical job, teachers perform the political function of control, which entails both serving the interests of capital and contributing to the political domination of the future working class.
    In addition to this the technical job of teaching itself has be-
come structured in such a way that its very performance places
teachers in relations of political dominance over pupils which are
virtually identical to the relations of political dominance existing
between (capitalist) controllers and workers. Thus on a second
and closely related count, teachers – as bearers of relations of
political dominance – once again perform the function of political
control on the behalf of capital.
    Four caveats, however, must now be put to those conclusions.
First, we have been speaking in this chapter about teachers-in-
general or teachers taken collectively. This clearly does not pre-
clude the possibility that some individual teachers are playing
down the political function here ascribed as far as they are able
to (especially with regard to maintaining relations of political
dominance over pupils in schools) or even that some teachers are
doing their level best, again within schools, to subvert rather
than reproduce capitalist social relations.
    Second, in laying the political function of the reproduction of
bearers of labour power directly at teachers' feet we are not, of
course, claiming that they alone perform this function; nor (as
previously indicated) are we suggesting that teachers (or schools)
are always successful, or that they meet with no opposition or

resistance along the way. We shall consider the matters of failure and resistance at a later stage.

Third, it must be recognised yet again that the political function we have identified is not related to teaching per se, but
rather to teaching within a particular context or set of conditions.
It is eminently possible to teach without engaging in reproducing
bearers of labour power, without performing the function of political (class) domination, and without bearing relations of political
dominance over those whom one teaches. This matter too will be
taken up further at a later stage.

Finally, the entire emphasis of this chapter has tended to play
down the instructional function of schools and teachers, or to
treat that function only in relation to matters of control, and with
regard to passing on the general skills and knowledge required
by workers in general. There is, of course, much more to school
instruction than that; and so far our account of the function of
teachers is lop-sided through being incomplete in that area. What
is needed to balance and complete the picture is an examination of
the ideological function of teachers; and it is to this which we now
turn.

Chapter 5
The ideological identification of teachers

INTRODUCTION

Ideology, like politics, can be seen in terms of dominance and subordination, but this time in the realm of consciousness. Ideological struggle is a struggle for domination of consciousness, and this itself entails two factors: promulgation of 'ideas', and the establishment, maintenance and legitimation of particular social conditions (including institutions) which both determine and 'justify' the particular form of consciousness (or 'ideas') in question.

Ideological struggle is all around us: but just as political struggle is most commonly recognised in terms of party struggle, ideological struggle is most commonly recognised in clashes of 'schools of thought' directed towards the establishment of dominant ways of thinking, and consequently of acting. In university departments behaviourists clash with psychoanalysts, structuralists battle with functionalists, and idealists lock horns with realists and existentialists. Throughout the world the religious argue with the non-religious; and among the religious Christians, Jews, Moslems and Hindus each promulgate certain theories and bring about certain sets of social conditions which incorporate and 'justify' these theories. In the field of education, progressive and traditional theorists struggle to have their respective ideas accepted and put into practice; and even the various football codes struggle to influence consciousness (and consequently swell their following and gate receipts). But the central struggle, in Marxist theory, is of course the class struggle in which capitalists and workers strive for ideological domination.

Now once again, as we found with political struggle, there is no such thing as neutrality in the basic ideological struggle. Just as with political issues, the very performance of a technical job within the social division of labour itself entails an ideological function (although often a far less obvious one) in that it is either assisting capitalists to maintain or increase domination over the workers, or in that it is assisting workers to achieve (ideological) dominance over the capitalists. An analysis of the ideological identification of teachers, then, is once again an attempt to determine their location in the class struggle; this time in terms of whose interests they serve at the ideological level through the performance of their technical job. Clearly, then, our task in this chapter is much the same as that undertaken in the previous one; and since only the focus of investigation has

changed we shall employ the same method of attack, moving from
an examination of the ideological function of the State through to
schooling and finally to teachers. Our overall tapestry should
then be sufficiently complete in that the individual threads, presented sequentially and abstractly, and thus hanging loosely,
will be seen to come together as a unified whole.

THE ROLE OF THE STATE

The function of the State, with regard to ideology, has been
well expressed in a now classic statement by Marx and Engels:[1]
    The ideas of the ruling class are in every epoch the ruling
    ideas: i.e., the class which is the ruling *material* force of
    society, is at the same time its ruling *intellectual* force. The
    class which has the means of material production at its disposal,
    has control at the same time over the means of mental produc-
    tion, so that thereby, generally speaking, the ideas of those
    who lack the means of mental production are subject to it. . . .
    Insofar, therefore, as they rule as a class and determine the
    extent and compass of an epoch, it is self-evident that they do
    this in its whole range, hence among other things rule also as
    thinkers, as producers of ideas, and regulate the production
    and distribution of the ideas of their age: thus their ideas are
    the ruling ideas of the epoch. . . .
        each new class which puts itself in the place of one ruling
    before it, is compelled, merely in order to carry through its
    aim, to represent its interest as the common interest of all the
    members of society . . . it has to give its ideas the form of
    universality, and represent them as the only rational, univers-
    ally valid ones.
Or in other words, the State, which (we recall) represents the
narrow interests of the ruling class, has the function of dis-
seminating ruling-class ideas, and of legitimating them by ensuring that they are accepted (i) as being in the interests of all,
and (ii) as representing the only rational, universally valid ideas
around.
    The ideological function of the State, then, is the establishment
of hegemony – which, in its broadest terms, means ensuring that
the relation between capital and labour remains unthreatened by
obtaining voluntary submission on the part of labour to the forms
and processes of capitalist production (i.e. by having labour
accept the theoretical and practical representations of capital as
being in the interests of all and as being the only rational, universally valid representations of the world). Now in some contrast
to the establishment of political domination, a large part of this
particular process is undertaken by individual capitalists themselves, the most obvious of whom are the small select band who
control the media where the expression of ruling-class ideology
is presented in the form of 'unbiased journalism' generated under
the aegis of 'freedom of the press'. And since the interests of

these individual capitalists and those of the State largely coincide, the State has little else to do in this area except exercise gentle control where necessary (not too many nipples in the Sunday papers, please) and also provide support where necessary.

The State's direct intervention in the establishment of hegemony comes in its provision of and support for both informal and formal institutions. An example of an informal institution is the family, and the State offers support for the family in many ways. It provides child-endowment payments. It encourages wives to stay at home undertaking 'domestic duties' by granting the family unit a tax concession where this occurs. It makes funds far more easily available to family units, as the experience of most single people who have tried to get a home loan will attest to. It encourages family units in subtle ways through things like building regulations – try approaching the State with plans for building a thirty-bedroom commune and you're likely to come up against all sorts of covenants. It legalises 'Family Trusts', and through a whole variety of laws protects family interests. It even intervenes in schooling to ensure that only the 'right' attitudes about the family are taught, as recent events in Queensland bear witness to when the State Government banned the teaching of SEMP and MACOS material in schools.[2]

Examples of formal institutions are things like the legal system, the church, and schooling. The legal system, from the highest court down to the most junior policeman, is entirely State provided and State controlled; and it is here that laws are formulated and enforced which ensure both the interests of capital and the maintenance of a particular kind of social stability under the outer guise of proclamations about impartiality, justice for all neutrality, and serving the public interest. The church too is a relatively autonomous and ostensibly neutral institution; but where it furthers the interests of capital (in the form of promulgating the 'correct' values, providing a fetishised centre of unity, etc.) it complements or acts for the State, and so receives massive State support – rate-free land, tax and other economic concessions, licence to incorporate its own schools, legal protections, and overall ideological backing to the extent that State and church lines often become difficult to distinguish. For instance, the motto of the agencies of political power in the USA is 'In God We Trust': which implies that the State at least tries to do God's bidding or work according to God's ways, and it is, of course, the Church which teaches what these are and so ostensibly guides State action. Similarly, in the UK the monarch to whom parliament is responsible is head of the Church of England, which by a series of extensions results in the same representation – the State's ways are God's ways. And where the Church, or elements within it, oppose the interests of capital, it is not uncommon to find State (and Church) support withdrawn and even the institution of repressive measures: radical priests and bishops in the third world have recently found themselves victims of State repression, and as such have received little support from their own church,

just as the Italian clergy who sided with the socialists against
the fascists and nazi occupation in the 1930s and 1940s found
themselves at odds with the Pope.

These formal institutions perform an extremely important social
function: one far wider than their particular overt operation
tends to display. They are largely instrumental in disguising
what interests are being served and how these interests are
being served; such that the interests of capital become represented as the interests of all, and the service of capital becomes
undertaken by ostensibly impartial bodies for ostensibly common
ends. Thus what we tend to see are police making arrests strictly
according to the letter of the law, people represented in courts
by lawyers and given a fair trial, the clergy relating the contemporary loss of moral values to a breakdown in the family unit,
and schools awarding certificates as rewards for cognitive attainments demonstrated in the most fair and rigorous of examination
procedures: that is, situations where all appears to be fair and
above board; where all appear to be served equally and impartially; and where the interests of capital, let alone the direct
intervention of capitalists or their agents, are conspicuously
absent. Now things would not appear this way if (say) employers
took direct charge of children, controlled and formed them for a
minimum of ten years, and then employed them in specific sectors
of the work-force according to how they turned out (which is
why it is important that schools do the forming, and award the
employment-related certificates). Nor would they appear this way
if capitalists made the laws (directly), employed police privately
to enforce them, and set up their own courts to try and punish
offenders. The State's institutionalised legal and educational
systems, by making and enforcing laws, and by controlling and
sorting children for employers, not only serve the ideological
function of making it all appear fair, but also allow the capitalists
and the direct agents of capital to remain in the background,
either unseen, or seen only as detached recipients of what a fair
and humane system has delivered up to them for further fair and
humane treatment. Both aspects are vital to obtaining that voluntary submission to the existing state of affairs which is nothing
more nor less than obtaining voluntary submission on the part of
labour to the forms and processes of capitalist production.

This double-disguise factor is the crux in understanding the
ideological functioning of State institutions, and having brought
it to the fore we can now examine one particular State institution
in some detail – namely schooling.

THE LEGITIMATION OF SCHOOLING

The central thesis of this chapter, which has yet to emerge, is
that the major function of schooling is constituting individual
ideological subjects who will voluntarily submit to the existing
social relations under capitalism. Now schooling, of course, could

not undertake or succeed in such a function unless the schooling process itself was legitimated - unless schooling was displayed as being the interests of all, and unless the ideas or knowledge and skills that schooling purveys were displayed and accepted as the only universally valid knowledge and as the most worthwhile knowledge (and skills) available. It is important, therefore, that we consider the various ways in which schooling is legitimated such that it can, consequently, perform its ideological function. Let us begin with a general overview.

In the first place, a very positive picture of schooling is presented through the common equation of 'schooling' and 'Education'. Education is represented as a good thing, and since schooling is usually represented not merely as the place where you get this Education but the only place where you get it, it follows (in the ideological representation) that schooling is necessarily a good thing, and the more of it the better. So strong is this constantly reinforced ideological representation, that the notion of schooling as being essentially good for people has rarely been challenged in this century (by respectable critics rather than school dropouts, of course), at least up until the time when Illich fired his first broadsides in 1971.[3] Along with this, schooling is represented as an instrument or extension of the State (which it is): but just as the State is represented as the neutral guardian of common, national interests, so too has schooling been ideologically represented as offering free Education for all in the service of the common interests of all. Further, free secular compulsory schooling is commonly represented as having been instituted in the interests of the working class and/or as a response and concession to working-class demands; whereas the facts of the matter are that the introduction of State compulsory schooling destroyed many worker-based educational ventures, brought about a further loss of control by the working class over Education, and in form ended up being not exactly what the working class was struggling for. Finally, State schooling is still represented, and accepted, as being free and secular, when in fact it is not, nor ever has been, either of these things.

Now within the overall canvas of this rather glowing picture of schooling certain specific aspects have tended to be especially highlighted, and so it is particularly imperative that we consider more closely four of the central legitimating pillars of schooling. (We shall find that in each instance the classic ideological manoeuvre of mingling things which clearly are the case with things which are not so clearly not the case has been employed to present an overall distorted misrepresentation.)[4]

(a) *Equality of opportunity*
Schooling is commonly represented as a clear (often the clearest) manifestation of equal opportunity for all in a democratic society, and on the face of it this does appear to be so. All children, regardless of race, creed, colour, religion, social background etc. are now offered a place in schooling; and once placed they

are offered roughly equal curricula, and roughly equal access to
school resources (including teachers). In order to progress or
graduate they all sit for the same or very similar exams, and
their performance on standardised examinations then becomes a
measure of how well they have grasped their opportunity. Nothing, it would appear, could be more fair or more equal.

And yet a mountain of studies show that this is not so.[5] Somewhere along the line schooling discriminates against females,
blacks, certain ethnic groups, and children of the lower socio-
economic classes. Possibly the most damning statement available
comes from an unexpected source; from the predominantly
bourgeois context of the Coleman Report:[6]

> One implication stands out above all: That schools bring little
> influence to bear on a child's achievement that is independent
> of his background and general social context: and that this
> very lack of independent effect means that the inequalities
> imposed on children by their home, neighborhood, and peer
> environment are carried along to become the inequalities with
> which they confront adult life at the end of school. For equality
> of educational opportunity through the schools must imply a
> strong effect of schools that is independent of the child's im-
> mediate social environment, and that strong independent effect
> is not present in American Schools.

It is not present in Australian or British schools either. This,
along with a myriad of similar studies and reports, indicates that
schools reinforce rather than ameliorate social inequality, and
preserve and deepen the differences children bring to school
with them on their very first day.

Now one explanation for this is that schooling, being structured
by capital, offers the same differential opportunity as that generally provided within capitalist social relations. Another explanation, and one very much favoured by educational reformers,
is that schools have erred through not being aware enough,
but that proper research and rethinking will point the way to
overcoming the problem.[7] A third explanation is that schools are
relatively powerless to bring about an independent effect in children who simply do not have the basic capacity to do very well;
and it just happens to be the case that blacks, certain ethnic
groups, and most children of the lower socio-economic class are
naturally and inherently inferior to their respective counterparts.
This leads us to our second area of consideration.

(b) *The meritocratic theory*
Even if it were accepted that schooling was the bastion of equal
opportunity for all, it by no means follows automatically from this
that schools ought to be turning out all people as equals. Equality
of opportunity, it can easily and reasonably be argued, implies
equal chances but not equal outcomes; and just as it is incumbent
on schools to offer all children equal opportunity, so too is it
incumbent on schools to produce unequal outcomes - to develop
and reward children differently but fairly on the basis of their

individual capabilities and intellectual merit.

Here we have the bare bones of the meritocratic theory. In more fleshed-out form, it claims that children differ in general mental ability or intellectual merit, that the relevant differences can be measured by standardised tests of cognitive or mental ability, and that the demands of school work increase in direct proportion to this particular merit such that the more able one is the longer one can stay on at school mastering increasingly difficult and more demanding content. It is then taken to follow that this intellectual merit is a reliable indicator of a person's productive value, and that schooling thus fairly and properly selects the more able people for the more intellectually demanding jobs: jobs which in turn bring with them high social status, economic and other privileges, and increased life chances along many dimensions. The end result of this is that merit, as measured by school performance, tends to become indicative of personal merit in a far wider sense, such that a large range of opportunities open up for those who have demonstrated particular capabilities at school.

Now both aspects of the meritocratic theory (which we shall deal with more or less separately in this and the following subsection) do have prima-facie validity. As far as the first aspect is concerned it is the case that people differ in mental abilities, just as it is the case that school grades are highly correlated with scores on general mental ability tests, the most common of these being IQ tests. This, however, is by no means the end of the matter; and the whole basis of the meritocratic theory can be seen to crumble when we consider just two issues.

First, even if we accept that it is a certain sort of cognitive ability (or intellectual merit) which is rewarded in schools (and we shall have qualifications to raise about this as we proceed), it most certainly is *not* the case that all those possessing that cognitive ability or intellectual merit are rewarded by schools. There is now considerable evidence available which shows that children from the middle and upper socio-economic classes stay on at school longer than those children of the lower socio-economic classes who have similar scores of cognitive ability; and also that post-school success (as measured in terms of income) correlates highly with years of schooling - and thus with socio-economic background - but hardly, if at all, with intellectual merit as measured by IQ tests and other tests of cognitive ability.[8] To put that another way, the chances of a cognitively gifted lower socio-economic class child staying on at school and then getting a high-paying 'intellectually demanding' job, are far less than those of either a similarly gifted or a less-gifted middle or upper socio-economic class child doing so. Consider, for instance, the figures brought forward in the 'Statistical supplement to the 17th Report 1978-79; Universities Central Council on Admissions' as reported in 'The Times Educational Supplement' of 5 October 1980 (p.3):

> the percentage of candidates applying for university from
> families of unskilled parents fell from 1.4 in 1977 to 1.2 in 1979
> despite an overall increase in applications during this period

from 132,000 to 142,000. Successful applicants from this class
fell from 1.2 per cent in 1977 to just 1.0 per cent in 1979.

Families where parents are classed as being in professional
or intermediate occupations (above skilled non-manual) provided 60 per cent of the applicants in 1977 and 62 per cent in
1979. Acceptances were 62 per cent and 63 per cent respectively.
Similarly, recent Australian figures show that children of professional parents have a twenty-seven times greater chance of
entering law school and a twenty times greater chance of entering
medical school than children of the working class.[9] There is,
however, no evidence to indicate that for each intellectually gifted
lower-class child there are twenty or twenty-seven similarly
gifted children whose parents are professionals (nor is there any
evidence to show that the particular cognitive attainments deemed
necessary for entry to law or medical schools are, in fact, necessary actually to practise those professions).

The plain fact of the matter is that large numbers of 'intellectually meritorious' children from the working class are not being
selected into those jobs (of which law and medicine are but
examples) which are allegedly more difficult and responsible and
requiring of 'intellectual ability', and which certainly offer greater
financial remuneration, simply because these children are not
receiving the requisite grades in school. But what appears to be
the case is that the cognitive ability or general merit, expressed
in terms of 'intelligence' and 'diligence', which is rewarded by
success at school is defined in such a way that it is virtually
equivalent to coming from a privileged background, i.e. having
highly schooled parents with similar ambitions for their children,
high socio-economic circumstances, books in the home, a quiet
room of one's own, and a supportive home environment with one
parent in full-time domestic duties relieving the children of having to undertake distracting chores like cooking, washing and
cleaning. It is reasonable to assume that a child in such a situation would surely have a better chance at school than one with
similar ability or merit but who shared a room with a sibling,
lived in a house devoid of books but dominated by TV, could not
afford cribs and encyclopedias, received little positive parental
support, and had to cook for the family most nights. The distinct
possibility emerges that what is rewarded in and by schooling is
that which has been structured by capital, and that the real
measure of merit involved in the chain of success - longevity
at school → appropriate grades → high-paying job - is largely a
matter of choosing the right parents. If this is the case then not
even equal chances are being offered.

Second, although it is the case that school grades correlate
highly with scores on general mental-ability tests, it is also the
case that neither of these factors correlate at all well with any
other factor, or with what McClelland refers to as 'any other be-
haviors of importance'.[10] What we have, then, is a somewhat
vicious cycle of self-fulfilment: school grades and tests of intellectual merit predict each other but nothing else. Doing well at

school, then, is really indicative of having only those particular
merits and abilities which enable one to do well at school, and
not of possessing the more generalised personal merits commonly
associated with those who have done well at school. In fact school
grades and scores on general mental ability tests do not, as is
commonly supposed, correlate highly even with the ability to
perform particular jobs well, and are thus poor predictors for
future employment – which leads us into our third area of consideration.

(c) *Preparation and selection for employment*
While schools do not directly prepare their charges for employment in the sense of providing mainly job-oriented skills and
knowledge, they do engage in a large degree of indirect preparation. For instance, length of schooling (plus attendant certificates) is a crucial factor in determining what jobs are open for
any applicant, and pupils do have to go to school for a requisite
number of years to get (or have any chance of getting) any particular job. Thus, on the face of it, schooling is a necessary pre-
requisite for employment and a necessary preparation for employment; and the more years of schooling the better the employment
prospects.
It does not, however, take much reflection to realise that this
actually says little about schooling per se. Employers do not have
to select employees according to length of schooling and school
certification, and even when they do they do not always expect
the school graduates to have learned job-specific skills at school:
initial employment is commonly complemented by much on-the-job
training, and even university graduates in medicine, law and
teaching have to do a number of years of on-the-job residency,
articles, or probation before certification and entry to the profession is complete. That employers do tend overwhelmingly to
select employees according to length of schooling and school
certification says far more about social relations as structured by
capital than it does about schooling. In fact it points almost exclusively to a structure; to little more than the established way
in which things are done. Schooling certainly is a necessary pre-
requisite for employment, but only because employers use schooling attainments as a major criterion in choosing employees.
Now this in itself would not be a bad or unusual thing if, in
fact, the meritocratic theory held; that is, if it were the case that
scholastic performance did measure some independent form of intellectual merit, if all of comparable intellectual merit were similarly rewarded or marked out by schooling, if intellectual merit
did determine a person's productive value, and if intellectual
merit (as measured by scholastic achievement) did determine the
type of job a person was capable of performing. But, as indicated
earlier, none of these propositions accurately represents the
state of affairs that actually exists. It has now been very
thoroughly documented that at best there is only a very weak
relationship between schooling credentials and job performance

(even at the higher vocational level as with medicine, engineering etc.), for most jobs there is no relationship at all, and that in the case of some jobs the relationship is negative. (11) The actual result of this is that large numbers of people have to put up with incomes and life chances that are far below those enjoyed by others when in reality there is no difference between the two groups regarding their 'intellectual capacity' to do the jobs which provide high income and favourable life chances. And as far as employers are concerned, it would appear as though they might do equally as well if they picked employees (or university entrants) out of a hat!

We might ask, then, why employers continue to employ on the basis of schooling credentials and attainments?

Three serious suggestions have been put forward. The first is that employers are irrational and/or ignorant of the facts. Certainly studies of employers' motives and methods indicate that rarely do they question the meritocratic theory, and even more rarely do they check out (in retrospect) their employees' actual work performance against their qualifying credentials.[12] Second, it has been proposed that employers, as bearers of the ideological context which contains the meritocratic theory, accept that theory unquestioningly, and in doing so continue to reinforce both the theory and the objective conditions which give rise to it. Finally, it has been suggested that what employers are actually seeking is 'character types', and since school certificates contain an affective factor, employers, by focusing on ostensibly cognitive certificates, are able to choose people with appropriate 'characters' for placement in particular jobs. Along with this it has also been suggested that, out of the common pool of (say) Higher School Certificate holders, employers are then able to pick the particular people they want on other grounds - namely sex, race, religion, and social background.[13]

Motives will, of course, vary from employer to employer, and at this stage nowhere near enough is known for us to make any definite conclusions as to why employers are so largely guided (and led) by school credentials. We can conclude, however, that the meritocratic theory serves a very strong ideological function in making job allocation appear to be fair, with each person appearing to get his or her rightful lot. This would not be the case if jobs were allocated by lottery or according to shoe size - which would appear to be just as reliable as predictors - in which case some sort of social unrest might be expected. We can also ponder, in a wry sort of way, about the very future of schooling if employers did face facts and ignored school credentials.

Before turning to the fourth legitimating pillar of schooling, two general points should be made about the ones already discussed. First, what we have in each case are theoretic rationales which are called into question by a massive and ever-growing body of evidence. And yet the rationales are still commonly accepted while the evidence is largely ignored. Second, the rationales of 'equality of opportunity' and the meritocratic theory place the onus for success or failure, either in school or in terms of getting a good job, quite squarely on the shoulders of the individual. They thus shift the focus away from objective structural social conditions, and make it appear as though 'every man [really] is the maker of his own fortune'.

(d) *Worthwhile knowledge*
The final aspect we shall consider in the legitimation process of schooling is the ideological representation that schools pass on worthwhile knowledge; and concomitant with this that only schools pass on worthwhile knowledge; and that schools pass on the only worthwhile knowledge.

Well, it is of course true that schools pass on knowledge. It is not, however, the case that only schools could pass on this knowledge. But within the overall structure of contemporary social relations under capitalism two things are virtually ensured: first, compulsory schooling keeps children at school, and thus away from other sources of knowledge; and second, resources for transmission of knowledge are overwhelmingly concentrated in schools. Thus the 'fact' that only schools pass on (worthwhile) knowledge is structurally secured, and schooling itself thus becomes structurally secured, and consequently valued because of its place in the structure.

Whether schools pass on the only worthwhile knowledge is largely a matter of definition. Schools certainly pass on the ideas generally legitimised as 'the only rational, universally valid ones', but even more important than this, schools pass on the knowledge necessary to pass school exams and gain school certificates. And since passing exams allows one to continue on with schooling and gain higher certificates, and since years of schooling and certification are highly instrumental in achieving future life success (as commonly defined), it is easy to see how 'school knowledge' comes to be regarded as worthwhile, and as far more worthwhile than other knowledge which does not lead to passing exams etc. Thus we can see that the notion of schools passing on the only worthwhile knowledge or the most worthwhile knowledge retains credibility only within the confines of a pre-set structure which ensures and secures the worth of school knowledge. (Theoretic attempts to push beyond the instrumentality of this situation tend to speak of the intrinsic worthwhileness of school knowledge – something like Arnold's 'best which has been thought and said in the world' – whereas 'instrinsic worthwhileness' is at best an ideological concept and at worst a vacuous one.)

In summary we can conclude that schooling is legitimised by being represented (ideologically) as the concrete embodiment of Education, as a site of equal opportunity for all, as a rewarder of merit defined in terms of intelligence and diligence, as a necessary preparatory phase for future employment, and as the only place where the most worthwhile knowledge is transmitted. On one level these things (or at least the last four of them) clearly *are* the case. What is not so clearly recognised as also being the case, however, is that schooling reinforces existing inequalities according to the overall needs and interests of capital, and distributes rewards according to similar criteria; and that schooling's place in job preparation, job selection, and the transmission of knowledge is structured and secured by social conditions rather than by any 'natural', intrinsically worthwile, or propitious features of schooling per se.

THE IDEOLOGICAL FUNCTION OF SCHOOLING

Before entering into a specific examination of schooling we must recall two things which were discussed in our second chapter. First, according to the Marxist problematic all conditions of social existence, including consciousness, are determined basically (but not solely) by the dominant mode of production. Thus in a capitalist society both formal and informal institutions, along with prevailing rhetoric, cultural manifestations, basic living conditions, and so on are determined (at least in part) both in form and content by the capitalist mode of production: and those which are legitimated are structured by capital to serve the interests of capital. Second, we recall that ideology has to be seen in two senses: (i) as a level of the social formation, i.e. as an objective social process which has definite theoretic, practical, and institutional forms; and (ii) as a distorted representation of reality which serves the interests of the ruling class. It follows from this that in a capitalist society the objective social-ideological process, along with its theory, practice, and institutions, as well as the prevailing distorted representations of reality, would all be structured by capital to serve the interests of capital. To live in such a society, therefore, is a matter of being immersed in and surrounded by, as well as actively participating in an objective social process which is both structured to serve the interests of capital and to disguise the very interests it serves.

Now the end result of living in, participating in, and passing through this objective social process is that people, who are essentially biological individuals, become constituted as ideological subjects bearing specific ideological representations of social reality and a relatively coherent set of norms, beliefs and attitudes relating to the dominant social relations. The central thing to recognise, then, is that human agency is performed by constituted ideological subjects rather than by bearers or prisoners of some incipient form of human nature. It is the ideological subject, and not some freely developed form or manifestation of human nature, who structures and interprets meaning, who recognises what is right and what is wrong, who accepts what is possible or impossible, and who judges what is true as opposed to fancy: it is the ideological subject, and not people who are naturally greedy or competitive, who 'freely' enters and perpetuates the existing acquisitive state of affairs: it is the ideological subject, and not some naturally lazy and apathetic manifestation

of humanity, who 'freely' enters the labour market as the willing
bearer of labour power.

Clearly, then, the reproduction of any existing social relations
is basically dependent on constituting biological individuals into
ideological subjects through their experience in a complex yet
coherent network of objective ideological processes. Now at this
point we should recall that the primary ideology in which the
(biological) person lives in capitalist society is that of the
bourgeois individual subject cherishing the qualities of individualism and uniqueness; and that this identity is constantly reinforced
in living and practising the rituals and exigencies of everyday
life (as structured by capital). Reproduction of capitalist social
relations, then, could be more accurately identified as being basically dependent on the constitution of biological individuals into
individual ideological subjects through experience in and of objective ideological processes. Schooling is one of these processes -
arguably the most important and pervasive of them all.

Schooling is a practical-theoretical-institutional ideological network; itself an objective social process, while also being part of
a larger more comprehensive social process concerned with adapting biological individuals into individual ideological subjects or
bearers of the general qualities required for overall social reproduction to take place. Schooling operates simultaneously at two
levels, those of process and content; and while these are, in fact,
totally interrelated, once more the mere logistics of writing impose
some degree of abstraction in that, in the first place, they must
be considered separately.

(a) *The process of schooling*
Schooling is something which everybody experiences, lives
through and participates in for a minimum of ten years; and
since the central features of the schooling process have been
introduced and discussed previously in this work we can proceed
by simply listing and recalling them. (We should also recall that
our focus on reproductive aspects is not to deny or overlook the
contested nature of much that takes place, or that within the
overall general pattern resistance does occur.)

Through their experience of the ideology of schooling pupils
generally come to recognise, bear, and accept as necessary, or
as part of the way things 'naturally' are, that:
(i) the control of the learning process must be in the hands of
others (experts) and be mediated through a hierarchy contain-
ing clearly stratified levels. That is, other people decide what
they (the pupils) should do and learn. Pupils thus recognise
that they cannot learn by or for themselves, or through lateral
learning experiences, and that they are unable to organise
their own worthwhile learning experiences let alone take control
of the schools by themselves. There must be an external media-
tor between the person and the work.
(ii) the learning process is a fragmented one, both socially and
technically: socially in that particular people have particular

roles, power, authority, status, and rights according to their
position and age; and technically in that learning follows institutional demands like timetables and bells rather than being
centred around pupils' interests, concerns, and motivation.
Pupils study what their teachers dictate, they do geography
when geography appears on the timetable, and regardless of
anything else they stop drawing their maps when the bell rings.
(iii) motivation and reward are extrinsic to the learning process.
Since the technical process is not based on intrinsic interests
other things are required to keep pupils working; and pupils
who wish to succeed strive for extrinsic factors such as grades,
marks, promotion, and teacher approval.
(iv) rewards are distributed unequally, but fairly in terms of
individuals' particular merit and application. Pupils, through
constant reinforcement (of both a practical and theoretical kind)
come to accept the meritocratic theory that those who succeed
do so in virtue of certain qualities and thus deserve to succeed;
they also consequently come to accept that those who fail in
school deserve to fail both there and in the outside world. Thus
they come to learn and accept their position within the social
hierarchy, to regard the attendant privileges, advantages and
disadvantages as just desserts, and to accept the right of the
successful to control and organise the unsuccessful (just as
they accept the law which forces them to attend school, and the
teachers' rights to run the place and give the orders).
(v) in order to get on one must conform to the rules and rituals
of the institution, as expressed in things like punctuality,
regular attendance, displaying correct manners and good behaviour, and overall obedience to technical and social dictates
(obeying, for instance, both bells and teachers); and that such
conformity is a highly valued personality characteristic. Most
pupils thus accept a compliant and passive relation to the process, along with a recognition of their incapacity to bring about
change (a recognition shared by those who choose not to be
compliant and passive).
(vi) what is taught in schools is essentially the most worthwhile
knowledge to have (regardless of whether one learns any of it
oneself) and thus things acquired out of school are of lesser
value, importance, and validity, at least in terms of future
social success and social status. Consequently, individual personal merit can be measured in proportion to the amount of
approved school content which has been mastered.
(vii) since equality of opportunity is offered to all, what actually
happens to any particular pupil is a discrete, personal and individual issue. Blame or praise, success or failure, are ascribed
individually and acquired individually; and in the long run the
only person or agency responsible is oneself.
Now the point should hardly need labouring that a minimum of
ten years' experience in that sort of process is highly likely to
assist (rather than guarantee or be universally successful) in the
formation of individual ideological subjects who are bearers of

particular values, attitudes and beliefs; who are well placed to
submit voluntarily to the existing social relations under capitalism
and the capitalist relations of production (both of which are structured in almost identical fashion to schooling – with hierarchical
control, fragmentation of the work process, extrinsic reward for
working, etc.); who would 'freely' enter the labour market as the
willing bearers of labour power; and who would accept the job
situations allocated to them by the needs of capital as their proper
and rightfully deserved ones.

(b) *The content of schooling*
Unlike universities, schools do not operate under the pretence of
seeking truth 'wherever it may lead'. The common rhetoric maintains that children need to grasp basic procedures before they
can become truly critical, and (in the fashion of J.S. Mill) that in
the earlier years of schooling especially they are too impression-
able and intellectually immature to be given a free rein. Thus
school curricula are fairly tightly structured, and although some
lip service is paid in senior years (which most pupils don't reach)
to developing 'critical thinking', curricula are also fairly tightly
controlled. It should thus come as no surprise to find that what
is contained in them reinforces the general ideological representations underpinning capitalism, and that material critical of the
capitalist system is either left out (especially in the junior years),
or in rare cases, as with the recent Queensland incident, deliberately excised.

The ideological nature of school curricula is not immediately
obvious simply because these curricula are part of the general
framework of thought dominant within a society, and that too is
similarly ideological. As Althusser puts it, although the school is
dominant in the overall ideological concert, 'hardly anyone lends
an ear to its music: *it is so silent!*'[14] The problem of identifying
the ideological nature of school curricula is very similar to the
problem of recognising that the earth is moving. Our own motion
as part of the moving earth is itself instrumental in producing perceptions of a stationary earth, and in order to recognise that the
earth is moving we must first be able to recognise how that movement is obscured or disguised for us by the fact that we are part
of the very movement in question. Similarly, in order to recognise
the ideological nature of school curricula we must first be able to
recognise how that ideological nature is obscured or disguised for
us by the fact that we are 'moving' (thinking, acting, and representing the world to ourselves) within the very same ideological
context. To take Althusser again:[15]

> those who are in ideology believe themselves by definition out-
> side ideology: one of the effects of ideology is the practical
> *denegation* of the ideological character of ideology by ideology:
> ideology never says, 'I am ideological'.

The important point to note, then, is that school curricula within
capitalist schools do not have to make a special point of supporting and legitimating capitalist social relations: all they have to do

is pass on the generally accepted views of history, science and geography; present the generally accepted best of English (and other) literature; present other 'neutral' subjects like mathematics and science; and pass on the accepted views and values about democracy, the nature of freedom, and so on. These, however, can be shown, through detailed investigation, to consist of ideological support for the status quo.

There is neither space nor point for going into the detailed investigations required, however, for the matter holds generally. Nevertheless, in order to indicate the sorts of things which might be revealed, perhaps just a little needs to be said. An analysis of mathematics curricula (especially in the junior school) will quickly pick up the subtle emphasis on things like profit, discounting and capital accumulation. In science, acceptable scientific method is generally defined in such a way as to support positivist and empiricist approaches, and consequently to devalue the products of the Marxist and Freudian research programmes. Neo-classical economics, and not political economy, is taught in schools. History still bears strong influences of racism, covert support for imperialism, and a focus on the 'great men' who shaped events, and it is rarely if ever presented coherently as a record of class struggle. And an interesting recent study has shown that, with regard to the English literature as taught in high schools, the overwhelming majority of works chosen for study (which are not restricted to works originally written in English) have been written under capitalism; that even those critical of capitalism accepted it as a necessarily given 'deep structure' rather than a historical mode; and that the vast majority of books set have as their central theme the struggle of an individual with a complex and/or unintelligible society in an apolitical context where the only intermediary group between the individual and society is the family.[16] Clearly there's little real danger of developing a consciousness critical of capitalism or bourgeois individualism there.

The content of schooling obviously supports and complements the process of schooling, even though there are occasional disjunctures and contradictions. Ruling-class ideas are disseminated and legitimated such that once more we find schooling assisting to a large degree in the formation of individual ideological subjects who are bearers of particular values, beliefs, knowledge and skills, and who are again (this time on a slightly different count) well placed to submit voluntarily to the existing social relations under capitalism and to the capitalist relations of production.

We see, then, that schooling, through both its process and content, is instrumental in constituting individual ideological subjects who are well placed to submit voluntarily to the forms and processes of capitalist production and 'freely' enter the labour market as willing bearers of labour power; and that schooling, under the banners of 'equality of opportunity' and 'serving the interests of all', assists in disguising which interests it is serving and how it is serving them. It should also be noted that schooling serves yet another ideological function; the obvious one of assisting in its

own legitimation. With this behind us we can now turn to the part
which teachers play in the process.

THE IDEOLOGICAL FUNCTION OF TEACHERS

As we noted in the previous chapter, teachers are the effective
agents in schools, and so once again we could identify their function - this time their ideological function - as paralleling the ideological function of schooling. But if this were taken as the end of
the matter, then once more it would be an unsatisfactory end, for
as with political considerations a great deal more can be gleaned
about teachers through examining the detail of their technical job
in the context of ideological criteria.

In our previous chapter we noted that politics was concerned
with relations of dominance and subordination. Ideology, too, is
concerned with dominance/subordination relations, but this time
in the area of knowledge (and commonly in the interaction of knowledge with power). Therefore, even if we accept that teachers,
as the effective agents in schooling, are agents of ideological
domination serving the interests of capital in the forming or domination of workers' (or future workers') consciousness (through
ideological struggle with children - especially working-class children) there is again much to be said and filled in concerning the
nature of the ideological dominance/subordination relations that
actually occur in, and make up, the teacher's work situation.

When Francis Bacon gave utterance to the claim 'Knowledge is
power' he was thinking in terms of dominance and control: dominance and control over the natural world. Under contemporary capitalism, however, the knowledge/power connection is directed to
other areas of dominance and control as well.

A major form in which the capitalist class maintains control over
the production process, and dominance over the workers in that
process, is by giving the workers the knowledge necessary for
the performance of their particular jobs (like how to operate specific machines) but excluding them from knowledge about the technical details of the production process, and of the place they play
in the overall functioning of that process. Excluding the direct
producers from knowledge about the total production process has
two major advantages for the capitalist. First, it reduces the
quantity and quality of skills that are required of the various individuals in the process, and thus cheapens the cost of labour
power required for production. Second, it concentrates control of
the process in the hands of management, for only they fully understand the production process and are able to make it work: and
this effectively prevents the workers from seizing control. The
best the workers can hope for is to stop production, by striking
or other means: without the requisite knowledge they cannot take
control of the production process. It is thus clearly to the advantage of capital to employ agents who have knowledge control or
knowledge power; and conversely people in this position function

as agents of capital and are dominant over the working class which
lacks this knowledge (of the production process). And very often
the subordination of the workers on the basis of special knowledge
held by management merges into the legitimation of political domination by management; because they know more they are put in
charge, and once in charge they have to be obeyed: that is, they
have to be obeyed basically because they know more. Now, how
does this apply to teachers?

Teachers possess three areas of specialised knowledge, all of
which, as we shall see, are of particular value to the State, and
which taken together (in variable balance) are the source and
justification for teachers' marginal economic privilege. First, they
have knowledge of fundamental aspects underlying the teaching-
learning process. They know something of child psychology, and
of the sociology of the classroom. They are conversant with learning theory, teaching techniques, principles and practices of motivation, and so on. This we shall refer to as teaching process
knowledge. Second, they have knowledge of the workings of the
schooling process, like how to order library books or science
material, what to do in case of an accident, how to obtain travel
passes for pupils, and how to arrange excursions or inter-school
sporting contests. This we shall call schooling process knowledge.
Finally they have knowledge of the particular content which they
are employed to teach, or more simply, content knowledge.

Now as was the case with political power, teachers rarely if
ever exercise any aspect of this three-fold knowledge power over
other members of the work-force, and so technically they aren't
in any active or direct relation of dominance there (although more
has to be said about this later). However, again as with political
power, teachers do exercise all three aspects of knowledge power
over their clients, the pupils; such that once again we can identify teacher-pupil relations as being extremely similar to the
general ideological relations between controller and worker. Once
more we recognise teachers as carrying out the task of control
and surveillance, this time in the area of knowledge, where they
now emerge as bearers of ideological relations of dominance - and
so once again as agents of capitalist domination - controlling not
their fellow workers but those whom they allegedly serve.

Now there might appear, on first glance, to be a major difference between teacher-pupil relations and controller-worker relations as far as knowledge power or knowledge domination goes. In
the work situation management deliberately keep certain knowledge from the workers (and in doing so also secure their own
jobs); whereas the school situation is commonly characterised by
the deliberate attempt to pass on knowledge, and teachers are
often depicted as people trying to put themselves out of a job
through the very act of handing over their knowledge.[17] Now
since the two situations do appear to differ it becomes important
for us to look more closely at the technical job of teaching, especially with regard to the place of the three types of knowledge
power, and with regard to which knowledge it is that teachers

do try to pass on to their pupils.

The second of these issues is easily settled: it is content knowledge which teachers pass on (which itself has considerable ideological significance, as our previous discussion has shown), while both teaching process knowledge and schooling process knowledge are quite deliberately kept from both pupils and the public at large. So teachers are most certainly not putting themselves out of a job through the sharing out of all their skills and knowledge. But how do the three types of knowledge interrelate to make up the technical job of school teaching? In examining this issue we would also do well to consider which of these types of knowledge might lay claim to being expert, or esoteric, or both.

Let us begin by considering teaching abstractly. Teaching is an activity performed by a person (T) with the intention of transmitting a certain body of content (C) to another person (P), such that P learns C or comes to know C. For teaching to occur, then, two necessary conditions must apply, which together can be regarded as sufficient:

1. T must know C (and P must not know C since you can't teach people that which they already know). Or, as we put it before, the teacher must have content knowledge.
2. T must employ processes consistent with the intention: that is, processes designed for the purpose of or thought to facilitate P's learning of C. Again, as in our earlier terminology, the teacher must have process knowledge to guide the teaching activity.[18]

We see, then, that the possession by T of both content and process knowledge is necessary for teaching to occur (although T must engage in some relevantly related activity before teaching actually does occur). But let us now consider these two areas of knowledge more closely in terms of whether they need be expert or esoteric.

There are two things we can note about content knowledge. First, whether it is expert and/or esoteric depends upon the actual teaching situation itself. Teaching someone that $2 + 2 = 4$ requires neither expert nor esoteric knowledge on the part of T; whereas teaching someone how to differentiate an equation does require that T possess knowledge which, under present conditions, could be regarded fairly as both expert and esoteric. Second, regardless of the actual situation itself, the content knowledge involved is always relatively expert and esoteric as far as the pupil is concerned since, by definition, it is something which the pupil does not know. We can thus conclude that the teacher is always in a relation of possessing expert esoteric content knowledge over the pupil, whereas that same content knowledge may be either mundane and commonplace or highly developed and esoteric in the wider social context.

As far as process knowledge is concerned we find once again that whether it is expert and/or esoteric depends largely upon the actual teaching situation, although in a different way from that relating to content knowledge. Very broadly, there are two types of process knowledge. On the one hand there is process knowledge which is nothing more than common sense (and thus by definition neither expert nor esoteric). Most of the teaching which goes on in the world, and which has gone on throughout history, is performed by people who have never come in contact with teaching or learning theory, who have no 'professional expertise' whatsoever, and yet who not only intend to bring about learning in others but also succeed in doing this to an extremely admirable degree. There is no evidence to suggest that the human race was severely handicapped in passing on skills and knowledge for those millions of years before the professional learning theorists arrived; and today (as always) children (and adults) are taught an enormous amount by other children, parents, and a whole host of people who possess nothing more than common sense as far as teaching processes are concerned. On the other hand, however, there is a body of expert and esoteric teaching process knowledge which has been developed largely by educational psychologists over the last century and which teachers (and usually only teachers) are introduced to as part of their pre-service training. Now, although many would argue variously that this expert esoteric knowledge is nothing more than common sense dressed up in scientific jargon, that it does more harm than good, or that it is irrelevant in that 'teachers are born, not made', we must at least admit of its existence and of its place in the armoury of professional teachers. This particular teaching process knowledge, however, can also be divided broadly into two types. First, there is that part which is directed only at facilitating P's learning of C, and thus focuses on the particular problems of the pupil and on the means by which the content can be most effectively transmitted. Examples of such processes (which I shall call PR_1) are the relating of teaching method to pupils' specific learning difficulties, the use of concrete operations for pupils who have not reached the Piagetian stage of formal operations, employing carefully graded examples in developing mathematical knowledge, and the judicious use of maps in teaching geography. Second, there is process knowledge which is directed mainly towards establishing conducive conditions whereby the former type might be employed effectively. Included here would be motivation techniques, ensuring that pupils are not distracted, and even gaining and maintaining pupil attention (these shall be referred to as PR_2). Now the issue before us is that of determining in what teaching situations we might expect to find the application of either common sense teaching process knowledge or one or the other of the two types of expert-esoteric teaching process knowledge.

The question can only be answered in generalisations. First, as suggested earlier, most teaching is carried out by common sense processes; and we would expect to find expert-esoteric process knowledge applied mainly, if not entirely, by professional teachers in their classroom work (although much of this would surely be based on common sense processes). Second, it would appear reasonable to assume that the need to apply expert teaching pro-

cess knowledge would increase in direct proportion to the difficulties inherent in the actual teaching situation at hand, and also
that the particular expert teaching process knowledge employed
should be related to the particular difficulties encountered. For
instance, teaching a child what that child wants to learn when he
or she wants to learn it, might not be expected to call up the
use of expert-esoteric process knowledge, and if it did then only
that type which we have called PR_1. Teaching a dyslexic child to
read, however, would in all likelihood demand intense usage of
very particular expert process knowledge of type PR_1, although
that in itself might not be sufficient. And pressing thirty children
simultaneously through an obligatory curriculum according to timetable demands might similarly demand the use of other particular
aspects of expert process knowledge, especially PR_2 types (although once again these in themselves might not be sufficient).

If we now take this discussion out of the abstract realm and
relate it to the concrete reality of the schooling situation we find
interesting things opening up for us. Consider, first, the matter
of the teacher's content knowledge. It should be abundantly if
perhaps paradoxically clear that there is nothing special, expert
or esoteric about the entire corpus of knowledge which is transmitted during the compulsory period of schooling; that is, the
period roughly corresponding with elementary and junior secondary schooling. Universal compulsory schooling means that everybody is confronted with this content; and even though teachers
are not, of course, universally successful in transmitting all of
this content to all of their pupils, it is a cornerstone of the
institutionalisation of schooling itself that all people should come
to know at least this much. The content which teachers transmit
in the first ten years of schooling is content which all adult members of the society are expected to have confronted in practice,
and which at least in theory they are expected to have learnt;
it is thus the very opposite of expert, special or esoteric knowledge. Elementary and junior-secondary teachers, therefore, could
hardly be regarded as the guardians or possessors of expert or
esoteric content. Unlike the general non-teacher population they
do not have the luxury of forgetting or discarding school knowledge, and they must, of course, keep abreast of developments in
theoretic practice (like learning the new maths which most of today's parents did not learn at school) but their content knowledge
is really esoteric and/or expert only in relation to their pupils'
knowledge.

Once we move beyond junior-secondary schooling (and into the
non-compulsory part) things change dramatically. The further we
move the more teachers' content knowledge becomes specialised,
expert and esoteric; at the higher levels of secondary schooling
(and even more so at university) things are so specialised and
esoteric that most teachers do not know the content of other
teachers' disciplines; and it is the very rare history teacher who
could take over a colleague's mathematics or French class. At this
level the teacher's content knowledge is expert and esoteric, both

in a general sense and in relation to pupil knowledge.

Consider now teaching-process knowledge. Schooling is a place (as hinted at above) where large groups of children are pressed simultaneously through obligatory curricula according to time-table demands. Now it is especially in this sort of situation that the teacher must know something of motivation theory and techniques since the pupils are unlikely to be intrinsically motivated by the content. Similarly, it is in this situation that the teacher must know something of disciplinary techniques since here pupils are likely to become diverted. And the teacher must know things about teaching groups of pupils since the child is not alone; and be conversant with remedial techniques since the whole class is expected to master certain content in a specific time. Thus we see that one major aspect of the particular expert teaching-process knowledge which teachers require here (and which is often er-roneously generalised as a requirement for all teaching) is direc-ted in the main to aspects of control or 'putting things over' with-in a basically unconducive context. 'Putting things over' within the context of schooling (as previously defined) requires more than careful explanation, small steps, graded examples, and skilled diagnosis of errors (PR_1): it requires also the maintenance of control, and thus the knowledge and adoption of teaching pro-cesses (PR_2) which will ensure and secure control as far as pos-sible. The particular teaching-process knowledge required by teachers, and consequently given to them in pre-service training, is very largely related to the conditions under which they teach and the amount of control required in those conditions. In ele-mentary and junior-secondary teacher-training courses teaching-process knowledge (both PR_1 and PR_2) far outweighs content knowledge; for senior secondary-school teachers the balance is completely reversed, and the process knowledge involved is dir-ected mainly towards the PR_1 type; while training in teaching processes, especially of the PR_2 type, is virtually unheard of for university teachers where possession of content knowledge is usually sufficient in getting a job.

The point we are seeking is simply this. Effective teaching re-quires the ability to 'put things over', and outside of the school-ing situation this commonly occurs without the implementation of specific expert teaching-process knowledge. Where expert teaching-process knowledge is required, and employed, is in the schooling and classroom situations (although not only there, of course); but once we move to these situations we find that the teaching process knowledge required and instilled is concerned both with facilitating learning (PR_1), and especially with gaining and maintaining control (PR_2). The expert teaching-process knowledge which teachers possess, then, is in part concerned with the effective transmission of content knowledge to children, and in part concerned with gaining and maintaining control. And since neither aspect of teaching-process knowledge is shared with or passed on to children (or to non-teachers) it is this knowledge, rather than content knowledge, which is determinant of relation-

ships of ideological domination over those who do not share it –
with one aspect of teaching-process knowledge (type PR_2) also
predominant in the establishment of relations of political domination over pupils.

Much the same, of course, goes for schooling-process knowledge
which has far less, if anything, to do with transmission of content; and which, by allowing the teachers to run the school and
at the same time preventing the pupils from running it, establishes
the teacher in relations of both political and ideological domination
over the pupil. It is in this regard that the teacher-pupil relation
most closely resembles the management-worker relation. The pupil,
like the worker, is given certain knowledge (just as the worker was
taught how to operate a machine) but is denied knowledge of the
operation of the production process and thus becomes subordinate
to, and at times in need of, the person who knows more – more,
that is, about the operation of the process. But in schools that
person also happens to be the one who knows more about content,
and who was employed on the basis of content knowledge and
teaching-process knowledge rather than schooling-process knowledge.

We are now in a position to outline the peculiar situation of
teachers. Of the three areas of knowledge which a teacher posses-
ses it is content knowledge along with teaching-process knowledge
of type PR_1 which are always necessary and which together can
be regarded as sufficient for teaching. (Schooling-process knowledge can be sufficient for administration, and many administrators,
like school principals, are commonly and loosely referred to as
teachers even though they don't teach.) It is content knowledge
along with teaching-process knowledge of type PR_1 which 'makes'
a teacher and which basically qualifies a person to teach. Now if
teachers were in the business of only transmitting content knowledge they would be performing an ideological function in constituting consciousness but, since they would be sharing this knowledge they would not necessarily be in a relation of ideological
dominance (and this especially so if they were not set up as the
only source of the knowledge to be shared). Further, if in transmitting content knowledge teachers made use of expert processes
only of type PR_1, then once again they would not necessarily be
in a relation of ideological dominance over pupils. In schools, however, or at least in schools as they are presently constituted, the
nature of the content knowledge transmitted or shared does serve
to place teachers in dominance relations, since what is transmitted
to or shared with pupils is instrumental in the future dominance
of the large majority of them.[19] But of even greater importance is
the fact that the teaching-process knowledge employed is geared
also toward issues of control and the establishment of conditions
whereby content can be transmitted, such that in the very act of
transmitting their content teachers assume a position of ideological
and political dominance – the ideological aspect based on their
knowledge of the processes in question (PR_1 and PR_2) and the
political aspect based on the implementation of the PR_2 processes,

which are an integral part of the technical job of teaching in
schools. (Interestingly, at the higher non-compulsory levels of
schooling, both the nature of the content transmitted and the
methods by which it is transmitted become less associated with
ideological (and political) dominance, as if teachers are already
beginning to shed dominance relations over one sector of the
future work-force as well as preparing that sector to perform its
own future dominant function.)

We see, then, that on three different counts teachers in schools
function as bearers of ideological relations of dominance and as
agents of capitalist domination. First, they transmit content which
will be instrumental in the ideological dominance of the future
working class. Second, their teaching-process knowledge becomes
directed largely towards the ideological (and political) dominance
of their pupils. Finally, their teaching-process knowledge and
schooling-process knowledge, which are integral aspects of the
technical job they perform, are employed towards the function of
control and surveillance, and are not passed on either to the
pupils or the public. And on all counts the specific knowledge
they possess as teachers is of particular value to the State.

A teacher is an authority, in history, mathematics or whatever
(and possibly also with regard to the PR_1 processes concerning
transmitting this content to others) first and foremost. But schoolteachers are especially equipped with particular PR_2 teaching-
process knowledge related to class and individual control such
that conditions might be brought about whereby content knowledge
might be transmitted effectively in that setting; and they are *then*
invested with legal powers which widen and complement the previous control power. Or in other words the teacher is placed in
authority (made up of legal and teaching process factors) by virtue of being an authority (in relation to content and teaching-
process factors); with the ensuing political and ideological power
being derivative from the teacher being an authority in the first
place. Now it is the common factor, from which both senses of the
'teacher as authority' derive in part, which is largely the source
of the trouble. In the investment of the teacher as an authority
into the teacher in authority a change occurs in the point, emphasis and function of teaching-process knowledge, such that it is
not only within the overall technical job of school teaching that
the functions of instruction and control become integrated in the
manner discussed in our previous chapter – the case is rather
that control also becomes integrated with instruction within the
instruction function itself; and given this double integration it is
little wonder that in teaching the functions of instruction and
control get hopelessly mixed up. The end result of this is that
we find pupils in schools acquiescing to teachers' political power
(e.g. obeying an order to get into line) basically because, with
all the intermediary steps removed, the teacher is a relative expert
(vis-à-vis the pupil) in science or reading and the PR_1 type means
of transmitting this content to others; just as we find teachers
unable to transmit their content without, at one and the same time,

entering into relations of political and ideological dominance
(which are counterproductive to Education) simply through the
adoption of certain PR_2-type teaching procedures (if in no other
way) and so performing the function of control and surveillance.

We see, then, a very close parallel between this and the general
work situation. The instruction of children on the basis of special
knowledge held by teachers merges into the legitimation of political and ideological domination by teachers - because teachers
know more than children (more, that is, about the content which
it is their job to pass on, and along with this certain PR_1-type
procedures for passing that content on - and here teachers differ
from most management), they are placed in charge of the schooling process; and once in charge they have to be obeyed on the
basis of their superior knowledge not of the content but (as with
management) on the basis of their superior knowledge of the
overall production process: knowledge which is not shared with,
but rather secures the teacher's political and ideological domination of the child.

Before concluding this section one small point should be noted.
So far we have considered teachers only within their workplace,
but if we look outside of that workplace we find that in certain
situations they are given superior social status and privileged
treatment vis-à-vis most members of the working class (like
special respect in small towns, easier access to community projects and to committee status in general, easier access to the
media through 'Letters' columns and interviews, and privileged
treatment from such diverse places as banks, bookshops and
sporting organisations). To the extent that this occurs, then to
that extent do teachers share in the direct ideological domination
of the working class.

CONCLUSION

Teachers are employed by the State, which has the general ideological function of establishing hegemony, or obtaining voluntary
submission on the part of labour to the forms and processes of
capitalist production. Teachers are employed in schools, which
have the primary ideological function of constituting biological
individuals into individual ideological subjects who will freely
enter the labour market as willing bearers of labour power. In
so far as teachers assist in, or are the agents of these processes,
which they perform through the very function of transmitting
content within the context of the schooling process (and they
are the source of the knowledge pupils must have to 'get on',[20]
while also possessing and guarding that knowledge related to the
schooling process which ensures that they shall remain in control
of the process) then to that degree are they agents of capital
(almost certainly unwitting ones) serving the ideological function
of capital by contributing to the formation of consciousness conducive to maintaining and reproducing capitalist social relations.

In performing their technical job teachers are also performing the function of ideological control; once more serving the interests of capital, this time contributing to the ideological domination of the future working class.[21]

In addition to this the technical job of teaching itself has become structured in such a way that its very performance places teachers in relations of ideological domination over pupils which, in most respects, are extremely similar to the relations of ideological dominance that exist between (capitalist) controllers and workers. As was the case with political considerations, we see once more that teachers, on two closely related counts, are bearers of relations of ideological dominance, and again perform the function of control (this time of ideological control) on behalf of capital.

Teachers are very unlikely to see it that way. On the other hand, however, they are also very unlikely to come out in direct opposition to the school's ideological function. Let us simply note four reasons why.

In the first place, existing social relations have been so structured that teachers themselves have to be highly schooled, and this greatly increases the likelihood that teachers will be well-constituted ideological subjects, bearing dominant ideological relations, and motivated on account of their own personal success (at school) to reproducing the conditions of their own making. Second, the very act of becoming a teacher is likely in itself to entail support for the overall structure and ideologically perceived function of schooling: some people do enter teaching for the deliberate purpose of subverting the system, but people generally do not become part of structures they are fundamentally antagonistic to. Third, once in the schools, teachers have to survive and also get results, and so they are most unlikely to give up their political and ideological power. They are more likely to exercise it, and thus support the function of the school. Finally, although not exhaustively, teachers have to justify themselves to themselves: and this is likely to entail extolling schooling as a good thing, which in turn would entail teachers becoming subject to the very illusions which they serve, and in practice serving the same illusions which they are subject to.

We can conclude by reiterating that teachers are ideologically dominant over pupils (and in a weak and occasional sense ideologically dominant over other workers) and through their ideological dominance they perform the function of capital. They are also ideologically distinct from the working class in the same way that managers are, in that their work and status is legitimised and rewarded on the basis of the expert specialised knowledge which is deemed necessary for carrying it out.

Notwithstanding all of this, however, two caveats must still be put (similar ones were found at the end of the previous chapter).

First, laying the ideological function of constituting individual ideological subjects who are willing bearers of labour power directly at teachers' feet is again not to suggest either that only teachers (or schools) perform this function, or that they are always successful or that they meet with no resistance. The issues of failure and resistance will, as suggested before, be given attention in due course.

Second, it must be recognised even yet again that the ideological function we have identified is not related to teaching per se but rather to teaching within a particular context or set of conditions. Teachers will always have more content knowledge than pupils, but there is no reason why they cannot teach in relations devoid of ideological agency, dominance, or struggle; nor need their teaching be connected with constituting ideological subjects well placed to enter capitalist production relations.

Chapter 6
The class location and class position of teachers

Having examined the economic, political and ideological identification of teachers we are now almost adequately placed to consider their class location under contemporary corporate capitalism. Only one thing causes us to hesitate; namely that the preceding discussion virtually demands that a slight modification be made in the original definition of 'classes' put forward earlier. Our original definition of classes identified relations to the dominant mode of production as the key factor, and this much, of course, still holds. Our ensuing discussion, however, has continually highlighted the increased complexity of contemporary social relations and also the increased (and increasing) emphasis now falling on political and ideological factors in determining and maintaining social relations. A slightly broadened definition of classes is thus needed; one which takes into account the totality and complexity of contemporary social relations.

Such a realisation is anything but new. Lenin, for instance, insisted on the centrality of relations to the mode of production when he defined classes as 'groups of people one of which can appropriate the labour of another owing to the different places they occupy in a definite system of social economy'; but he widened his definition slightly in order to account better for the appropriation which takes place in situations more complex than slavery, feudalism, or entrepreneurial capitalism. Classes, Lenin saw as groups of people:[1]

differing from each other by the place they occupy in a historically determined system of social production by their relation (in most cases fixed and formulated in law) to the means of production, *by their role in the social organisation of labour,* and, consequently, by the dimensions of the share of social wealth of which they dispose and the mode of acquiring it.

It is that emphasised section which we wish to encompass; for in doing so we can shift from a mechanistic view of classes as people simply sharing an economic location to a view which recognises class groups as, in the words of Therborn, 'acting human supports of particular relations and forces of production'.[2] This shift in perspective from victim to bearer of social relations is consistent with and anticipated by our previous discussion, and gives proper attention to the active (political and ideological) function which people perform in the maintenance, reproduction, or transformation of the social relations of production.

With that slight amendment in mind let us now consider the class location of teachers; i.e. their relation to the means of production, and their role in the social organisation of labour, under contemporary corporate capitalism (or as put earlier, their location within the contemporary class structure as agents within an ongoing production process on the basis of their real economic, political and ideological relations in that process).

THE CLASS LOCATION OF TEACHERS

The purpose of this section is to draw together, and derive an overall conclusion from, the relevant material discussed in the previous three chapters; and in order that we do not become laboriously repetitious the first of those tasks will be undertaken in an extremely brief and schematic way.

Teachers basically are workers: they are salaried labourers contracted to perform specific activities; and in common with the working class they have little occupational independence, little control over the labour process, and no access to the means of production. They are, however, unproductive labourers, outside of the valorisation process, and they do not directly produce surplus value. They belong to that stratum of unproductive labour which is employed by the State to maintain the overall conditions of capitalist production; and thus, even though they share many characteristics with the working class, they do not belong to the working class.

Economically, teachers are positioned between the capitalists and the working class, and bear features common to both. They belong to a middle class, positioned between the global function of capital and the function of the collective labourer, sharing both functions.

Teachers perform the function of the collective labourer through their direct contribution in the work of organisation and coordination of the labour process. This task is carried out mainly through sharing content knowledge with pupils, and thus transmitting to each new generation the skills and knowledge which will (initially) enable them to take their varied places in the work-force, whether as production-line workers, lawyers, or senior management. Within the 'orthodox' problematic this is seen as the main function of teaching, and even though we are giving little space and attention to this function, it is of course recognised that teachers expend a great deal of their time and effort in transmitting content knowledge to pupils. What is also recognised, however, is that the skills and knowledge transmitted serve the overall interests and conditions of capitalist production, that it is ideologically loaded, and that it serves to raise both productivity and the future exploitation of future productive workers. Thus even within the realm of performing the function of the collective labourer teachers are also performing the function of control and surveillance and are thus serving particular political and ideological functions.

Now the mere fact that teachers belong to a middle class supported out of surplus value produced by the working class could
be regarded as sufficient to give them, as employees of the capitalist State rather than as teachers per se, an objective (if un-
spoken or unarticulated) interest in the continued exploitation
of the working class. The entire middle class 'lives off' the labour
of the working class, and they are thus, as Marx noted, 'a burden weighing heavily on the working base'[13] whose political interests coincide with the directly exploiting class. On this count
alone we find the objective political location of the middle class
coinciding with the interests of capital, and the middle class
in general providing political support for the capitalists (to whom
their economic fortune is objectively connected) rather than the
working class (on whom their economic fortune is directly dependent). But within the middle class teachers are particularly supportive of the political interests of capital. Unlike (say) clerks,
accountants, or bank personnel, teachers through performing
their technical job actually serve the political interests of capital
in an extremely important and pervasive way.

Teachers are in the business of constituting individual ideological subjects as willing bearers of labour power for capital;
and whether those bearers are headed for the factory floor, the
directors' seats, or somewhere in between, the overall process is
still service of the economic, political and ideological interests of
capital.

Teachers act as political agents of capital, or perform the global
function of capital, through their work of control and surveillance: specifically through acting as bearers of relations of political dominance over pupils; through performing police-type and
bureaucrat-type activities; by controlling the schooling process;
through inculcating particular norms, habits, values and attitudes in pupils; and through their role in the certification and
selection processes of schooling. The objective political location
of teachers within capitalist social formations is clearly right
alongside the capitalist camp - more so than with most of the
middle class who are in much the same general area because of
the coincidence of objective economic and political interests.

The coincidence between ideological interests and economic
interests among the middle class is not as clear cut as it is regarding political interests, but then again it is not absent. As we
noted earlier, in the context of the 'orthodox' problematic to
'rise' from the working class requires accepting certain factors
to be inferior, and abandoning them, as other values, ideals and
so on are embraced. Now there is nothing amiss in picking out
the same actions from the Marxist problematic (what would differ
would be certain conceptualisations and interpretations); and
what we find is that the middle class (in Marxist terms) has made
similar adaptations: it has, in general, rejected certain ideological
supports of the working class (regardless of whether individual
members ever embraced them or not), and it has accepted, or is
moving towards accepting, the ideological interests of capital.

A clear example here is the embracement, at an extreme level, of consumption relations; or participation in the 'conspicuous consumption' required to establish 'orthodox' middle-class status in the public eye. At a far less certain level of generalisation it can be suggested that the objective ideological interests of the middle class in general coincide with those of the exploiting class. And once again we can recognise that, within the middle class, teachers are particularly supportive of the ideological interests of capital: again their technical job, unlike most technical jobs among the middle class, serves the ideological interests of capital in a direct and pervasive way.

Teachers act as ideological agents of capital, or perform the global function of capital, again through their work of control and surveillance: specifically (this time) through acting as bearers of relations of ideological domination over pupils; through legitimising school knowledge as being most worthwhile and the only rational and universally valid knowledge; through promoting ruling-class norms and grading accordingly; through promoting ruling-class ideological representations of schooling - or generally through their agency in the establishment of hegemony or in making ruling-class ideas prevail (which entails the formation of 'willing' bearers of labour power 'freely' entering the labour market as structured by capital, regardless of which level they enter at). The objective ideological location of teachers (within capitalist social formations) is once more to be found right alongside the capitalist camp (although possibly not as close as with the political location); and again more so than with most of the middle class found in the same general area through the coincidence of objective economic and ideological interests.

In summary: as far as economic relations are concerned, teachers belong neither to the capitalist class nor the working class, but on all aspects of economic relations they stand very close to the working class, while some aspects actually coincide with working-class relations; in terms of both political and ideological relations, teachers stand very close to the capitalists and assist capitalist domination of the working class. Teachers belong to neither of the major opposed groups in contemporary class struggle, and they are in the contradictory position in that, while their objective economic conditions very closely approximate those of the working class, their political and ideological relations within the ongoing production process support the capitalist class in its domination of the working class.[4] It would be of more than passing interest to line this location up against the broader 'social function' which teachers have performed since the beginnings of compulsory universal schooling: teachers have battled to improve the individual and collective conditions of the working class - there can be no doubt about that - but they have done so generally within the existing constraints of capitalism. Or in other words, and herein lies the basic contradiction underpinning both their social function and their technical job, they have sought to make things better for the working class while at the same time supporting and reproducing the social relations underlying capitalism itself.

THE CLASS POSITION OF TEACHERS

It is of the utmost importance that we stress yet again that in examining the class location of teachers we have been seeking an objective determination of their location within a class structure on the basis of their real (economic, political and ideological) relations in a production process. This is not to be confused with class position, or the alignment taken up by agents at particular stages of the class struggle. There is, of course, a very strong connection between class location and class position, but the connection is neither directly causal nor exclusively determinant: as we have already noted, workers at times take up capitalist positions, and capitalists at times take up working-class positions. Now if this is so then we could reasonably expect fundamentally non-aligned groups, like teachers, to be even more fickle, or at least be more amenable and likely to make adjustments in their class position in accordance with other determining factors. (For teachers, one extremely important factor is the way their class identification and interests are represented to and by them in the 'orthodox' problematic - see pp. 35-7. Fundamentally non-aligned groups are of particular importance in class struggle: they can change the whole direction of the struggle depending on which position they take, and thus it is very much in the interests of each of the major opposed classes to court them, and to win them over at strategic times. For instance, the rise and fall of the Allende government in Chile was very largely influenced by the changing allegiances of the police and the military.[5]

The class position of any fundamentally non-aligned group cannot be determined in the abstract. At any particular time and place the class position taken will be determined by a multitude of concrete conditions, and neither they nor their interactive effects can ever be foreseen accurately. What we can consider in a general manner, however, are the basic interests of groups as they relate to known concrete and objective conditions; and in this way predictions and suggestions can be made in terms of what position a group ought to take in the face of existing and clearly predictable conditions. As far as teachers are concerned, there is much that we can identify in terms of their interests in aligning either with the capitalist class or the working class, as long as we remember that these interests will not magically turn into action without the presence of other clear and objective factors. Let us consider, then, what teachers have to gain and what they have to lose in serving, respectively, the capitalist class and the working class in terms of those contemporary and future objective conditions which can be clearly identified.

Teachers have much to gain by serving capital. Teachers are presently dependent for their employment on the State as representative of capital in general, and so their immediate jobs are at stake. And should any decide to resign and cease serving capital (or not enter the service, and thus not serve capital in the first place) the vacancies will be filled quickly enough from the now-vast reserve army of unemployed teachers. (That teachers are dependent on the State for employment does not mean, however, that they have to be dependent on a State which represents capital in general - but why hang out for a social revolution when there's a job to be had now?) Second, teachers have a privileged economic position since they receive a wage component connected with performing the function of the collective labourer, and a revenue component for acquiring knowledge which is part of their source of value to the State, and which is paid as a reward for the important political and ideological functions (legitimated by the knowledge differential) that teachers perform for capital. It is, of course, very much in teachers' immediate objective interests to preserve this privilege; and along with it any aspect of social privilege that might accrue to them through their relations of political and ideological domination (privileged treatment by the police, the media, lending organisations etc.). Third, it seems feasible that teachers in general get a personal buzz out of being in control of others (the pupils) in the workplace. It is of some interest that, out of all the studies that have been done on 'reasons for teaching' and teachers' personalities, very little has been discovered (or sought) concerning this variable. Finally, although not exhaustively, there is much in the theoretical ideological rationalisations surrounding the notion of 'upward mobility' which makes it appear advantageous (at least on the surface) for social groups to aspire to, and thus support and align themselves with the ruling interests: certainly agents of capital who are also supportive of capital are under far less threat in times of ruling-class offensive; i.e. when capital has the offensive in the class struggle. There are always advantages in being on the winning side, which in itself provides some justification for running with the leaders.

But what do teachers have to lose by serving capital? Basically they stand to lose further control over their own work, and they face even further erosion of the opportunity to Educate. These are very large issues, but they shall have to be put aside temporarily for there is a less obvious but more fundamental thing which teachers stand to lose - namely just about everything they have gained over the last fifty years or so with regard to status, self-determination, prestige and 'professionalism'. Teaching has come about as far as it can go in these areas under corporate capitalism - in fact it reached this point about a decade ago - and the thing that looms largest for teachers in the contemporary situation, and in terms of clearly observable trends, is increasing proletarianisation. This matter has been considered once before; it must now be returned to in further detail.

In our earlier discussion we examined proletarianisation basically in terms of a process of devaluation of labour power from skilled

to average labour power - a process arising out of the contraction
of capital into fewer and fewer hands along with the continued
division of labour; and one resulting in lowered living conditions,
progressive loss of control and growing alienation in the workplace, and a drift from prestige employment to average or unquali-
fied employment. At a broader level proletarianisation can also be
regarded as pointing to what Mandel has described as:[6]

increasing alienation, increasing subordination of labour to demands that no longer have any correspondence to the special
talents or fulfilment of the inner needs of men.

Proletarianisation comes about mainly from the needs of capital
to reduce production costs, which it can do most effectively by
the introduction of technology to replace human labour power and
by devaluing the labour power still required from skilled to
average levels. Consider a few examples. Twenty years ago the
sort of computer usable in an average commercial office cost, on
a yearly basis, the equivalent of the annual salaries of 400 junior
employees (e.g. typists, clerks). Today, however, with the
dramatic decreases in the costs of such technology, the cost of
running the same computer has dropped to a mere 7 per cent of its
original costs, while labour costs for the same employees are almost five times higher. Thus the annual cost of the computer is
now equivalent to the total annual salaries of less than six employees, and this figure is continually falling.[7] And as the advert-
isements state, the machines never go on holidays, take a coffee
break, or make mistakes. It is clearly to the ever-increasing
advantage of capital to replace cumulatively high-costing labour
power with such technology. The latest official estimates in New
South Wales indicate that word-processors will eliminate 50,000
typing positions between 1978 and 1981, thus employing a small
number of new highly skilled operators, but leaving 25 per cent
of all current typists either unemployed or employed in lower
skill-level jobs (making coffee, running messages etc.).[8] Similarly,
telecommunication technicians who once applied specialised talents
have been reduced to the mundane and alienating tasks of replac-
ing faulty sub-systems (identified automatically) - click out, click
in - while the faulty sub-systems are sent off to Taiwan to be
repaired.[9] And even such diverse areas as motor mechanics and
medicine are similarly affected, with sophisticated machinery doing
the skilled work and diagnosis, leaving human labour to do the
routine matters prescribed and then clean up. As noted earlier,
in the continued rationalisation of the labour process (in the
interests of capital) no one escapes proletarianisation to some degree or other (and in its wake, class struggle, as far as the working class is concerned, can easily tend towards a struggle to
maintain already established conditions, rather than struggle to
improve them, let alone to take control of the means of production).

With that general background behind us let us now consider the
specific case of teachers. There are four basic factors underlying
the proletarianisation of teachers, all of which are closely interrelated. First we have the overall proletarianisation process which

teachers can hardly escape being caught up in. Second, there is
the brute fact which must be faced that liberal education, progressive education, or any Education concerned with the full
personal, intellectual and/or cultural development of people has
had its heyday and is on the way out. Third, for the first time
since the institution of universal compulsory schooling teachers
are now quite dispensable as far as possessors and transmitters
of 'school' knowledge goes - teachers are now in competition with
cheaper, more efficient and less fallible sources and transmitters
of content. And fourth, there is the State's financial role with
regard to schooling. Let us begin with this last issue.

It is both a logical and a practical necessity for the State continually to reduce the cost of reproduction of bearers of labour
power; and since schooling is the major institutionalised site for
the reproduction of bearers of labour power in general it follows
that the State will always seek ways of making the schooling
system simultaneously cheaper and more productive. Now since
the State is committed ideologically to universal compulsory schooling (and probably also to more of it for everyone) and since
teachers are not going to accept erosion of their pay or working
conditions without a fight, the State (at least at present) cannot
take the easy ways out like modifying compulsory schooling, directly increasing class sizes, and paying teachers less. What the
State has to do, and obviously is doing, is to change the nature
of schooling to make it more productive; and, tied in with this,
change the nature of the technical job of teaching in order to
extract more value in exchange for the work performed. And this
whole process must, of course, be rationalised ideologically such
that it is represented as being in the interests of all, and especially as being advantageous to pupils.

As far as changes in the nature of schooling go, clear trends
have already emerged in all advanced capitalist States. First,
there has been a redirection of expenditure; away from social
democratic concerns like the compensatory programmes for the
disadvantaged which were a highlight of the 1960s, and away
from areas such as the liberal arts (areas which seem fairly central to the production of Peters' 'educated man', or Whitehead's
or Nunn's ideal products); and towards an emphasis on instilling
basic skills, increasing job-relevance, and boosting technical
education. Ideals of 'liberal Education' are luxuries associated
with 'boom periods' of capital expansion, and in the current
world-wide crisis within capitalism they have, not surprisingly,
been put aside in practice (although some theory still lingers on)
in favour of producing children who have clearly marketable skills,
in much the same way as ideals of progressive education were
put aside in the USA in 1957 when the appearance of Sputnik
demonstrated clearly who was winning in the technological race.
The purpose of this redirection of expenditure is to make schooling both directly and indirectly more productive for capital; and
among the rationalisations given are that standards have dropped,
that compensatory programmes inevitably fail, and that liberal

curricula tend to produce people who are unemployable.

Second, there has been, and will continue to be, a redirection of expenditure towards more cost-efficient schooling practices, which inevitably affect and modify the role, function, and technical job of the teacher within the production process. Certain trends are already obvious; others can be predicted with a high level of confidence.

Attempts are already being made to increase the accountability of teachers in terms of their effectiveness not in providing a broad, general liberal Education, but in terms of achieving highly specific learning and behavioural objectives. Central to such attempts are moves to fragment instructional content further through newly produced modules which require pupils to cover predetermined information, on which performance is discretely measurable, in specified time periods. The production of such modules, or packaged units, is one of the two major growth areas in the industries serving schooling; and the use of these modules (usually graded, sequenced, and complete with self-testing material) is almost certain to increase dramatically. So too is the use of computers in schools (the other major growth industry - recently referred to as a bonanza in the 'Education Market').[10]

Computers are already 'in', and plans for their vastly increased usage are already well under way.[11] In Australia, which lags well behind the UK and the USA, we have already witnessed an enormous proliferation of their use in both elementary and secondary schooling, and the Victorian Education Department confidently predicts that: 'Every secondary school in Victoria should have access to computing facilities in five years.'[12] The New South Wales Education Department, having now recognised that it can place a computer in every one of its high schools at a cost of less than 2 per cent of its annual recurrent budget[13] (and remember that computer costs are falling while teachers' salaries are rising), is very likely to follow suit; while on the outskirts computer suppliers are engaging in fierce lobbying and competition to win schooling tenders and contracts.

Now the use of modules and computers is, of course, ideologically represented as a 'breakthrough' in assisting pupils to learn;[14] but what effects will they have on teachers and the technical job of teaching? Let us consider just two things.

First, modules and computer programmes emphasise a product-oriented relationship between teacher and pupil; with teachers guiding pupils (or merely checking pupils' progress) past modules, units, or programmes, and thus 'manufacturing' the pupil-product in much the same way as a car is manufactured on a factory production line. The pupil can then be handed over to quality controllers - in the form of standardised tests (which, not coincidentally, are being reinstated) - where the quality of the teacher's product, manufactured technologically, can be measured. Clearly the nature of the production relations in the learning exchange thus undergoes large changes.

Second, and of far more importance, pre-packaged units and

computers seriously threaten the very basis of teaching itself. In our earlier discussion we highlighted the point that it is the possession of content knowledge, along with a particular form of process knowledge, which 'makes a teacher'; and that the teacher's legal and de facto political and ideological power, along with the establishment of relationships of political and ideological dominance, were derived from the teacher being initially and primarily an authority in these areas. It is the possession of this content knowledge and PR_1-type process knowledge which 'legitimises and justifies' teachers performing the function of control and surveillance as part of their technical job of teaching in schools. Now with modules and computers around the teacher as bearer of content knowledge could become significantly devalued: such that it could no longer be the teachers who are required to possess the content knowledge to be transmitted to pupils. In fact, teachers might be required to do no more than select pre-packaged material, or even worse, display or plug in what others have selected, as their contribution to the transmission of content knowledge. In this respect teachers will not only lose what independence they had over the content to be transmitted, and the prestige, status and so on accruing to the possessor of expert knowledge, but they will also experience changed working conditions entailing deskilling and devaluing of their expert process knowledge of type PR_1 as well - all of this resulting in a new technical job, and consequently an overall change in the function they perform.

Teachers will not, of course, sit around all day doing nothing while pupils learn from modules or computers. What will happen is that as teachers have less to do with, and less control over, the instruction process, they will have more to do with other tasks: tasks concerned with routine maintenance of the schooling process (recording, filing and other paper work) and with the overall control of pupils (organisation, discipline, checking that equipment is not damaged, inculcation of values and attitudes). Here we see a classic form of proletarianisation: the introduction of new technology calls for new expert skills from a small number of teachers (those concerned with designing and programming) while at the same time a general devaluing of skilled labour power as well as de-skilling is brought about within teaching itself. As this occurs what we shall find is a literal dehumanising of the instruction process, and a 'humanisation' of the control process; with teachers' content-knowledge power being played down (or removed) along with their PR_1-type process knowledge, while their general control powers are increased and reinforced. Teaching activities will become routine in the instruction area - selecting modules or computer programmes, setting them up, marking their tests, recording and filing results and progress charts - and vastly increased in the control area: put bluntly, teachers can expect progressively to lose control over instructional activities and to perform less of them, and to become more and more like figures of administration. For those whose status is based on possessing expert content and PR_1-type process knowledge, this is clearly proletarianisation.

But it is not, of course, only the new technology that will bring this process about. As we noted in our third chapter, certain changes in production relations can be expected whereby the teacher will become more accountable for the production of more tangible but less 'idealistic' results. Apart from some teachers who will still be charged with passing on advanced knowledge to select groups of children, teachers in general are likely to find themselves in the position of passing on less knowledge more effectively to more children. Teachers in this position would require less content knowledge, and more knowledge of processes related to control (PR_2); and thus even without the new technology we could expect to find devaluation of the possession of expert content knowledge among teachers. (In Australia the training of secondary-school teachers is being literally heaved out of universities: regardless of the complex reasons for this, the move is a clear expression of the belief that secondary teachers no longer require a university education.)

But with the devaluation of possession of content knowledge and PR_1-type process knowledge teacher power in schools will have to be legitimated and justified in some other way and on some other grounds. There is only one real possibility here; and that is justification in terms of control features and schooling-process knowledge. Teachers, therefore, are likely to be given and assume functions very similar to those of low-level management in industry: they will be in charge because they know how things work and how to make them work. Basically, they will have a different job, a new function, and possibly a changed class location.

As capitalism continues in its contractive phase we can expect a continual rationalisation of educational services, within which the privileged position and relative advantages which teachers now hold will gradually be eroded as they move further away from instructional activities and more towards the function of control and management. This is not to say that they will completely lose economic, political or ideological privileges, although some aspects of present ideological domination will disappear. But the basis for these privileges will change. Economic privilege will be bestowed for the work of political and ideological control; and in order to maintain this privilege teachers will experience a new and increased intensity of work, and a new type of work concerned less with direct instruction and more with direct administration and control, itself subject to more administration and control from above. When teachers are no longer the sole possessors of content knowledge, and no longer do the teaching (or employ that expert and esoteric teaching process knowledge - both PR_1 and PR_2 - which they currently have at hand) they don't really have much to fall back on: they are at worst dispensable, and at best well placed for proletarianisation. Teachers will not, of course, become members of the proletariat while they are still employed by the capitalist State, but we can reasonably expect a shift in their location towards that of the proletariat. The nature of their exchange relations and work situation will more closely approximate that of the proletariat in that their economic oppression will increasingly approximate, in form, the economic exploitation of productive labourers; and their ideological distinction from the working class will lessen: their political function in the service of capital and their ideological dominance over the working class, however, will increase, yet paradoxically these will have a weaker base and a more tenuous justification. Actually the whole situation of teachers under contemporary capitalism is paradoxical and tenuous: while there certainly are immediate advantages to be had and maintained by supporting capital, that very support will itself contribute to the long-term worsening of conditions. By supporting capital, teachers are engaging in the process of their own proletarianisation.

The above discussion should not be taken as indicating a headlong rush towards proletarianisation. The process is an historical one and its speed and intensity will depend upon many specific aspects in the development of capitalism. One of these aspects is the amount of resistance teachers put forward, and in this area it is clear that while teachers support capital they cannot put up effective resistance where it really counts. Teachers can continue to defend things like their salary structure, but they are relatively powerless to do anything about the decisions which affect them in a major way like massive cuts in educational spending or major redirections in educational expenditure. When capitalist governments make such moves they are not going to be diverted by teacher protests, and the only possible long-term reaction for teachers still in support of capital is to adjust to the new conditions.

Before entering into this discussion of proletarianisation we noted that by serving capital teachers stood to lose the opportunity to control their own work, and that they faced further erosion of their opportunity to Educate. The first of these issues has already been covered in passing, and we have demonstrated (in this chapter and elsewhere) the continuing loss of control confronting teachers in the work situation under capitalism. The second of these issues, however, requires a little further consideration.

Schooling is primarily in the business of socialisation, or the reproduction of bearers of labour power; and within this process teachers perform two functions simultaneously and in a totally integrated way. On the one hand, they perform the global function of capital through their work of control and surveillance, mainly through their agency in transmitting the hidden curriculum to pupils. On the other hand, they perform the function of the collective labourer, mainly through instructional activities concerned with transmitting the overt curriculum to pupils; or, put another way, through transmitting content knowledge to pupils. Now even though the content and context of schooling, or the

'what' and 'how' of teaching activities cannot be totally separated
out from each other, we can still recognise certain things about
their separate natures. First, if Education is in any way associated
with schooling then the association must come through the
teacher's instructional activities and passing on of knowledge
(although not all, or all aspects of, teacher instruction would
count as being Educative). Second, as we have already seen,
socialisation, or the reproduction of bearers of labour power, is
not Education; and where it takes place in conjunction with Educative activities (as in schools) it interferes with them and is
counter-productive to Education. The point to come out of this is
the simple one that teachers have the potential to Educate only
through performing the function of the collective labourer; more
specifically, only through their instructional activities: activities
which can be undertaken in a context devoid of control and surveillance, and where the teacher does not bear relations of political and/or ideological dominance over pupils.

Now we have already seen that the Educative activities of
teachers are presently frustrated in that they take place within
the context of schooling, which is dominated by requirements of
socialisation and control; within the context of capitalism which
severely limits the number of people who can be Educated; and
more broadly within the context of a class society itself wherein
teachers function, in part, in the political and ideological interests of the dominating class, even while trying to serve the personal interests of their pupils.[15] If we now add to this our latest
realisation, namely that teachers under capitalism are going to
instruct less and control and administer more, then it becomes
frighteningly clear that teachers will be progressively giving up
that part of their technical job wherein Educating is possible,
while taking on more and more of those aspects of their technical
job which are frustrating of Education – thus the further erosion
of the opportunity to Educate. This does not mean, of course,
that there will no longer be any Educated people about; it simply
means that teachers will have less to do with producing them –
less than they do even now.

Before concluding this section we should note what teachers
have to lose and to gain by opposing the interests of capital and
siding with the working class in the class struggle (it ought to
be remembered that there can be no such thing as neutrality or
'fence-sitting' in this area). At the immediate individual level
there are jobs to be lost, or at least put at risk. At a wider level
there are privileges to be lost (privileges, we might add, which
neither teachers nor anyone would have in a classless society).
These sorts of losses should not be considered lightly; they are
in fact very, very substantial.

But what is to be gained? Before answering that we must recognise what aligning with the working class entails. Such an alignment would, of course, be concerned with improving the conditions
of the working class under capitalism, but real alignment could
not stop at that point – the point where all social democratic and

welfare services stop. Taking the side of the working class is
taking its side in the class struggle, for the ultimate end of class
struggle, namely the overthrow of the capitalist system. Now
given that understanding, what is to be gained?

First, and most obviously, the overthrow of the capitalist
system, and the exploitation and oppression that goes with it.[16]
And second, the opportunity to teach (for teachers will most
certainly be needed in a socialist system) without the fear of
impending proletarianisation, without performing the function of
capital, and without the particular work of control and surveillance which necessarily accompanies teaching at the present. If
Marx and Engels were right in that:[17]

> In place of the old bourgeois society, with its classes and class
> antagonisms, we shall have an association in which the free
> development of each is the condition for the free development
> of all,

then we shall also have an association in which teachers, as possessors of expert content knowledge along with expertise of the
PR_1-type in transmitting this, but no longer serving capital, no
longer performing the function of control and surveillance, and
no longer bearing relations of political and ideological domination
over pupils, can carry out their instruction function in a context
devoid of the antagonisms accompanying class relationships - that
is, in an Educative context and towards the Education of all: for
where the free development of each is the condition for the free
development of all, then the free Education of each becomes the
free Education of all.

That is easily said; so easily said that it creates a false impres-
sion. If all teachers were to rush out immediately and join up with
the working class right now, it is hardly likely that capitalism
would be overthrown tonight, let alone in our lifetimes. And it is
hardly likely that teachers are going to do this just because it is
suggested to them in a book that it might be a good thing to do
(not that it can be done like that anyway). Class struggle is
complex and dynamic, and for fundamentally non-aligned groups,
like teachers, class position is a shifting and varying thing. What
position such groups take up in the basic struggle between capitalists and workers depends upon a myriad of ideological factors
and a myriad of objective existential factors deriving from their
work situation and from their life situation in general; but it also
depends heavily on the nature of the basic class struggle itself
and where the offensive lies there. No fundamentally non-aligned
group can come independently to revolutionary politics. The proletariat is the only potentially revolutionary group; and it would
be sheer utopianism to suggest that a group like teachers, who
are not members of the working class and who enjoy clear immediate advantages under capitalism, would suddenly join with the
proletariat in the absence of a strong and active revolutionary
working-class offensive. The common adaptation for such groups
in times of ruling-class offensive is to run with the hounds, secure
their own advantages, and dabble in the politics of reform - which

has been the thrust of teachers' movements in general throughout this century.

For those content to dabble in such reform - 'dabble', because political and ideological activity undertaken through the proper channels must tend towards ineffectiveness in overthrowing the ruling class since the channels themselves favour ruling-class objectives - this is the end of the book. For those who feel a moral responsibility and a serious desire to put an end to inequality, exploitation and oppression among people, to change people and the world for the better, and to bring about conditions conducive to Education - tasks to be undertaken in common by workers and teachers, although not exclusively by them - an optional chapter follows.

Chapter 7
Revolutionary strategy for teachers

INTRODUCTION

A common criticism levelled at Marxist analyses is that generally they fail to tell us what to do NOW. The problem, however, lies with the critics, not the Marxists. Marxism is not utopian, and it has no blueprints for the future, because it recognises that future (historic) events will influence and interact with future theory and vice versa, such that while the general direction can be pointed to, neither the path to the goal nor the actual nature of the goal itself can be mapped out in fine detail in advance. The process of historical transformation transforms the human agents who engage in it; and the theory underlying transformation is continually tested, and if necessary modified, as the transformational process proceeds. Clearly, then, since it is continually transforming human agents who achieve (and constitute) goals through the long-term interplay of theory and practice, future historical transformation has to be lived and experienced in order to be understood. Future events, experiences, resultant modifications to theory and practice, and the transformed actions of transformed people cannot be prophesied in advance, nor can the processes or goals of transformation be theorised about in the abstract. This does not mean, however, that nothing can be said; and the purpose of this chapter is to lay out some feelers and some starting points for teachers concerned to undertake revolutionary practice.

People often face the prospect of revolutionary practice with justifiable despair, once they recognise both their powerlessness as individuals ('What can I possibly do that would be effective against the whole system?') and the daunting fact that revolutionary practice has to be undertaken largely within the (economic, political and ideological) constraints of the very system to be overthrown. Individual powerlessness suggests hopelessness; working within the system suggests counter-productivity in that people are, at one and the same time, sustaining that which they seek to overthrow. The pessimism and despair, however, arise partly through perceiving the situation in the context of bourgeois ideology, and they can at least be mitigated if a different conceptualisation is adopted.

The individual, as a solitary individual, can do very little indeed; and if we conceive of ourselves as solitary individuals then our options must immediately close in a dramatic fashion. If, however, we conceive of ourselves as historical agents engaged in class struggle and historical transformation; that is, as members of historically determined groups collectively undertaking historical action; then the options open up again. Our place in history, and what we can achieve, depends primarily on how we see ourselves: and thus the starting point for revolutionary practice must be to divest ourselves of all notions concerned with bourgeois individualism ('What can I do?', 'Look after No. 1', 'I'm all right Jack', etc.) and to go in bearing class consciousness.

But go in where, when, and to do what?

The answer here is to go into the existing situation, immediately, but to recognise that historical transformation is a dialectical process, a tension-filled participatory transformation of existing conditions rather than a mighty explosion triggered off from some external point. Paul Willis describes the situation admirably:[1]

practitioners have the problem of 'Monday morning'. If we have nothing to say about what to do on Monday morning everything is yielded to a purist structuralist immobilising reductionist tautology: nothing can be done until the basic structures of society are changed but the structures prevent us making any changes. There is no contradiction in asking practitioners to work on two levels simultaneously – to face immediate problems in doing 'the best' (as far as they can see it) for their clients while appreciating all the time that these very actions may help to reproduce the structures within which the problems arise. Within the doom the latter seems to place the former there are spaces and potentials for changing the balances of uncertainty which reproduce the living society. To contract out of the messy business of day to day problems is to deny the active, contested nature of social and cultural reproduction. . . . To refuse the challenge of the day to day – because of the retrospective dead hand of structural constraint – is to deny the continuance of life and society themselves. It is a theoretical as well as a political failure. It denies the dialectic of reproduction. . . . There is no reason why we cannot ask those whose *work* is social and caring to operate under the tension and irony of the relationship between two levels in their activity.

The question remains of what do we do, and how do we do it?

THE POINT OF REVOLUTIONARY ACTIVITY

Revolutionary activity has a double focus. The overall aim is to take control of the means of production; and for teachers specifically this means taking control of the schooling process and sharing that control with others involved in the process, especially pupils, parents, and all members of the community served by the school. Taking control, however, requires that existing forms of control be overthrown. Now as we have seen, it is the State which exercises the general control which protects the interests of capital: thus the second (and allied) focus must be to divest the State of its power, to break up existing agencies, and to take over State power and exercise it in the interests of all. It is the State which is the ultimate prize of class struggle. But it is also within the State's political and ideological agencies, institutions and formations that class struggle takes place. Thus, as Poulantzas (and others) have put it, the State is both the site and the stake of revolutionary class struggle. Now exactly the same holds with regard to schooling: schooling is both the site and the stake of struggle. Control of schooling is the prize, and it is through the contribution of activities broadly within schooling (through direct experience with its day-to-day ideology) that it shall be won, if it is to be won. Thus the necessity of on-site revolutionary activity (which may be identical with some reform activity in substance, but which would differ markedly in point) - but not the sufficiency.

THE SCHOOLING-STATE RELATIONSHIP

The history of educational theorising glows perennially with visions of bringing about a better society through reforming or restructuring schooling, and nowhere is this seen more clearly than in the progressive education movements which flourished in the first half of this century. But the visions, of course, are nothing more than quaint ideals or ideological confusions. Schooling does not bring about new social orders or new social relations: schooling responds to prevailing social orders, or to be more precise, to ruling interests within prevailing social relations. This does not mean that schools are not open to criticism, or that there are no others with interests in them. The faults and weaknesses of schooling are very open and very clear, and schools have never been regarded or presented as perfect institutions. But the aspects that theorists and reformers look to - like regimentation, inequality, stifling of creativity, the competitive ethos and so on - are not accidental features which can be patched up or excised; rather they are basic structural features built in to schooling, which serve the reproduction of the capitalist mode of production, and as such they shall remain as basic structural features, albeit in possibly ameliorated forms, while capitalism remains the dominant mode of production. Put bluntly, the basic schooling process cannot be fundamentally changed independently of changing the mode of production of which that process is an integral part.

Now, it might appear as if this conflicts with what was said in the previous section about the necessity of on-site activity; and that schooling might best be left alone while we go about changing the mode of production first. Such a view, however, derives from a mistaken, atomistic view of social relations. Schooling, like other institutions, is thoroughly integrated with the general social relations of production: it neither has an independent existence, nor can it be taken in isolation. It is rather the case that any struggle to change fundamental social relations is at one and the same time a struggle to change the form, function, and process of schooling,

and struggle so to change schooling is part of the struggle to
change the mode of production. The struggle for schooling, however, cannot be finally successful in advance of, or independently
of, success in the broader struggle. We must recognise that there
is a world of difference between engaging in struggle and being
there, either temporally or spatially, when the final death blow
is delivered; and if the latter is to be achieved then the former
must be engaged in on all fronts. Class struggle in schools has
to be seen as an integral part of general class struggle, not as a
fight for an independent victory.

THE SPACE AND OPPORTUNITY FOR STRUGGLE

As we noted earlier, class struggle must be fought within an
overall context already structured by ruling-class interests and
ruling-class ideology, and it is for this reason that many victories
turn out to be little more than reformist gains still located in the
same largely untouched structure. It is also for this reason, as
we have again noted, that many despair of any possibility of
engaging in truly revolutionary activities: as if it were the case
that there was nowhere to put the thin end of a revolutionary
wedge in the first place. This is simply not so. Two particularly
promising places for beginning, or placing the wedge, are within the contradictions that necessarily exist within capitalist social
relations, and side by side with the historically produced resistance areas which can be located in capitalist societies. Let us
consider each of these as they specifically relate to and are manifested in schooling.
   The objective form of the various ideological (and political)
institutions within the State is shaped (as we have seen) by previous class struggle; while the institutions themselves are the
sites of ongoing contemporary struggle. Now even though these
institutions generally support the ruling class and help to ensure
its political and ideological dominance, they do so not because of
lack of opposition but rather in tension with the internal opposition already in existence. Ideological institutions are constituted
of contradictory elements, and as such they are never totally
reliable or uncompromisingly functional for the ruling class. For
instance, Christianity serves capital very well in the inculcation
of a vast range of attitudes concerned with individualism, obedience to authority, and inaction regarding the ways of the State.
At the same time, however, it turns some people right off these
attitudes. And at the same time again it produces in some people
a central concern for the oppressed, and commitment to personal
sacrifice which, when manifested in the likes of Paulo Freire,
causes more than just embarrassment for capital. Now given that
ideological processes are made up of internally contradictory
elements (and thus cannot function with complete smoothness),
it is clear that resistance and opposition are possible: existing
contradictions can be emphasised and highlighted with consider-

able effect, and they thus provide excellent places for the positioning of wedges.

Contradictions abound within the ideology of schooling, and between the ideology of schooling and the real needs of the capitalist State. At the very centre of these are the issues of whether schooling should be directed towards Education or socialisation, and the conflicts between the ideology of Education and the present demands on capital regarding the reproduction of labour power. Within schooling itself we find the stress on critical thinking and developing individual judgment lined up against the pupil's need to gain teacher approval and to pass external exams. Schooling is also caught between overt declarations of fostering individuality and individual talent, and covert requirements to routinise and regiment the entire process: it is committed to fostering beliefs in certain human rights while denying those very rights to the pupils in whom the beliefs are being fostered; to developing autonomy in pupils within a teacher-controlled situation; to making curricula relevant for pupils' needs while following the dictates of distant curriculum boards; to promoting ideals of equality of opportunity while actually trading on and reinforcing inequalities; and so on. Now teachers can, with a large degree of safety, highlight these contradictions for pupils (and others) and also work on them themselves. Teachers would be at little risk in explaining to pupils the dangers involved in presenting a radical, independent, intelligent critique of a novel to external examiners and also how this relates to the teacher's own position in the classroom. Teachers could, with much justification, give special attention to pupils with unsupportive home backgrounds, and explain why this is necessary to the other pupils (and if need be, to parents). And no teacher with an ounce of subtlety is going to be fired for bestowing human rights on children, making them autonomous, attending to their needs, fostering critical thought, or encouraging and practising truthfulness. Further particular strategies will be explored in a later section: the general point to recognise here is that it is possible to expose the internal contradictions of schooling, and the contradictions between the prevailing liberal theory of schooling and the real external demands made on it, and to use these towards an overall subversive end – all within the acceptable bounds of classroom teaching. The founding fathers were right: schooling is a two-edged sword. Even the most reactionary of teachers are, through the very process of teaching children to read and write, enhancing the revolutionary impact of those children while also reproducing bearers of labour power; and we can truly wonder at what the full impact of a revolutionary teacher might be in using the accepted means, processes and content of schooling primarily for revolutionary ends.

The recognition that ideological processes do not work with perfect smoothness or efficiency further suggests to us that within any social system there are likely to be resistance groups who have been largely unaffected by dominant ideology and who

will continue to resist its effects. Willis, for instance,[2] has shown
that the dominant ideology of schooling fails to penetrate all
layers of society, and that certain sections of the working class
actually penetrate (in part) the ideology of schooling. This rever-
sal is directed at both the theoretical ideology of schooling as
manifested in the overt curriculum, and at the practical ideology
of schooling as manifested in school structures and processes,
both of which are rejected as irrelevant to perceived social reality.
Willis demonstrates how certain sections of the working class
create a counter-school culture within schooling – one which is
ideologically consistent with their future as unskilled wage
labourers – and thus to a large extent reproduce their own labour
power, with schooling being largely by-passed in the process.
The dominant forces operating in the reproduction of labour
power here are, so Willis claims, the culture of the workplace, the
home, and the neighbourhood, all of which are opposed to the
ideological representations of the school, and all of which the
school fails to have any serious effect over. The end result for
the children, however, is the same as that which we have identified above (pp. 90. 113) – the counter-school culture reproduces
willing bearers of labour power, and working-class kids get
working-class jobs which they accept (along with the attendant
lack of privilege) as their just desserts – and so in this respect
there is not much comfort for revolutionary teachers. Nor is there
much comfort in the dominant ethos of the counter-school culture,
based as it is on racism and sexism; and Willis himself is the first
to admit that we don't have a revolutionary vanguard here, nor
would we want this group, while it retains its dominant values, to
be a revolutionary vanguard. Where the ray of hope does lie in
Willis's research is in the identification of a going ally, alive and
well, which revolutionary teachers could join up with. There are,
however, three very large attendant problems. The first is to
find this group and to understand it (and here a great deal more
research is necessary) but it could be that this resistant culture
is larger and stronger than we even now suspect. The second
problem is that of gearing into the counter-school culture in an
attempt to increase its penetrative effects; and this leads directly
to the third problem. Increasing the degree of penetration of
the counter-school culture and helping it overcome the limitations
it does not penetrate means in effect opposing the basis of the
culture and engaging in much the same sort of conversionary
activity which schooling-in-general attempts and which is soundly
rejected. This throws particular difficulties back at teachers
since it is hardly likely that any counter-school culture would
seriously accept teachers as an ally in the first place, and this
especially so when those teachers come out in direct opposition to
the sexism and racism on which much of the culture is built. At
the very least, however, revolutionary teachers can be heartened
by the knowledge that schooling is not having a unilateral or
totally pervasive effect; and that the basis of resistance is actually
already there in the school. The problem for teachers is not how

to counter this, but rather how to link up with it.

We began this section by recognising that class struggle is largely fought within the constraints and context structured by ruling-class interests. We can end it by further recognising that a central part of class struggle itself is to change those constraints and to find new forms of effective political and ideological activity, just as those who formed the first trade unions or who engaged in the first illegal street march did.[3] Teachers will have to work largely through 'acceptable' means, but they should also attempt to stretch those means and seek out other avenues in which to undertake political and ideological struggle, thus increasing their overall space and opportunity. There is, of course, a higher element of risk involved here, but you can never really know what will work or what you can get away with until you try it.

THE NEED FOR COLLECTIVE ACTIVITY

Teaching is a solitary, isolated, individualistic job. Classroom teaching is carried out alone, and most of the problems that arise there tend to be seen as the teacher's individual problems rather than as things shared by all teachers or even many teachers. School staffs are small and do not tend to be the most cohesive of groups; and the problems they share and discuss tend to be problems associated with an individual school - what to do about the discipline problems in year seven, how to reduce noise around the library area, and so on. And teachers rarely meet on a wider basis. There are unions, and professional associations, both of which are poorly patronised by teachers, and which themselves are indicative of a 'disunited occupational group' since teachers traditionally join different unions or associations on the grounds of sex, academic qualifications, the type of school they teach in, the subject they teach, and their position in the school hierarchy.[4] Regular state or city or country-wide meetings of teachers are virtually unheard of. Teaching is largely a matter of individual teachers working alone in individual classrooms in isolated schools, and teachers' problems are largely private problems, or at least they are internalised as such. Teachers, as we have noted, commonly look to immediate factors as the measure of their competence and success, or the cause of their failure, and they carry on without an internal feedback system. The whole process is an extremely privatised one wherein it becomes difficult for a teacher to get beyond the real everyday concerns which operate at the individual level. Teachers are very badly placed to think, organise and act collectively because of the individual nature and the fragmented conditions of their work(fragmentation which also makes teachers far more vulnerable to supervisory control).

Radical change and revolutionary strategy, however, will not come out of individual classrooms or isolated schools. For teachers to act effectively in this area they must act collectively, not simply because of the strength unity provides, but also because of the very need to see problems in their widest possible context, and to share experiences and plan strategies with the widest possible group. There are three avenues already open for teachers to do this; two of which can be effectual; and one avenue not as yet open, or at least not widely so, which is also necessary for effective collective teacher action.

The avenues already open are the teachers' unions, the trade-union movement in general, and professional associations. Teachers' unions are an extremely important site for teacher struggles, but by themselves they are not enough. Teachers' unions are basically concerned with securing and improving the conditions of teachers within the prevailing system, which is a necessary and vital task and one which all teachers should be actively involved in. The problem with such unions, however, is that their strength is also their limitation. Their credibility and bargaining power is based on the acceptance of a particular context, and the concessions they gain lie within the parameters of that context. Teachers' unions, especially the larger ones, are unlikely to be revolutionary in nature. Their concerns are more of a reformist kind - getting the best possible deal for teachers under capitalism rather than organising concerted action to overthrow capitalism. This is not, of course, to belittle such efforts which themselves can be an important part of class struggle, and which can also work in the direction of gaining control of the means of production: successful struggles against the inspectorial system, in getting teachers appointed to curriculum boards, and in abolishing some external examinations, *have* resulted in teachers gaining some further degree of control over the production process, but as yet not a significant degree. The activities of teachers' unions are vital, but taken alone they are not sufficient.

The second existing avenue is the trade-union movement in general, and most of what has been said about teachers' unions also applies there. But why should teachers be concerned with the trade-union movement in general as well as with their own specific unions? There are two central reasons. First, involvement in a wider context broadens the teachers' perspective of what class struggle is all about, how it affects other workers, and what strategies are being employed. Second, as we noted earlier, fundamental changes in schooling cannot be brought about independently from fundamental changes in society as a whole, and the concerns of teachers have to be seen as part of an overall common concern. Involvement with the trade-union movement in general can assist in linking concerns and in coordinating action. One of the most successful instances of militant teacher action in New South Wales became successful largely because other unions came in behind a struggle over school staffing and virtually crippled a major port.[5] Teachers, on the other hand, are not renowned for their propensity to 'go out' in support of other workers' struggles. A stronger linkage between teachers and working-class movements could highlight areas of common concern for both sections and lead to more unified action.

The third existing avenue for teachers consists of the professional organisations which have proliferated during this century.[6] These, however, are usually narrow in scope and are relatively apolitical. Their main concerns appear to be promoting the 'professionalism' of teachers, looking after narrow sectional interests, and publishing journals mainly concerned with classroom issues like new advances in drama teaching or evaluation of the use of coloured rods in elementary-school mathematics. Such associations might have value for the teacher, but they are not centres of serious political or ideological concern or struggle.

The avenue as yet not generally available for teachers is one whose primary concern is with the politics and ideology of schooling, and which is open to all affected by schooling - teachers, students, pupils and parents alike.[7] An organisation of this type could have a large beneficial and complementary effect to the work being done in unions. It would be untrammelled by concerns which take up much union time (e.g. salary claims) and its base would be broader yet more cohesive than union bases - broader in that non-teachers would be admitted; more cohesive in that it would attract people with one central concern, and in that its theoretical and practical activities would be directed at one overall end. Teachers engaging in collective action would do well to inaugurate and encourage the development of such groups, and to participate in those already in existence. They have one further advantage as well: being non-institutional and non-formal they offer opportunities to act in ways not dominated or prescribed by bourgeois ideology or politics - thus participation in such groups also becomes learning and training for living under new social relations.

To conclude on a pessimistic but realistic note; the lack of a disposition towards collective action is a serious impediment for teachers, and one which shows little sign of being easily overcome. To suggest collective action on three fronts for a group which has difficulty in making it on one is asking a lot.

IMMEDIATE STRATEGIES

Breaking up State power, taking control of the schools, finding out how to use existing contradictions and how to link up with resistance groups, and engaging in union and other collective activity all take time: they are all long-range projects. Meanwhile, Monday morning draws closer and closer: what can be done at that point? Actually a great deal. Monday-morning activities, however, are limited or determined for each individual teacher by the objective conditions under which that teacher works, and by the particular concrete existential concerns of each particular workplace. What follows here is nothing more than a set of general principles or suggested starting points which are not meant to be exhaustive or prescriptive for every teacher in every workplace.

The suggestions should also be seen as being totally interrelated, and the order of their presentation has no connection with their relative importance.

Don't quit (unless you can serve the class struggle better in some other place). If you opt out you will be replaced immediately, and almost certainly by a teacher with less interest in rocking the schooling boat than you have.

Teach your pupils well. Although you are, on the one level, training them to serve the interests of capital, they also need the basic skills you can offer them in order to combat capitalism should this desire and opportunity arise for them.

Don't refuse to be an agent in the reproduction of bearers of labour power by going to the extent of disqualifying your pupils from getting jobs. They need jobs as much as you need yours, and there are thousands of unemployed people ready to take any jobs left vacant.

Promote class consciousness wherever possible. Use what freedom and control you have over the curriculum to introduce the working class and the concept of class struggle into schooling. This can be done in a subtle manner in all subjects and at all levels. Don't dig out the 'hard core' material; it isn't necessary and it could get you into trouble. Kids don't have to be confronted with 'The Communist Manifesto': a *sensitive* reading of Dickens will do very well. And you don't have to take kids to see Godard movies when highly respectable commercial releases like 'Norma Rae', 'Blue Collar', 'Harlan County', and 'Bread and Chocolate' (a comedy!) are around.

Expose fetishised centres of unity (including sexism and racism) for what they are, and don't assist in promoting them yourself. Register objections to sex-segregated schooling, 'houses', competitive intra-class groupings, etc.

Don't promote a competitive ethos in your classroom. Encourage cooperative activities and the sharing of knowledge, and develop consciousness of collective activity and collective power.

Break down existing discriminative roles. Give girls 'boys' jobs' to do, and vice versa. Don't reward the top academic students with special privileges.

Be honest about the very basis of schooling. Use your curriculum freedom to promote discussion of such things as equality of opportunity and the meritocratic theory in social science or civics lessons, or anywhere. Let the kids in on the reality of the situation they are experiencing, and what jobs they are heading for, and why.

Be honest about your own role. Don't try to come over as the 'kids' friend' too early; and admit that when the crunch comes you will have to revert to the role of oppressor. But explain why. Don't fool kids into thinking you're all in the same boat, and don't pretend to working-class affiliation. The kids might have a better sense of class consciousness than you.

Use the openings in the curriculum and the rhetoric about personal development and critical thinking to promote discussion about the pupils' own problems, concerns and interests. Listen to kids and learn from them.

Help make pupils more aware of the way authority structures and economic systems influence their lives. This can be done in lessons on respectable topics such as pollution, trade, etc.: in fact, anywhere.

Be as honest as conditions will allow about your political views and your stance on specific matters; e.g. wear anti-uranium badges if that's what you believe in. Explain your reasons for the stances you take rather than engage in missionary activity. If you're not allowed to talk about your views, wear badges, etc., tell the kids *that*, and explain why you put up with it.

Work towards building up the self-esteem of each child as a worthwhile contributory agent in the process of historical transformation. Give kids as much control in the classroom as is possible.

Attempt to establish democratic managerial bodies (school councils) which have real control over the day to day affairs of the school.

De-mystify the schooling process and encourage pupil and community access to it. Train pupils to use duplicators etc., and to carry out the bureaucrat activities discussed above, thus increasing their knowledge and control of the process. Let them know how the school is run, why there is overcrowding, etc.

Encourage contact with workers in their job situation. Take kids on work experience programmes and let them see what it's really like.

Try to influence other teachers to join you in your efforts.

Just keep cutting away with the 'wrong' edge of the sword they handed to you; but never lose sight of the real point of your activities - namely victory in the class struggle. Recognise that reformist achievements are only a step along the road, not the goal.

Above all, don't get fired in the process. If you do, not
only do you cease to be effective within the school, but it's
certain that your replacement will be very carefully selected.

CONCLUSION

In the final analysis what you will be able to achieve is dependent upon four factors. First, it's a matter of 'where your head
is at'; that is, a matter of personal commitment, goals and the
level of theory and understanding you have achieved. Commitment and action are always theory-guided, and there is no
substitute for serious reflection and understanding, which
eventually has to be interrelated with practice. A book such as
this can take you only so far - reflection on and discussion of
your own practice is the key to further practice (although
such reflection might, and probably will, turn you back to
books periodically - try the ones in the Select Bibliography for
starters). Second, effective practice is directed against concrete
existential, objective conditions; and these will determine what
ought to be done, what the priorities are, and how much can
be done. What is a pressing problem in one situation may not
be significant in another situation: what one teacher can 'get
away with' may not be possible for another teacher in a different school. Strategies can neither be planned nor carried out
in an abstract form: they must be tailored to actual concrete
situations, and so will vary as those situations vary. Third,
what can be practised and/or achieved is dependent generally
on the overall conditions of the class struggle and where the
offensive lies there: in times of ruling-class offensive one often
has to be content to settle for smaller gains or even minimal
losses. An understanding of the nature of contemporary class
struggle can assist in setting realistic expectations, as well as
in providing consolation in the face of genuine frustrations.
Finally, it all goes back to economic determinants, since it is the
economic instance - the process of production within the dynamic context of the overall mode of production - which is determinant (although not necessarily dominant) with regard to
material circumstances and forms of existence, including consciousness.[8] This, however, doesn't mean sitting back and doing
nothing until the economic instance, or economic conditions, are
right, for the very point of class struggle is to change the economic instance and make economic conditions right. What it does mean
is that what can be achieved along with the amount of support one
gets from people with similar ideas, and conversely the amount of
derision or resistance to be faced from those in opposition, are
variable factors determined largely by economic conditions (taken
in the wide sense adumbrated above). There are favourable times
and unfavourable times for achieving tangible results; and if immediate successes are not readily forthcoming this should not be
cause for despair or resignation - practice which brings no im-

mediate tangible success can itself be the momentum for bring-ing about conditions more conducive to success.[9]

Notes

CHAPTER 1 TEACHERS AND EDUCATION

1 F.A. Cavenagh, 'James and John Stuart Mill on Education', Cambridge University Press, 1931, p. 133.
2 T.P. Nunn, 'Education: Its Data and First Principles' (3rd edn), London, Edward Arnold, 1945, p. 12.
3 A.N. Whitehead, 'The Aims of Education', New York, Williams & Norgate, 1929, p. 1.
4 D.H. Lawrence, 'Fantasia of the Unconscious', London, Martin Secker, 1923, p. 67.
5 R.M. Hutchins, 'The Conflict in Education', New York, Harper & Row, 1953, p. 70.
6 R.S. Peters, What is an Educational Process? in R.S. Peters (ed.), 'The Concept of Education', London, Routledge & Kegan Paul, 1969, p. 9.
7 See, for instance, F. Musgrove and P.H. Taylor, Teachers' and Parents' Conception of the Teacher's Role, 'British Journal of Educational Psychology', vols. 35-6, 195-6, pp. 171-8.
8 In R.C. Edwards et al. (eds), 'The Capitalist System', New Jersey, Prentice Hall, 1972, pp. 123-4.
9 In J. Rich (ed.), 'Readings in Philosophy of Education', California, Wadsworth, 1972, pp. 117-18.
10 The ideological force arises from the actual relation that does exist to the daily practice of schooling, wherein some activities either are Educative (thus our use of 'very little') or are indistinguishable in outward form from Educative processes.
11 For more detailed discussion of this issue see K. Harris, 'Education and Knowledge', London, Routledge & Kegan Paul, 1979, ch. 1.
12 R.S. Peters, 'Ethics and Education', London, George Allen & Unwin, 1970, p. 154.
13 P.H. Hirst and R.S. Peters, 'The Logic of Education', London, Routledge & Kegan Paul, 1970, p. 110, my italics.
14 'Function' is being used in a quite specific sense. See below, pp. 27-8.
15 For excellent discussion on this issue see P. Willis, 'Learning to Labour', Farnborough, Saxon House, 1977.
16 I argue this more fully in K. Harris, Peters on Schooling, 'Educational Philosophy and Theory', 9, 1, April 1977, pp. 33-48.
17 The particular ways in which these regulations have been tightened or changed has, of course, varied from country to country.
18 Interestingly, as unemployment has increased, these communes have recently received indirect government support: the unemployed have been encouraged (if only in word) to join them.
19 The distinction between receiving a weekly wage and a salary is, in some contexts, an extremely important one. See p. 35.
20 See p. 133; and the discussions on proletarianisation (pp. 65-7, 133-8).
21 R.S. Peters, 'Ethics and Education', pp. 74. 167, my italics in each case.
22 D.H. Lawrence, Education of the People, commissioned by 'The London Times' in 1918, but first published posthumously in E.D. McDonald (ed.), 'Phoenix', London, William Heinemann, 1961. The quotation is from 'Phoenix', pp. 588-90.

CHAPTER 2   CLASSES AND CLASS STRUGGLE

1   For more detailed discussion of this point see K. Harris, 'Education and Knowledge', London, Routledge & Kegan Paul, 1979, ch. 1.
2   See I. Lakatos, Falsification and the Methodology of Scientific Research Programmes, in I. Lakatos and A. Musgrave (eds), 'Criticism and the Growth of Knowledge', Cambridge University Press, 1970. The term 'problematic' is not Lakatos's.
3   The capital 'S' is used to emphasise the fetishised nature of this institution and to show that our conception is not the standard bourgeois conception.
4   See O. McKevitt and G. Douglas, The Occupational Background of Intending Teachers, 'Australian Journal of Education', 17 (1), 1973, pp. 69-79.
5   D.S. Anderson, 'The Development of Student Teachers', Paris, OECD, 1974, p. 20.
6   George Bernard Shaw, 'Pygmalion', Act 1.
7   See G. Grace, 'Teachers, Ideology and Control', London, Routledge & Kegan Paul, 1978, chs 1 and 2.
8   For discussion of teaching as a vocation see E. Altman, Teaching as a Vocation: A Reappraisal, 'Education For Teaching', 82, 1969-70, pp. 28-33.
9   See, for example, D. White, The Profession of Teaching, in P. Boreham et al. (eds), 'The Professions in Australia: a Critical Appraisal', St Lucia: Univ. of Queensland Press, 1976, pp. 156-68. See also H. Cox and J. Elmore, Public School Teachers: a Sociological View of their Status, 'Contemporary Education', 47, 4, Summer 1976, pp. 244-7.
10 See P.M. Leigh, Ambiguous Professionalism: A study of teachers' status-perception, 'Educational Review', 3 (1), 1979, pp. 27-44.
11 K. Marx, The Holy Family in T.B. Bottomore (ed.), 'Karl Marx: Selected Writings', Harmondsworth, Penguin Books, 1956, p. 75.
12 An exact figure is difficult to obtain because occupational categorisations in Census Reports tend to be imprecise on important variables, and the categorisations are difficult to translate into Marxist categories. This problem will confront us again as this work proceeds: see especially p. 107 and ch. 5, n. 9., p. 158.
13 The terms are used interchangeably in this work.
14 The word 'levels' is potentially misleading. In the context in which it is being used it suggests neither a hierarchy of layers nor even discrete and separable layers. Engels spoke of 'instances', but this terminology is also not without its problems.
15 For discussion of the establishment of universal compulsory schooling as a *ruling-class* victory see below, pp. 80-2. It was not, however, an unequivocal ruling-class victory: see p. 146.
16 K. Marx and F. Engels, The German Ideology, in R.C. Tucker (ed.), 'The Marx-Engels Reader', New York, W.W. Norton, 1972, pp. 136-8.
17 Fort St High School; commonly recognised as one of the two leading State High Schools in NSW up until abolition of the selective school system in 1962. The motto formed the basis of the principal's weekly address throughout the five years I attended the school.

CHAPTER 3 THE ECONOMIC IDENTIFICATION OF TEACHERS

1   G. Carchedi, On the Economic Identification of the New Middle Class, 'Economy and Society', 4 1, February 1975, p. 17.
2   K. Marx, 'Capital', Moscow, Progress Publishers, 1974, vol. 1, p. 476.
3   Ibid., p. 477.
4   I. Gough, Marx's Theory of Productive and Unproductive Labour, 'New Left Review', 76, Nov.-Dec. 1972, pp. 47-74.
5   P. Baran, 'The Political Economy of Growth', Harmondsworth, Penguin Books, 1976. The quotations are from p. 144 and p. 145 respectively.
6   E. Mandel, 'The Leninist Theory of Organisation', London, International Marxist Group, 1971, p. 14.

7   In Carchedi, On the Economic Identification of the New Middle Class, op. cit., pp. 1-86.
8   What follows is our extrapolation; not an analysis performed by Carchedi himself.
9   Carchedi, op. cit., p. 63.
10 Ibid., pp. 59-66.
11 See pp. 69-70 and ch. 4. in general.
12 J. O'Connor, 'The Fiscal Crisis of the State', New York, St Martin's Press, 1973, p. 116.
13 We recognise here part of the broader fundamental contradiction between the ideology (including the practice) of teacher training and the objective conditions of the job of teaching.

CHAPTER 4 THE POLITICAL IDENTIFICATION OF TEACHERS

1   F. Engels, 'The Origin of the Family, Private Property, and the State', New York, Pathfinder Press, 1975.
2   It is not, of course, *only* the State which adapts working-class victories to serve the needs of capital; nor is it only the State which grants concessions to workers or implements welfare schemes for them. Many individual capitalist firms engage in all or some of these policies. In the final analysis, however, it is the State which legalises working hours and holidays, and which supports the concessions and schemes offered by individual firms.
3   Quoted in S. Bowles and H. Gintis, 'Schooling in Capitalist America', New York, Basic Books, 1976, pp. 108-9.
4   G. Grace, 'Teachers, Ideology and Control', London, Routledge & Kegan Paul, p. 16.
5   Ibid.
6   Ibid., p. 11.
7   L.C. Deighton (ed.), 'The Encyclopedia of Education', New York, Macmillan 1971, vol. 9, p. 72.
8   Ibid., vol. 9, p. 64.
9   I. Illich, 'Deschooling Society', Harmondsworth, Penguin Books, 1973, p. 32; and E. Reimer, 'School is Dead', Harmondsworth, Penguin Books, 1972, p. 35.
10 D.H. Lawrence, 'Phoenix 11', London, Heinemann, 1968, pp. 578-81.
11 The simplistic, misleading picture is clearly exemplified in Bowles and Gintis's elaboration of what they call the 'correspondence principle'; see 'Schooling in Capitalist America', pp. 130-2. My own oversimplification and error appears most notably in 'Education and Knowledge', London, Routledge & Kegan Paul, 1979, pp. 142-4. For valuable corrective work produced by the University of Birmingham Centre for Contemporary Cultural Studies see especially 'On Ideology', London, Hutchinson, 1978; P. Willis, 'Learning to Labour', Farnborough, Saxon House, 1977; and S. Hall and T. Jefferson (eds), 'Resistance Through Ritual', London, Hutchinson, 1976. Unfortunately the work produced by the Centre has, in my opinion, been flawed mainly through a basic and unresolved confusion regarding the nature and interrelationship of culture and ideology; and while I accept it as a valuable corrective in some areas I do not feel that it tells sufficiently (as yet) against the accounts it attacks or the similar overall approach taken in this book.
12 The latest full scale Australian study shows that, even with increased unemployment and the need for credentials both keeping children at school longer than ever before, less than one-third complete secondary schooling. See P. Meade, 'Youth, Education and Life Chances', Sydney, School of Education, University of New South Wales, 1979.
13 R.S. Peters, 'Ethics and Education', London, Allen & Unwin, 1970, p. 252.
14 In New South Wales school pupils sitting for the Higher School Certificate are awarded a 'Higher School Certificate'. Irregular students (mainly mature students studying at technical colleges, which is really another

form of schooling) who pass the same exams are awarded a 'Certificate of Attainments'.

15   See S. Bowles and H. Gintis, 'Schooling in Capitalist America', pp. 131-41.
16   See, for example, ibid., pp. 109-24. See also Select bibliography, Sections G and H.
17   R.C. Rist, Student Social Class and Teacher Expectations: The Self-fulfilling Prophecy in Ghetto Education, 'Harvard Educational Review', 40, 3, August 1970, p. 449.
18   An interesting reaction among employers in times of high unemployment is to reject those applicants who are either not sufficiently literate and/or who do not display the 'right' attitudes on interview, and then to blame the schools – and teachers – for the unemployment problem. As 'The Australian' put it, in very bold type: 'The first reason why the school-leaver is unable to get a job is his teacher' (14-15 January 1978).
19   R.M.W. Travers (ed.), 'The Second Handbook of Research on Teaching', Chicago, Rand McNally, 1973.
20   E. Reimer, 'School is Dead', p. 23.
21   M. Deutsch, Minority Groups and Class Status as Related to Social and Personality Factors in Scholastic Achievement, in M. Deutsch et al. (eds), 'The Disadvantaged Child', New York, Basic Books, 1967.
22   P.V. Gump, The Classroom Behavior Setting: Its Nature and Relation to Student Behavior, Final Report, Project 2453, Lawrence, Kansas, Midwest Psychological Field Station, University of Kansas, 1967.
23   See, for example, P. Goodman, 'Compulsory Miseducation', Harmondsworth, Penguin Books, 1972, p. 32.
24   A. Morrison and D. McIntyre, 'Teachers and Teaching', Harmondsworth, Penguin Books, 1969, pp. 110-11.
25   P. Marsh, E. Rosser and R. Harré, 'The Rules of Disorder', London. Routledge & Kegan Paul, 1978, p. 38.

CHAPTER 5   THE IDEOLOGICAL IDENTIFICATION OF TEACHERS

1   K. Marx and F. Engels, The German Ideology, in R.C. Tucker (ed.), 'The Marx-Engels Reader', New York, W.W. Norton, 1972, pp, 136-8.
2   For valuable discussion of this action see J. Freeland, MACOS and SEMP in Queensland: a case study in ideological class struggle, 'Intervention', 12, 1979.
3   For other material see Select bibliography, Section D.
4   For examples of this manoeuvre see K. Harris, 'Education and Knowledge', pp. 100-5.
5   See Select bibliography, Section H.
6   J.S. Coleman et al., 'Equality of Educational Opportunity', Washington, US Government Printing Office, 1966, p. 325.
7   For this sort of approach see C. Silberman, 'Crisis in the Classroom', New York, Vintage Books, 1971.
8   See again S. Bowles and H. Gintis, 'Schooling in Capitalist America', New York, Basic Books, 1976, pp. 109-24; and Select bibliography, Sections G and H.
9   See the figures compiled by D.S. Anderson and J.S. Western, Social Profiles of Students in Four Professions, 'Quarterly Review of Australian Education', 3 (4), December 1970, pp. 3-28. Manipulation of the figures in Tables 3 and 8 (p. 10 and p. 16 respectively), and taking the categorisations of 'skilled', 'semi-skilled' and 'unskilled' as representative of the working class, generates the proportions indicated, viz 27:1 for law, and 20:1 for medicine.
10   D.C. McClelland, Testing for competence rather than intelligence, in A. Gartner et al. (eds), 'The New Assault on Equality: I.Q. and Social Stratification', New York, Holt, Rinehart & Winston, 1974, p. 165.
11   See especially I. Berg, 'Education and Jobs: The Great Training Robbery', Harmondsworth, Penguin Books, 1973.
12   Ibid, pp. 83-93.

13   See S. Bowles and H. Gintis, 'Schooling in Capitalist America', pp. 53–101, pp. 13–48.
14   L. Althusser, 'Lenin and Philosophy', London, New Left Books, 1971, p. 155.
15   Ibid., p. 175.
16   J. Davies, The H.S.C.: Preparation for What?, 'Radical Education Dossier', 5, February 1978, pp. 15–20. This study was restricted to curricula in Victorian High Schools, and would probably reward replication elsewhere.
17   See, for instance, P.H. Hirst and R.S. Peters, 'The Logic of Education', London, Routledge & Kegan Paul, 1970, p. 124. Presumably it is only continued procreation by the population at large which keeps successful teachers in employment.
18   Those still interested in conceptual analysis might argue that, through not entering a condition requiring that P learns C, I am speaking of 'teaching' only in a 'task' sense and ignoring the 'achievement' sense. My concern is not to become involved in this sort of discussion; but rather to examine what teachers actually do.
19   Teachers, virtually by definition, will always be in a position of possessing more knowledge than their pupils, and will thus have knowledge-domination over pupils. This, however, need not necessarily result in the establishment of dominance relations, since dominance relations derive from the nature of the exchange (which includes the function which the exchanged knowledge serves).
20   Where this knowledge is not esoteric non-teachers rarely keep up to date with it; and parents (even if they are an adequate source) often 'abdicate' from teaching, or see their role as complementing that of the 'expert teacher'. For instance, most parents can read and teach their children to read, yet quite deliberately leave the task up to the teachers; and few parents who do possess 'school knowledge' exclude their children from school and do the teaching themselves.
21   Teachers play a further ideological role in so far as they disguise the class nature of the social production of the very knowledge they purvey.

CHAPTER 6 THE CLASS LOCATION AND CLASS POSITION
OF TEACHERS

1   V.I. Lenin, A Great Beginning, in 'Collected Works', Moscow, Progress Publishers, 1965, vol. 29, p. 421, my emphasis.
2   G. Therborn, The Travail of Latin American Democracy, 'New Left Review', 113–14, Jan.-April 1979, p. 75.
3   K. Marx, 'Theories of Surplus Value', Moscow, Progress Publishers, 1968, part 2, p. 573.
4   It will be recalled that our exclusion of unproductive labourers from the working class (p. 59) was more or less arbitrary. With the full class identification of teachers now behind us it can be seen that, in their case, very little hangs on the decision.
5   This is not to suggest, of course, that teachers either could or would have an effect anywhere near as immediate as the police or the military.
6   E. Mandel, The Changing Role of the Bourgeois University, in T. Pateman (ed.), 'Countercourse', Harmondsworth, Penguin Books, 1972, p. 16. The original is in italics.
7   For extended discussion of computers and schooling see 'Radical Education Dossier', 11, Autumn 1980. For support of these figures see the 'Sydney Morning Herald', 16 October 1979, p. 3.
8   'Technological Case Studies: Employment Effects of Technological Change', Central Planning and Research Unit, N.S.W. Department of Industrial Relations and Technology, 1978.
9   The going 'joke' at the moment is that it takes only one man and a dog to maintain a modern telephone exchange. The dog guards the exchange, and the man feeds the dog.
10   'Australian Financial Review', 14 January 1980, p. 14.

11   See 'Radical Education Dossier', 11, Autumn 1980, pp. 5-10.
12   'Sydney Morning Herald', 25 March 1980, p. 26.
13   A. Weaving et al., 'Computers and Teaching in Australia', Canberra,
     Australian Advisory Committee on Research and Development in Education,
     Report No. 6.
14   The representation is ideological in that it disguises the real interests which
     are being served while pointing to aspects which, at least on the face of it,
     probably are the case. It might be that modules and computers do help
     people to learn; and as far as this aspect is concerned we would have no
     objection to them. The position taken in this book is not a 'Luddite'
     one. It is not technology per se that is being argued with, but the way it
     is being employed and the uses to which it is being put. Technology can
     liberate people: under capitalism the general tendency is for it to hasten
     dehumanisation and proletarianisation of the workers and the new middle
     class.
15   It should be of particular interest for the reader now to compare the 'ortho-
     dox' identification of the social class of teachers (pp. 30-7) with the Marx-
     ist identification which has followed in terms of the light which each throws
     on the social function of teachers, and on the contradictions and problems
     teachers face in their day-to-day work, especially with regard to their
     represented role as Educators.
16   Teachers, being economically oppressed themselves, also have a *direct
     objective interest* in ending the basis of that oppression - namely the capi-
     talist system.
17   K. Marx and F. Engels, The Communist Manifesto, in R.C. Tucker, 'The
     Marx-Engels Reader', New York, W.W. Norton, 1972, p. 353.

CHAPTER 7 REVOLUTIONARY STRATEGY FOR TEACHERS

1   P. Willis, 'Learning to Labour', Farnborough, Saxon House, 1977, p. 186.
2   Ibid., pp. 119-69.
3   We have here two good examples of the State adapting policies originally
    won by the working class to serve the needs of capital (see p. 77). By
    legalising both trade unions and some street marches the State is able to
    maintain its 'image' of democratic neutrality and serving the interests of all,
    while at the same time being provided with movements it can respectively
    (but not universally) manipulate, bash, or ignore. The part that some
    unions have played, often through State manipulation, in 'selling out' the
    workers should not be lost sight of as well.
4   See P.M. Leigh, Ambiguous Professionalism: A study of teachers' status-
    perception, 'Educational Review', 3 (1), 1979, pp. 27-44. I have added the
    last two criteria to his categorisation of the grounds whereby teachers
    join different unions or associations.
5   Maritime unions became involved in the Warilla High School strike in 1975.
6   In Australia over 100 teacher organisations are officially registered: among
    these basically non-political Associations outnumber unions by about eight
    to one.
7   I am most certainly not thinking of PTA groups, Parents and Citizens organ-
    isations, Mothers Clubs, or their like.
8   The economic instance, or process of production, is not necessarily always
    dominant, but it *is* determinant of which level or instance will be dominant
    in any social formation. On this issue see N. Poulantzas, 'Political Power
    and Social Classes', London, New Left Books, 1973.
9   Until recently I believed that to employ non-sexist language over a sustained
    piece of prose would result in an ostentatious straining of the English
    language. I have now come to believe that this is not so; and that provided
    certain constructions are avoided, non-sexist language can be employed in
    a manner whereby it does not call attention to itself. The entire text of
    this book has (I believe) been written in non-sexist language. If the reader
    failed to notice this in passing then an important point has been made; and

hopefully others might no longer be deterred from attempts to remove sex-ism from their writings on the grounds that such endeavours must lead either to strained constructions or to a form of inverted sexism (where female rather than male constructions are used). Comments would be most welcome.

Select bibliography

The central criterion for including works in this bibliography has been their relevance to the argument developed in the text. Some consideration has also been given to availability and to level of difficulty.

Books - especially books of readings - can rarely be categorised as neatly as a bibliographer would desire; and it must be recognised that the placement of books within the following sections has at times involved matters of judgment which could be questionable. Some books (mainly collections of readings) have been listed in multiple sections. Readings within collections have not been listed individually.

SECTION A WRITINGS OF MARX AND ENGELS, INCLUDING COLLECTIONS

Engels, F., 'The Origin of the Family, Private Property, and the State', New York, Pathfinder Press, 1975.
Marx, K., 'Capital' (3 vols), Moscow, Progress Publishers, 1974.
Marx, K., 'Grundrisse', Harmondsworth, Penguin Books, 1977.
Marx, K., 'Surveys From Exile', Harmondsworth, Penguin Books, 1973.
Marx, K., 'The First International and After', Harmondsworth, Penguin Books, 1974.
Bottomore, T., and Rubel, M., 'Karl Marx: Selected Writings in Sociology and Social Philosophy', Harmondsworth, Penguin Books, 1974.
Feuer, L., 'Marx and Engels: Basic Writings on Politics and Philosophy', London, Fontana Books, 1972.
Fischer, E., 'Marx in His Own Words', Harmondsworth, Penguin Books, 1975.
McLellan, D., 'The Thought of Karl Marx', London, Macmillan, 1972.
Tucker, R.C., 'The Marx-Engels Reader', New York, W.W. Norton, 1972.

SECTION B CLASSES AND CLASS STRUGGLE

Blackburn, R. (ed.), 'Ideology in Social Science', London, Fontana Books, 1973.
Carchedi, G., 'On the Economic Identification of Social Classes', London, Routledge & Kegan Paul, 1977.
Connell, R.W., 'Ruling Class: Ruling Culture', Cambridge University Press, 1977.
Giddens, A., 'The Class Structure of Advanced Societies', London, Hutchinson, 1973.
Hunt, A. (ed.), 'Class and Class Structure', London, Lawrence & Wishart, 1977.
Johnson, T., What is to be known? The Structural Determination of Social Class, 'Economy and Society', 6, 1977.
Nicolaus, M., Proletariat and Middle Class in Marx, 'Studies on the Left', VII (1), Jan.-Feb. 1967.
Poulantzas, N., 'Political Power and Social Classes', London, New Left Books, 1973.
Poulantzas, N., On Social Classes, 'New Left Review', 78, 1973, pp. 27-54.
Poulantzas, N., 'Classes in Contemporary Capitalism', London, New Left Books, 1975.
Therborn, G., 'What Does the Ruling Class Do When it Rules?', London, New Left Books, 1978.
Walker, P. (ed.), 'Between Labor and Capital', Boston, South End Press, 1979.
Wedderburn, D. (ed.), 'Poverty, Inequality and Class Structure', Cambridge University Press, 1974.

Wright, E.O., Class Boundaries in Advanced Capitalist Societies, 'New Left Review', 98, 1976.
Wright, E.O., 'Class Crisis and the State', London, New Left Books, 1978.

SECTION C   MARXIST ANALYSES: ECONOMICS, THE STATE, WORK

Althusser, L., 'For Marx', London, New Left Books, 1969.
Arrighi, G., Towards a Theory of Capitalist Crisis, 'New Left Review', 111, 1978.
Baran, P., 'The Political Economy of Growth', Harmondsworth, Penguin Books, 1973.
Baran, P., and Sweezy, P., 'Monopoly Capital', Harmondsworth, Penguin Books, 1968.
Blackburn, R. (ed.), 'Ideology in Social Science', London, Fontana Books, 1973.
Braverman, H., 'Labour and Monopoly Capital', London, Monthly Review Press, 1974.
Clarke, J., et al., 'Working Class Culture', London, Hutchinson, 1979.
Connell, R.W., 'Ruling Class; Ruling Culture', Cambridge University Press, 1977.
Cornforth, M., 'Dialectical Materialism' (3 vols), London, Lawrence & Wishart, 1976.
Cornforth, M., 'The Open Philosophy and the Open Society', London, Lawrence & Wishart, 1977.
de Brunhoff, S., 'The State, Capital and Economic Policy', London, Pluto Press, 1978.
Edwards, R.C. et al. (eds), 'The Capitalist System', New Jersey, Prentice Hall, 1972.
Geras, N., Althusser's Marxism: an Account and an Assessment, 'New Left Review', 71, 1971, pp. 57-86.
Gough, I., Marx's Theory of Productive and Unproductive Labour, 'New Left Review', 76, 1972, pp. 47-72.
Gough, I., State Expenditure in Advanced Capitalism, 'New Left Review', 92, 1975, pp. 53-92.
Gough, I., 'The Political Economy of the Welfare State', London, Macmillan, 1979.
Holloway, J., and Picciotto, S. (eds), 'State and Capital: A Marxist Debate', London, Edward Arnold, 1978.
Jessop, B., Recent Theories of the Capitalist State, 'Australian Left Review', 68, April 1979.
Laclau, E., 'Politics and Ideology in Marxist Theory', London, New Left Books, 1977.
Mandel, E., 'Marxist Economic Theory', London, Merlin Press, 1968.
Mandel, E., 'The Formation of the Economic Thought of Karl Marx', London, New Left Books, 1971.
Mandel, E., 'Late Capitalism', London, New Left Books, 1975.
Mandel, E., 'Revolutionary Marxism Today', London, New Left Books, 1979.
Mandel, E., 'The Second Slump', London, New Left Books, 1978.
Miliband, R., 'The State in Capitalist Society', London, Weidenfeld & Nicolson, 1969.
O'Connor, J., 'The Fiscal Crisis of the State', New York, St Martin's Press, 1973.
Ollman, B., 'Alienation', Cambridge University Press, 1976.
Pateman, T. (ed.), 'Countercourse', Harmondsworth, Penguin Books, 1972.
Poulantzas, N., 'The State in Capitalist Society', London, New Left Books, 1973.
Poulantzas, N., 'Fascism and Dictatorship', London, New Left Books, 1973.
Sheehan, J., 'The Economics of Education', London, Allen & Unwin, 1973.
Sweezy, P., 'The Theory of Capitalist Development', London, Monthly Review Press, 1968.
Wirth, M., Towards a Critique of the Theory of State Monopoly Capitalism, 'Economy and Society', 6 (3), 1977.
Zaretsky, E., 'Capitalism, the Family, and Personal Life', London, Pluto Press, 1976.

SECTION D   CRITIQUES OF SCHOOLING: NON-MARXIST

Flude, M., and Ahier, J. (eds), 'Educability, Schools, and Ideology', London, Croom Helm, 1976.
Gartner, A. et al. (eds), 'After Deschooling, What?', New York, Harper & Row, 1973.
Goodman, P., 'Compulsory Miseducation', Harmondsworth, Penguin Books, 1972.
Graubard, A., 'Free the Children', New York, Pantheon, 1972.
Henry, J., 'Essays on Education', Harmondsworth, Penguin Books, 1972.
Holt, J., 'How Children Fail', Harmondsworth, Penguin Books, 1973.
Holt, J., 'Freedom and Beyond', Harmondsworth, Penguin Books, 1973.
Holt, J., 'Escape From Childhood', Harmondsworth, Penguin Books, 1975.
Illich, I., 'Celebration of Awareness', Harmondsworth, Penguin Books, 1973.
Illich, I., 'Deschooling Society', Harmondsworth, Penguin Books, 1973.
Jackson, P., 'Life in the Classrooms', New York, Holt, Rinehart & Winston, 1968.
Kohl, H., '36 Children', Harmondsworth, Penguin Books, 1971.
Kozol, J., 'The Night is Dark and I am Far From Home', New York, Bantam Books, 1977.
Kozol, J., 'Death at an Early Age', Harmondsworth, Penguin Books, 1971.
Marsh, P. et al., 'The Rules of Disorder', London, Routledge & Kegan Paul, 1978.
Moore, A., 'Realities of the Urban Classroom', New York, Doubleday, 1967.
Postman, N., and Weingartner, C., 'Teaching as a Subversive Activity', Harmondsworth, Penguin Books, 1972.
Reimer, E., 'School is Dead', Harmondsworth, Penguin Books, 1972.
Silberman, C., 'Crisis in the Classroom', New York, Vintage Books, 1971.
Wright, N., 'Progress in Education', London, Croom Helm, 1977.

SECTION E   MARXIST CRITIQUES OF SCHOOLING

Apple, M., 'Ideology and Curriculum', London, Routledge & Kegan Paul, 1979.
Blackburn, R. (ed.), 'Ideology in Social Science', London, Fontana Books, 1973.
Bourdieu, P., and Passeron, J.C., 'Reproduction: in Education, Society and Culture', London, Sage, 1977.
Bowles, S. and Gintis, H., 'Schooling in Capitalist America', New York, Basic Books, 1976.
Brown, P. (ed.), 'Knowledge, Education and Cultural Change', London, Tavistock, 1973.
Carnoy, M., 'Education as Cultural Imperialism', New York, David McKay, 1974.
Castles, S., and Wustenberg, W., 'The Education of the Future: The Theory and Practice of Socialist Education', London, Pluto Press, 1979.
Dale, R., et al. (eds), 'Schooling and Capitalism', London, Routledge & Kegan Paul, 1976.
David, M., 'The State, The Family and Education', London, Routledge & Kegan Paul, 1980.
Davies, B., 'Social Control and Education', London, Methuen, 1976.
Feinberg, W., and Rosemont, H., 'Work, Technology and Education', Illinois, Univ. of Illinois Press, 1975.
Flude, M., and Ahier, J. (eds), 'Educability, Schools and Ideology', London, Croom Helm, 1974.
Freire, P., 'Pedagogy of the Oppressed', Harmondsworth, Penguin Books, 1972.
Freire, P., 'Cultural Action For Freedom', Harmondsworth, Penguin Books, 1972.
Freire, P., 'Education: The Practice of Freedom', London, Writers and Readers Cooperative, 1974.
Gleeson, D. (ed.), 'Identity and Structure: Issues in the Sociology of Education', London, Nafferton Books, 1977.
Harris, K., 'Education and Knowledge', London, Routledge & Kegan Paul, 1979.
Holly, D. (ed.), 'Education or Domination?', London, Arrow Books, 1974.
Norton, T.M., and Ollman, B. (eds), 'Studies in Socialist Pedagogy',

London, Monthly Review Press, 1978.

Pateman, T. (ed.), 'Countercourse', Harmondsworth, Penguin Books, 1972.

Rubinstein, D., and Simon, B., 'The Evolution of the Comprehensive School: 1926-1966', London, Routledge & Kegan Paul, 1969.

Sharp, R., 'Knowledge, Ideology and the Politics of Schooling', London, Routledge & Kegan Paul, 1980.

Sharp, R. and Green, A., 'Education and Social Control', London, Routledge & Kegan Paul, 1975.

Simon, B., 'Intelligence, Psychology and Education', London, Lawrence & Wishart, 1971.

Simon, B. (ed.), 'The Radical Tradition in Education in Britain', London, Lawrence & Wishart, 1972.

Willis, P., 'Learning to Labour', Farnborough, Saxon House, 1977.

Young, M.F.D. (ed.), 'Knowledge and Control', London, Macmillan, 1971.

Young, M., and Whitty, G. (eds), 'Society, State, & Schooling', Ringmer, The Falmer Press, 1977.

Young, M., and Whitty, G. (eds), 'Explorations in the Politics of School Knowledge', Driffield, Nafferton Books, 1976.

SECTION F IDEOLOGY AND SCHOOLING

Althusser, L., Ideology and Ideological State Apparatuses, in 'Lenin and Philosophy', London, New Left Books, 1971.

Apple, M., 'Ideology and Curriculum', London, Routledge & Kegan Paul, 1979.

Bernbaum, G., 'Knowledge and Ideology in the Sociology of Education', London Macmillan, 1977.

Bisseret, N., 'Education, Class Language and Ideology', London, Routledge & Kegan Paul, 1979.

Blackburn, R. (ed.), 'Ideology in Social Science', London, Fontana Books, 1973.

Bourdieu, P. and Passeron, J.C., 'Reproduction: in Education, Society and Culture', London, Sage, 1977.

CCCS, 'On Ideology', London, Hutchinson, 1978.

Dale, R., et al. (eds), 'Schooling and Capitalism', London, Routledge & Kegan Paul, 1976.

Flude, M., and Ahier, J. (eds), 'Educability, Schools and Ideology', London, Croom Helm, 1976.

Grace, G., 'Teachers, Ideology and Control', London, Routledge & Kegan Paul, 1978.

Harris, K., 'Education and Knowledge', London, Routledge & Kegan Paul, 1979.

Harris, N., 'Beliefs in Society: The Problem of Ideology', London, C.A. Watts, 1968.

Hirst, P.Q., Althusser and the Theory of Ideology, 'Economy and Society', 5 (4), 1976, pp. 385-412.

Karabel, J., and Halsey, A., 'Power and Ideology in Education', New York, Oxford University Press, 1977.

Laclau, E., 'Politics and Ideology in Marxist Theory', London, New Left Books, 1977.

Lawton, D., 'The Politics of the School Curriculum', London, Routledge & Kegan Paul, 1980.

MacDonald, M., 'The Curriculum and Cultural Reproduction', London, Open University, 1977.

Mepham, J., The Theory of Ideology in 'Capital', 'Radical Philosophy', 2, 1972, pp. 12-19.

Pateman, T. (ed.), 'Countercourse', Harmondsworth, Penguin Books, 1972,

Pateman, T., 'Language, Truth and Politics', Lewes, Jean Stroud, 1980.

Sharp, R., 'Knowledge, Ideology and the Politics of Schooling', London, Routledge & Kegan Paul, 1980.

Skillen, A., 'Ruling Illusions', Sussex, Harvester Press, 1977.

Stevens, P., Ideology and Schooling, 'Educational Philosophy and Theory', 8 (2), October 1976, pp. 29-41.

Young, M.F.D. (ed.), 'Knowledge and Control', London, Collier Macmillan, 1971.

SECTION G   EQUALITY OF EDUCATIONAL OPPORTUNITY

Block, N.J., and Dworkin, G., 'The I.Q. Controversy', New York, Pantheon, 1975.

Boudon, R., 'Education, Opportunity and Social Inequality', New York, John Wiley, 1974.

Bowles, S., and Gintis, H., 'Schooling In Capitalist America', New York, Basic Books, 1976.

Carnoy, M. (ed.), 'Schooling in a Corporate Society', New York, David McKay, 1972.

Coleman, J. et al., 'Equality of Educational Opportunity', Washington, US Government Printing Office, 1966.

Dale, R. et al. (eds), 'Schooling and Capitalism', London, Routledge & Kegan Paul, 1976.

Floud, J.E. et al., 'Social Class and Educational Opportunity', London, Heinemann, 1956.

Flude, M., and Ahier, J. (eds), 'Educability, Schools and Ideology', London, Croom Helm, 1976.

Gartner, A. et al. (eds), 'The New Assault on Equality: I.Q. and Social Stratification', New York, Harper & Row, 1974.

Ginsburg. H., 'The Myth of the Deprived Child', New Hersey, Prentice-Hall. 1972.

Jencks, C. et al., 'Inequality', New York, Basic Books, 1972.

Keddie, N. (ed.), 'Tinker, Tailor . . . The Myth of Cultural Disadvantage', Harmondsworth, Penguin Books, 1973.

Mosteller, F., and Moynihan, D.P., 'On Equality of Educational Opportunity', New York, Random House, 1971.

Persell, C., 'Education and Inequality', New York, Free Press, 1977.

Rist, R., 'The Urban School: Factory for Failure', MIT Press, 1973.

Roper, T., 'The Myth of Equality', Melbourne, NUAUS, 1970.

Rosenbaum, J., 'Making Inequality', New York, John Wiley, 1976.

Wedderburn, D. (ed.), 'Poverty, Inequality and Class Structure', London, Cambridge University Press, 1974.

Wexler, P., 'The Sociology of Education: Beyond Equality', Indianapolis, Bobbs-Merrill, 1976.

SECTION H   THE MERITOCRATIC THEORY

Barrow, F., 'Creative Person and Creative Process', New York, Holt, Rinehart & Winston, 1969.

Beauchamp, J., Some assumptions in university admissions, 'Selection for University', TERC, University of NSW, 1978.

Berg, I., 'Education and Jobs: The Great Training Robbery', Harmondsworth, Penguin Books, 1970.

Blakers, C., 'School and Work', Canberra, ANU Press, 1978.

Block, N., and Dworkin, G., 'The I.Q. Controversy', New York, Pantheon, 1975.

Blum, J., 'Pseudoscience and Mental Ability', London, Monthly Review Press, 1978.

Bowles, S., and Gintis, H., 'Schooling in Capitalist America', New York, Basic Books, 1976.

Collins, R., Functional and Conflict Theories of Educational Stratification, 'American Sociological Review', 37, 1972, pp. 1002-19.

Dale, R. et al. (eds), 'Schooling and Capitalism', London, Routledge & Kegan Paul, 1976.

Dore, R., 'The Diploma Disease: Education, Qualification and Development', London, Allen & Unwin, 1976.

Dunn, S., 'Public Examinations: The Changing Scene', Adelaide, Rigby, 1974.

Elton, C.F., and Sheval, L.R., Who is talented? An analysis of achievement, Research Report no. 31, Iowa City, Iowa, American College Testing Program.

Entwistle, N., and Wilson, J., 'Degrees of Excellence: The Academic Achievement Game', London, Hodder & Stoughton, 1977.

Fitzgerald, R., 'Poverty and Education in Australia', Fifth Main Report, Commission of Inquiry into Poverty, Canberra, 1976.

Gartner, A. et al., 'The New Assault on Equality: I.Q. and Social Stratification', New York, Holt, Rinehart & Winston, 1974.

Gezi, K. (ed.), 'Education in Comparative International Perspective', New York, Holt, Rinehart & Winston, 1971.

Gonzales, G., The Historical Development of the Concept of Intelligence, 'Review of Radical Political Economics', 11 (2), 1979, pp. 44-54.

Goodman, P., Pitiful Waste of Youthful Years, 'Times Educational Supplement', 16 July 1971.

Goodman, P., 'Compulsory Miseducation', Harmondsworth, Penguin Books, 1972.

Halsey, A. et al. (eds), 'Education, Economy and Society: a Reader in the Sociology of Education', New York, Free Press, 1961.

Harrison, B., 'Education, Training and the Urban Ghetto', Baltimore, Johns Hopkins Press, 1972.

Holland, J., and Richards, J., 'Academic and Non-academic Accomplishment: Correlated or Uncorrelated?', Research Report no. 2, Iowa City, American College Testing Program, 1965.

Hoyt, D., 'The Relationship Between College Grades and Adult Achievement', Research Report no. 7, Iowa City, American College Testing Program, 1965.

Hudson, L., 'Contrary Imagination', London, Methuen, 1966.

Husen, T. et al., 'Teacher Training and Student Achievement in Less Developed Countries', New York, World Bank, December 1978.

Jaffe, A., and Froomkin, J., 'Technology and Jobs: Automation in Perspective', New York, Praeger, 1968.

Jencks, C. et al, 'Inequality', New York, Basic Books, 1972.

Kamin, L., 'The Science and Politics of I.Q.', Harmondsworth, Penguin Books, 1977.

Karier, C., 'The Roots of Crisis: American Education in the Twentieth Century', New York, Rand McNally, 1970.

Klug, B., 'The Grading Game', London, NUS, 1977.

Levine, D., and Bane, M. (eds), 'The Inequality Controversy', New York, Basic Books, 1975.

Morrison, A., and McIntyre, D., 'Schools and Socialization', Harmondsworth, Penguin Books, 1971.

OECD, 'Selection and Certification in Education and Employment', Paris, 1977.

Pucel, D. et al., The Ability of Standardized Test Instruments to Predict Training Success and Employment Success, Minneapolis Project MINI-SCORE, Dept of Industrial Education, Univ. of Minnesota.

Renehan, W., 'The Predictive Validity of the 1964 Commonwealth Secondary School Examination', Melbourne, ACER, 1972.

Schultz, T., 'Investment in Human Capital: The Role of Education and of Research', New York, Free Press, 1970.

Squires, G., The Function of Education: Technical Training or Social Control?, 'Journal of Intergroup Relations', 5, 1, March 1976, pp. 37-54.

Wallach, M., Tests Tell Us Little About Talent, 'American Scientist', 64 (1) Jan.-Feb. 1976, pp. 57-63.

West, L., and Slamowicz, R., The Invalidity of the Higher School Certificate as a Tertiary Selection Device, 'Vestes', XIX (2), 1976, pp. 8-12.

Whiteland, J., The Selection of Research Students, 'Universities Quarterly', 21, 1966, pp. 44-8.

Zymelman, M., 'The Relationship Between Productivity and the Formal Education of the Labor Force in Manufacturing Industries', Harvard University, Graduate School of Education, October 1975.

Index

action, collective, 52-3, 148-50
adaptations, teacher, 24-6
administration, school, see bureaucrat-
type activities
age-specificity, 82-3, 92
alienation, 23, 133
alignment with working class, 139-41
Althusser, L., 85, 114, 159, 163, 165
Altman, E., 156
analysis of schooling, 9-10
Anderson, D.S., 33, 156, 158
'anyone can, therefore everyone can'
fallacy, 17-18
Arnold, M., 80, 110
associations, teachers', 149-50, 160
attendance, school, 82, 87-8, 92, 106-
8

Bacon, F., 116
Baran, P., 58, 156, 163
Barnard, H., 81
Bartlett, H., 80
bearers of labour power, reproduction
of: and certificates, 85; costs of,
89; and counter-school culture,
147; described, 81; by family, 79;
and schooling, 84-5, 89, 98, 124,
129-30, 138-9; as socialisation, 138-
9
Berg, I., 166
Borrowman, M., 81
Bourdieu, P., 85, 164-5
bourgeoisie, 39-40, 50-2; see also
class
Bowles, S., 157-9, 164, 166
bureaucrat-type activities of teachers,
84, 94, 96-7, 129, 136

capital: global function of, 61, 64-5,
128-30, 138; payment by, 56
capitalism, 21-4, 37-43, 59-62, 115-16,
140; changes in, 59-62
capitalist class, 21, 37-43, 60; see also
class struggle; ruling class
Carchedi, G., 56, 60-3, 67, 73, 156-7,
162
Carter, J.G., 81
Cavenagh, F.A., 155
certificates, 85-9, 103, 108-10, 129,

157-8
church, 53, 102
class groups in school, 91-2, 121
class, social: capitalist, 37-43, 60;
changes in, 39-42; consciousness,
51, 143, 151-2; definitions of, 30,
37-43, 127; location, 50, 53-4, 127-
31; Marxist concept of, 37-43;
mystification of, 52-3; position, 50,
127, 131-41; ruling, 37-47, 53, 60,
76, 101, 106, 111, 115, 130; and
state, 44-5; struggle, 29-54, 75,
140-8; and teachers, 30-7, 62-5,
75, 127-41, 160; unities, cross-,
53-4; value-ladenness of 'orthodox'
divisions, 34-5
cognitive: ability, 14, 106-7; attainment, see certificates
Coleman, J., 158, 166; Report, 105
collective action, 52-3, 148-50
collective labour, 59, 63-5, 138-9
common sense teaching-process
knowledge, 119
communality, 52-3, 148-50
communes, 19, 155
competition, 151
compulsory schooling, 31, 80, 92, 104,
120-1, 156
computers in schools, 133, 135-6, 160;
see also modules
consciousness, class, 51, 143, 151-2
content knowledge, 117-18, 120, 122,
128, 136-8
contradictions of teacher's position,
73, 130-1
control, teachers', 36, 73, 92-3, 121,
125, 128-30, 132, 137-9
'correspondence principle', 157
costs of schooling, 78, 89, 98, 135
counter-Educational function of school,
83-4
counter-school culture, 147
Cox, H., 156
cross-class unities, 53-4
curriculum: ideological nature of, 114-
15; obligatory, 82-3, 92; overt and
hidden, 138; packages, 71, 135-6,
160; see also schooling

169

Index compiled by *Ann Hall*